LOSING YOUR PARENTS, Finding Your Self

OTHER BOOKS BY VICTORIA SECUNDA

WHEN MADNESS COMES HOME

WOMEN AND THEIR FATHERS

WHEN YOU AND YOUR MOTHER CAN'T BE FRIENDS

BY YOUTH POSSESSED

HQ
755.86
.S43
2000

LOSING YOUR PARENTS,
Finding Your Self

The Defining Turning Point of Adult Life

VICTORIA SECUNDA

NEW YORK

KALAMAZOO VALLEY
COMMUNITY COLLEGE
LIBRARY

SEP 2 2 2000

Copyright © 2000 Victoria Secunda

All rights reserved. No part of this book may be used or reproduced in any manner whatsoever without the written permission
of the Publisher. Printed in the United States of America. For
information address: Hyperion, 77 West 66th Street, New
York, New York 10023-6298.

Library of Congress Cataloging-in-Publication Data

Secunda, Victoria.
    Losing your parents, finding your self : the defining
turning point of adult life / by Victoria Secunda.—1st ed.
        p.   cm.
    Includes bibliographical references and index.
    ISBN 0-7868-6312-9
    1. Parent and adult child.   2. Parents—Death—
Psychological aspects.   3. Adult children—
Psychology.   4. Adult children—Family relationships. I. Title.
HQ755.86.S43   2000
306.874—dc21   99-35867
                                          CIP

Designed by Ruth Lee

FIRST EDITION

10 9 8 7 6 5 4 3 2 1

For my sister,
NANCY

Contents

Acknowledgments

In the course of writing this book, it has been my privilege to work with, learn from, and be supported by many generous people.

To the men and women across the country who graciously filled out my parental loss questionnaire, sent me letters, and shared their memories and deeply moving personal stories in lengthy interviews, I am grateful beyond counting. I found these people through bereavement support group leaders and other mental health professionals, as well as through friends and colleagues who introduced me to interview subjects. These respondents constitute the heart of this book, and I can never repay them for their cooperation, candor, and above all, their trust. To protect their privacy, I have changed all names and identifying characteristics.

I am also indebted to the following researchers, clinicians, and other authorities who gave me interviews, sent me their writings, and in some cases, distributed my questionnaire:

Susan Battley, Psy.D., consulting psychologist and clinical associate professor at the School of Health Technology and Management at the State University of New York at Stony Brook; Michael Beechem, M.S.W., Ph.D., associate professor, Department of Social Work, University of West Florida; R. Benyamin Cirlin, C.S.W., executive director, Center for Loss and Renewal in New York City; Roselyn J. Deyo, L.I.S.W., coordinator of supportive services, NCJW/Montefiore Hospice, Beachwood, Ohio; Kenneth J. Doka, Ph.D., professor of gerontology at the College of New Rochelle, national grief counselor for the Hospice Foundation of America, and past president of the Association for Death Education and Counseling; Kenneth O. Doyle, Ph.D., psychologist, financial planner, and associate professor, University of Minnesota School of Journalism and Mass Communication; Paul R. Duberstein, Ph.D., assistant professor of psychiatry and oncology, University of Rochester School of Medicine, Rochester, New York; Edward J. Dunne, Ph.D., psychotherapist and investigator, New York State Research Foundation for Mental Hygiene, New York State Psychiatric Institute; Glenda Feinsmith, C.S.W., A.C.H.T., N.B.C.C.H., hypno-behavioral therapist and facilitator for grief and loss support groups at Gilda's Club and the Alzheimer's Association in New York City; Marilyn Frankfurt, C.S.W., family therapist, New York City; Jane Greer, Ph.D., marriage and family therapist, New York City; Gerald N. Grob, Ph.D., Henry E. Sigerist Professor of the History of Medicine, Institute for Health, Health Care Policy, and Aging Research and Department of History, Rutgers University, New Brunswick, New Jersey; Evan Imber-Black, Ph.D., director of program development, Ackerman Institute for the Family, New York City, professor of psychiatry at the Albert Einstein College of Medicine, and family therapist; Rea Kahn, R.N., M.P.S., support group coordinator, Alzheimer's Association, New York City; Karen Gail Lewis, Ed.D., A.C.S.W., faculty member, Johns Hopkins University and family therapist; John L. McIntosh, Ph.D., professor of psychology and graduate program director, Indiana University at South Bend; Jane L. Pearson, Ph.D., chief, Preventive Interventions Program, Adult and Geriatric Treatment and Preventive Interventions Research Branch, National Institute of Mental Health, chair, NIMH

Suicide Research Consortium, and adjunct assistant professor at Johns Hopkins University; and Susan Carole Vaughan, M.D., assistant professor of clinical psychiatry at the New York-Presbyterian Hospital, New York City.

For providing leads and sending literature and research, many thanks to Abby Ambinder, Ed.D., family counselor, Aging and Dementia Research Center, Department of Psychiatry, New York University School of Medicine; Alan L. Berman, Ph.D., executive director, American Association of Suicidology; Johnine Cummings, M.S.W.; Bonnie Detzel, editor in chief, *Surviving Suicide Newsletter*; Mariko Foulk, M.S.W., Turner Geriatric Clinic, University of Michigan Geriatrics Center, Ann Arbor; Susan Lakin, M.S.W., and Laura Malee, marketing/public relations associate, NCJW/Montefiore Hospice, Beachwood, Ohio; Ellen Nordberg; Thomas H. Otwell, Media Relations specialist, American Association of Retired Persons (AARP); *ProfNet*, which links journalists to various experts and professional organizations via E-mail; John Richardson, Office of Public Affairs, University of West Florida; Diane Swanbrow, News and Information Services, University of Michigan, Ann Arbor; Nicolle Ugarriza, Zynx Marketing Communications, Miami, Florida; and Debra Umberson, Ph.D., Department of Sociology, University of Texas at Austin. In addition, the reference librarians and other staff members of the Ridgefield Public Library were indispensable to this effort, gathering material, steering me through assorted Internet search anomalies, and answering my last-minute queries on the phone.

I am also grateful to Robert N. Anderson, Ph.D., Mortality and Statistics Branch, Division of Vital Statistics at the Centers for Disease Control/National Center for Health Statistics, who went above the call of demographic duty to pull together, calculate, and patiently explain national census data. Thanks also to Jennifer Reid in the Public Affairs Office at the center, and to Harry Rosenberg, Ph.D., chief of the Mortality Branch.

I owe a particular debt to Dennis P. Gehr, president of Dennis and Company, a consumer research organization in Stamford, Connecticut. Dennis helped me formulate my questionnaire and code the answers, and he then crunched my data, providing me with over three hundred tables of information. Without his informed cheerfulness, my study would not have been possible; he guided me throughout so that I might understand the complicated business of parsing, and interpreting, the data. My thanks also to Steve Davis, of Davis Coding, New York City, and to Janel Prospero, Pro-Tab, for their computational expertise.

Janice Papolos, a sublimely talented writer and dear friend, read every word of my manuscript—several times—summoning the courage to tell me where I had meandered and had committed literary carnage. She also cheered me on with constant telephone calls, without which I could not have managed. Her husband, psychiatrist and researcher Demitri Papolos, M.D., provided much needed knowledge and supportiveness.

I am also indebted to Valerie Enders, a psychoanalyst and cherished friend of long standing, and to Marilyn Frankfurt, a family therapist, writer, and new friend, for reading sections of the manuscript that deal with their fields of expertise. Their suggestions, sensitivity, and remarkable insights were invaluable.

Elaine Markson, my literary agent for nearly fifteen years, is the soul of calm, intelligence, wit, and understanding; she possesses an uncommon perceptiveness about the life and anxieties of a writer. I am blessed to have so esteemed and supportive an advocate and friend.

Robert Miller, publisher of Hyperion, is the godfather of this and my previous three books. When it comes to nurturing writers and championing them and their work, he is in a league of his own. For these and others of his many gifts, I am more appreciative than I can express, counting myself as the luckiest of authors. Jennifer

Barth, my editor, is also of the old literary school; her extraordinary eye and proddings, her professionalism, and her enthusiasm for this book, have, from first to last, been a joy. Peternelle van Arsdale, who became my new editor when Jennifer Barth moved to another company, shepherded the manuscript through production with graciousness and verve. I am grateful, as well, to Alison Lowenstein for her unfailing patience, good will, and quick responses. Thanks also to Jennifer Landers, Hyperion's director of publicity, who is a particular delight; no author ever had a more capable, tireless, and encouraging publishing comrade.

Without the forbearance, aid, and comfort of these treasured friends, I cannot imagine having endured the two years it took to research and write this book: Joyce Burland, Ph.D., and Sascha Burland, Teresa and Mike Capuzzo, Barbara Coats, Erik and Linda Rodgers Emory, Hank and Valerie Enders, Lesley and Dennis Gehr, Terry and Traug Keller, Mary Alice Kellogg, Judy and Aron Hirt-Manheimer, Barbara Manners and Morgan Weber, Herb and Shirley Mitgang, Jane Resnick, Gene and Shirley Secunda, Ada and Philip Quigg, and David and Jane Bryant Quinn.

Special mention must be made of the Connecticut Writer's Bloc (as we call ourselves), my fellow journalistic travelers, who provided their wisdom and understanding.

To the members of my immediate and extended family who bolstered me in this undertaking, my boundless love and appreciation.

But one person is deserving of my highest praise and admiration—my husband, Shel Secunda. He is my greatest champion, my most fearless critic, my first thoughtful reader, my nurturer and dearest companion in life. Because of him, everything is, and has been, possible.

Foreword:
"I've Lost My Reference Point"

When my mother died in 1993, I did not attend her funeral. My absence shocked her grieving friends and most of my acquaintances. The reasons for it were private and complex, understandable, perhaps, only to those who had observed our turbulent attachment over time.

My younger brother and sister, the only surviving witnesses to my childhood (my older sister had died the previous year), knew in grim detail the degree to which my mother and I had never gotten along. But they had had a relatively easier connection to her, had managed to appeal to her better, if not altogether untroubling, maternal self. Indeed, it could be argued that we had entirely separate mothers, wholly dissimilar childhoods, and thus, not the same mother to "lose."

Three children, three differing experiences—pretty routine, as families go. In our case, however, it was the *enormity* of these differences that would set the stage, would serve as preamble, for what became of my siblings and me, individually and collectively, when my mother was no longer among us. And none of that outcome did I foresee at the time of her death.

It was my indomitable mother herself who laid the groundwork for my unorthodox decision to be excused from her ceremonial departure from life. When informed in 1992 that she had what would soon become terminal cancer, she said to my younger sister, Nancy, "Don't tell Vicky." This was not intended to spare me but rather—and I'm guessing here—to spare herself. Given her precarious health, one could hardly blame her if she wished to avoid even the possibility of more distress.

Whatever her reasons, it felt to me like a shunning, a lost last opportunity for us to reach some kind of rapprochement. But in view of our long, difficult history together, I can't say I was surprised.

Certainly I was born at a bad time—the worst time—in her life, for at twenty-seven, she had a great deal to be angry about. Her first marriage, which produced one child (my older sister), had lasted but five years. Her second marriage, to my father, a chronic philanderer, was a disaster from the start. No female, including his daughter, was safe from his indiscriminate sexual attentions.

And yet my mother was crazy about him. Besotted. For in my father she found a mirror image of her young self. Both were beautiful, indulged only children; both were brilliant, possessed of a biting wit, capable of lobbing verbal hand grenades with such dazzling sophistication that even as they drew blood you had to admire the finesse of their delivery; both were much sought after in their Manhattan social set; both were alcoholics. And both found it preposterous to suppose that they weren't, each of them, the center of the universe.

This near-fatal attraction, which produced, in addition to me, my brother, crashed and burned throughout the first decade of my life. Divorce proceedings, initiated at last by my mother, precipitated a five-year custody battle in which my brother and I had to testify in court as to our parental preference (Mom).

In this marital brawl, my father gave his best shots. He could not believe that anyone would elect to leave him. But my mother was, in the end, the more formidable foe. Not even my uncommonly self-absorbed father could best her need, her *hunger*, to be found right.

In the company of such a mother, a child frantic for a comforting word—a child who also happened to capture the unsavory fancy of her father—was in for a rough ride.

Of my mother's four progeny, I was the one she seemed to single out for emotional target practice. Driven, she later said (although not to me), by "a force inside I can't stop," her anger toward me took the form of blistering humiliations, as inescapable as lightning.

My siblings did not seem to evoke in her so great a rage. My more introverted younger brother, who had life-threatening asthma and me to take the heat, was less imperiled. My shy older sister, who had her own fragilities (she would later develop a manic-depressive disorder), was frequently out of the house, visiting her father on weekends.

That left me to become the primary recipient of my mother's considerable frustration—the "strong" one, she often called me, who could "take it." I could not take it. I was a wreck.

The year I turned eleven, my mother's divorce finally came through and she married again, this time much for the better. The man she chose was every inch a "gent"—her highest praise for men—as well as her intellectual equal. Most important, he simply worshipped my mother, and with her produced her fourth and last child, Nancy.

As a *parent*, however, my stepfather was a man of next to no words or emotional expressiveness—except, that is, when he was fired up by a martini (unlike my mother, he could hold his liquor).

Then his frostiness would melt and he would regale us with hilarious stories of his childhood and assorted coming-of-age exploits.

It was during one such evening of rare family conviviality that my mother characteristically broke the happy moment by lacing into me. As a rule, my stepfather did not intervene at such instances. But on this occasion, even he could see that she had gone too far. He wheeled around toward my mother and bellowed *"Leave her alone!"* It was the only time my stepfather ever came to my rescue, and I never forgot it.

After his death in 1981, without him as a steadying force, my mother had no constraints. All her attention narrowed onto her children; she became increasingly demanding, intrusive. She did not know how to let up, saw no reason to, particularly with me.

Of my mother's children, I was the one most easily rattled by her reckless rhetoric. I had an exceptionally good ear for nuance, a nose for trouble. When it came to my mother, I was always tightly wound—braced. It took decades for me not to tremble at the sound of her voice on the telephone, the sight of her handwriting on an envelope.

And I gave her plenty of opportunities to pile on, right through my early adulthood. With a tenacity equal to my mother's, I was determined to persuade her to put down her dukes and take a measure of joy in me. I was not, she was fond of reminding me, the child of her choosing. But she was my *mother*, and I kept hoping she'd warm to the subject. I fervently wanted a mother to approve of me, to advise me and be on my side. Somehow we would put the past behind us and begin anew. We would become friends. (Well. Friendlier.) I didn't give up, no matter how bizarre her accusations. This, when her mother, my adored grandmother, died in January 1969:

"You killed Grandma."

"Oh. How'd I do that?"

"You asked her to make you a hooked rug for Christmas and she was up all night and that's why she got sick and died."

(I scream with laughter, now, recalling this absurd conversation. You had to hand it to us: My mother and I at least provided entertainment value.)

Round and round we went; thrust and parry; her rebuking phone calls and letters, my entreaties for her to lay off. Enthralled, I kept returning for more, blind to the possibility—my therapist had been telling me this for*ever*—that I would always be the outcast. It was my family role. And none of it mattered because I was, on paper anyhow, a grown-up. Clearly I was not even close.

Only in middle age did I begin to *get it*: As long as my mother still had so much power over me, I would never get out of the hole I had dug for myself.

By the time she reached her late sixties and I my forties, I had seen for myself how tough it is to be a divorced parent, and I had remarried happily. Little by little, the arguments between my mother and me struck me as increasingly pointless, indecorous. And then, as she closed in on eighty and I on the half-century mark, I simply stopped. Stopped wanting. Stopped defending. Seeing her only at Christmas, weddings, and funerals, when I would, with little difficulty, and no matter what she said or did, be courteous. Separate. Bombproof.

This fifty-year siege, this mother-daughter *thing*, was over.

It was at this juncture that my mother discovered she was gravely ill and directed Nancy to withhold the news from me. My levelheaded sister wisely chose to ignore my mother's request. It was important for the three of us—my brother, my sister, and me—in our own ways, to try to ease our mother's leavetaking and begin to sort out what would be left of us as a family when she was gone.

In my mother's last arduous months, she never asked for my

help. She had other options. The role of being her favorite child had a high turnover rate, a pattern that would hold to the end. In recent years, she and Nancy had often quarreled, and I was pretty much out of the picture.

There was only one child left to whom she could pledge allegiance—her son—and she summoned him to care for her in the waning weeks of her life. My brother, who had become devoutly religious, eagerly took on the job. He had a longing, I think, to come in from the cold, to make his peace with her, to become the child who was favored at the finish. He was that and more to her, and he took on the caregiving task with grace and nobility. My sister joined him in my mother's final days.

The last thing I wanted at this point was to cause my mother an ounce of anguish. Whatever had transpired between us was of no importance now. And since I knew that she was not alone—she had many friends, the best medical care, her other children by her side—I honored her wish that I keep my distance. The only help I could give was to my brother and sister, whom I periodically telephoned to lend moral support.

When the inevitable call came from Nancy to say that our mother probably would not live out the night, she said:

"What do you want to do?"

"I'm coming," I replied.

Whatever one's history, it is not every day that one's mother actually dies. I felt that attention of some sort should be paid by me while she was still alive, when surely it counted most. I was not at all certain that my presence would be welcome. But I had to risk it, had to extend one last olive branch. I did not want to be left with the remorse of the unfixable—a gesture unmade, at this of all times.

On the last evening of my mother's life, my husband drove me to the retirement community where she lived. I greeted my sister and brother, then anxiously entered my mother's bedroom. She was semicomatose, struggling for breath.

Nancy leaned close to my mother and said, "Vicky's here." My mother's eyes flew open, then clamped shut, a frown knitting her brows. Nancy discreetly withdrew as I sat on a chair next to the nearly spent woman who for so much of my life had terrified me. I could not wrap my brain around the two conflicting images, the *then* of my memory of her, the *now* of her dying. The fire-breather, all gorgeous, uncompromising heat and energy, now worn, inert, felled like a great tree.

And in those moments with her, not knowing what else to do, I stroked her arm—*Oh God, she hates being touched, is this okay?*—trying to give her some comfort. I imagined her opening her eyes and demanding to be lifted against her pillows to have one last talk to put things right between us. A deathbed epiphany. My end of the conversation would have been: "Why could you never meet me halfway? What was that all about?" Her end of the conversation: "Forgive me. I couldn't help myself. It was never you."

My mother did not open her eyes, and after a couple of hours, my husband and I went home. I later learned that she got up once in the night, with my sister's help, to go to the bathroom—stalwart to the last—then went back to bed. At 11:07 P.M., February 13, 1993, she died peacefully in her sleep. She was eighty-two.

I had been preparing for this event my whole life; as a child, I had recurring nightmares that she would die and leave me. And when it finally happened, for one day I felt some melancholy. Still, there was no big bang of grief—I had already done my grieving, years before.

And so I did not go to her funeral, a ceremony designed for those who would want to pay mournful homage—her other children, her grandchildren, her loyal friends—because I would have been out of place and because I had said all my good-byes. Instead I stayed home, feeling, more than anything, a sad sense of relief. We would never again disappoint each other.

What caught me by surprise, and was far more wrenching than the death itself, *was the ripple effect of her dying.* What I never saw coming—this is the part no one warned me about; what can happen long after the funeral is over—was the impact her demise would have on the grown children who survived her. For my siblings and I had not simply suffered a death in the family but, in a sense, a death *of* the family, at least as we had known it.

My mother's death blew a hole in our midst, and when the smoke cleared, nothing was familiar. It was as though I never really *saw* my siblings before. Always there had been our larger-than-life mother—the center of family gravity—in our line of vision, holding us together. All our dealings somehow were mediated by "Mom." Like spokes in a wheel, we couldn't reach each other without in some way going through her, the hub. She was the prism through which we viewed each other and ourselves: Who was "in," who was "out," what Mother said or hadn't said this week, who was going to visit, who wasn't, who had met her expectations, who had fallen short.

Now we were on uncharted ground. She had been the common denominator that defined us as a family. What, literally, would we do without her? What would we have to say to one another in the breach?

In my brother's case, and to my utter astonishment, nothing. Suddenly, and without explanation, my only full sibling, who for most of our lives had relied on me for sisterly affection—I was his "role model," he once said—closed the door on me and all our history together. My phone calls and letters to him went unanswered.

I cannot express how dreadful it was to realize that my mother's rancor toward me lived on in him. It was one thing to have lost my mother ages earlier; to lose my brother now was devastating. From his point of view, this rupture was, and remains, nonnegotiable.

In becoming my mother's last "best" child, my brother could not sustain a tandem love for me. Of her several children, it might be, in the all and all, that he was the most undone by our difficult beginnings, unable thereafter to put all the pieces back together. Or perhaps we never shared anything *but* blood—not enough, at all events, to allow for a real bond.

My husband says that in my youthful yearnings to have a sense of family, I never really saw my brother in my mother's long shadow. I never saw how completely opposite, how differently constructed we are. Now I see him. I have come to accept his need to keep a separate peace, far away from the family and any reminders of our origins.

In my sister's case, however, and to my great delight, the outcome has been extraordinary: The silver lining in all this has been our relationship—she and I are closer than we have ever been.

This did not happen overnight. While Nancy had understood, up to a point, my feelings about my mother, *she did not share them.* Indeed, in nearly every sense we had sprung from entirely separate contexts. I was born into my mother's wretchedly unhappy second marriage; Nancy was born over a decade later into my mother's contented third marriage, the one that took.

In the months after my mother's death, Nancy laid down a single ground rule between us: She would not discuss our mother. "I've lost my reference point," she said, shaken, bereft. "I'm trying to remember more of the good things so I can have a mother to mourn." And I was not about to deny her. Because she is the sibling to whom I was always closest, I did not, do not, want to do anything to fray

the single strand of affectionate kinship left to me from my childhood.

Nancy and I have rediscovered each other over the chasm left by
my mother's death. We have fashioned an entirely new bridge of
affection and mutual regard. She is now the relative to whom I turn
first with good news or bad. She has become the family switchboard,
keeping tabs on and dispensing bulletins to all the members of our
immediate and extended clan.

And I have stopped treating her as "the kid." Recently, I called
her for advice on my balky computer—she is a whiz—and she said,
chuckling, "You know, this is the first time you've ever asked my
opinion about anything. I was always the little sister."

For my part, I have become, by virtue of birth order alone, the
nominal "head" of the family. Each year at Thanksgiving, my husband and I serve a twenty-five-pound turkey to our assorted relatives;
Nancy is always there, my family anchor.

The six years since my mother's death have been the best years
between my sister and me. When we talk, we almost never revisit
the past. Instead we talk about politics, movies, her cats, our over-
lapping menopause, aging. We talk as old friends do, but with the
added bonus of genetic connection.

This was not possible while my mother lived.

One last benefit has accrued to the absence of my mother: It is now
possible also for me *to see her whole*. While she lived, I was so busy
shielding myself from her furies that the long-term advantages of
her sky-high standards were not on my radar. My mother had to
die—had to be still—for me to be able to step back and allow the
advantages to register in unencumbered hindsight. This new acuity
explains a great deal about the person I have become in the aftermath
of my mother. I can vividly recall things I hadn't thought about in
decades.

Like the times I stood with her at the subway entrance on the corner of Eighth Street and Sixth Avenue when I was a child, holding a tin can with a slit in the lid, in drenching rain or snow, collecting money for her many liberal causes. And the times she took us to hear Leonard Bernstein's concerts for young people and to see the New York City Ballet, my passion; she also bankrolled my years of dance and, later, voice lessons. She taught me to collect and reread fine books, to savor the deftly crafted phrase, to be my own most merciless critic—polishing, polishing a project until it is as perfect as I can make it.

It could have been, it is now safe to say, a lot worse.

And so I have changed, have tried to finish the job of putting all the pieces together and of growing up, as a direct result of my mother's death. There is, however, one caveat: A vestige of the bad times, a weakness that also has its roots in the long ago, lingers within me even now. I freeze whenever someone is cutting to me. A stranger would not know of this nanosecond of numbing as I quickly calculate how, or whether, to respond. A stranger would not know it because in ways that I am not proud of, *I am very like my mother*. I can "cut" with the best of them—locution is my turf, as it was hers—although I seldom do, because killing retorts fill me with punishing regret.

Perhaps this unsparing awareness, unclouded by my mother's presence, of the extent to which her good and not-so-good qualities live on in me, is simply where childhood ends. It would be nice to have acquired this awareness while she lived and to have shared it with her. It would be nice to have had a mother I could rely upon to be honest about herself and accepting of me, even as I became separate from her. It would be nice to have had a mother to miss and wish to have back, as I do my grandmother, every day of my life. But that is not the mother I drew. And I am not the daughter she had in mind.

To be sure, mine is not a mainstream inheritance; my husband—whose parents loved and championed him unfailingly, and he them—finds it nearly impossible to comprehend. Where he and I are on more common filial ground, however, is the aftermath of his parents' deaths. As he is the first to admit, while his parents lived he could not, even in middle adulthood, truly grow up. He had to have no fallback position, no one to see him as flawless, to be able to see himself realistically and to stand entirely on his own.

Such memories and ponderings are the genesis of this book. To be without parents in adulthood is a watershed event that happens, sooner or later, to almost everyone. And while each person's story, even within the same family, is unique, one can find certain similar themes among those who live on.

Through two years of research, and having conducted a study of people who have lost one or both parents in adulthood, I have discovered the ways in which my experience is not so different after all. No matter how loving, or ambivalent, or stormy the parent-child relationship, the grown children who survive nearly always undergo a transformation in the aftermath of parental loss and as a direct consequence of it.

It is when they find themselves in uncharted, unprotected territory—with no buffer between themselves and their own mortality—that adult children can, in ways they could not before, shape themselves and their futures. Out of their loss can come unforeseen gain. It's like what happens when you prune a tree: New "shoots" emerge.

And so I have learned from others, as well as for myself, what happens to the ones who are left behind—the changes in their family connections, their relationships, their aspirations, and their identities. Most important, I have learned what it means to be nobody's child and what benefits can be derived from that eventuality.

The result of that exploration is this book, which I dedicate to my sister, Nancy. She was there at our mother's ending, and continues on with me in this amazing new beginning.

—Victoria Secunda, Ridgefield, CT

Introduction
Childhood's End

On a crisp autumn afternoon last year, Richard and Sarah, a couple in their late forties my husband I have known for years, drove up from New York to spend the weekend with us. The Connecticut countryside where we live is at its fiery best in the fall, when the trees ignite with color; it was to witness this exuberant seasonal display—and, of course, to see us—that occasioned our urban friends' visit.

That evening, another close friend, Jessica, fifty-three, a divorcée who lives nearby—and whom Richard and Sarah were meeting for the first time—joined us for dinner. After the meal we settled into the living room to continue our relaxed conversation over coffee. Knowing that I was working on this book, my friends began to reflect upon their own experiences with parental death.

Sarah—who, with Richard, has two grown daughters—lost her mother in an automobile accident when Sarah was ten. "It's the worst thing that ever happened to me," she said evenly, "and I never really got over it. It has informed everything I have ever done, especially in terms of my kids. When they were little, I always felt this urgency to make them independent, to teach them everything I knew—just in case."

Not wishing to monopolize the discussion, Sarah politely turned to Jessica and inquired, "What about you? Are your parents still alive?"

"Sort of," Jessica replied, smiling wearily.

It had not been a good year for Jessica; in fact, this congenial evening was the first real respite she'd had in some time. She had had to move her parents, both in their eighties and in failing health, out of the house of her youth and into an acceptable nursing home, the arrangement of which had entailed months of exhausting leg-work.

I had met her parents often through the years and admired them enormously—her father, a political leftie whose writing career had been demolished in the 1950s by McCarthyism, was a man of beguiling optimism and wry wit; her vivacious mother, the life of every party, seemed never to age. And now they were falling apart—he from advanced emphysema, she from a series of strokes—requiring every spare minute of their only child's time to monitor their medical care and vanishing finances, and to be a reassuring presence. Jessica continued:

> I adore my parents, but I feel as if I'm in a tunnel with no light at the end. No matter what I do, I can't make it better for them— every day there's another crisis. Yesterday I had "words" with my dad's doctor, who's impossible to reach. Today, I tried to ingratiate myself to new members of the nursing staff because my parents are totally dependent on their goodwill. And as I left to come here, I suddenly realized that I can't carry all this weight—these lives and this pain—*for* my parents. I thought: Their lives are ending, and mine is not. I feel so guilty for saying this—I want my life back. But I don't want to let them down. I'm just incredibly torn. I have no sense of where I am.

As I listened to this disarmingly frank exchange between Sarah and Jessica, what struck me was not just the stark differences in their filial perspectives. Rather, the remarkable thing—perhaps because they were each too considerate to take the conversation down a rockier path—was what they did *not* say: that there are times you wish with all your heart you still had one or both parents, and there are other times when, despite a world of love for them, you wish you didn't.

It was apparent to me that Sarah could not fathom Jessica's conflicted anguish. Certainly, when it came to grievous loss, the two women were not in the same league; the sudden death of Sarah's mother so early in life was by any measure the more searing wound, its implications more catastrophic.

On the other hand, the parental loss Jessica ambivalently anticipated was one she would be expected to take in stride. She was, after all, middle-aged, at the top of her career, with children and a wide circle of friends to sustain her. Conventional wisdom dictated that after her parents died, followed by a brief period of mourning, Jessica would easily be able to move on with her life, relatively unchanged by the experience.

But as Jessica was to discover in the months ahead, it would prove to be quite the reverse: Her parents' deaths would change everything.

The Question of Timing

To be without parents in childhood is a cataclysm that most children dread—a heartbreak, for those who have experienced it, that never fully mends. For as tragic (and relatively rare) as untimely death is for a young parent, it is even more terrible for the offspring who

must somehow endure without that parent. Thus it is entirely understandable that when a young parent dies, the immediate sympathetic concerns of friends and relatives tend to cluster around the
children and their survival.

To lose one's parents in adulthood, however, is so "normal" as
to be ordinary—a commonplace event that happens when the offspring are more or less "ready" for it, and therefore, in the Darwinian
scheme of things, it is not a threat to their survival. Parents are
supposed to, and usually do, live long enough to ensure that their
progeny are reasonably self-sufficient, able to feed and support and
think for themselves. Seen in this evolutionary light, parental death
at this point in a child's life is not regarded as particularly calamitous.

It might be no big *Darwinian* deal for adult offspring to be
without parents. But it is an enormous *psychological* and *familial* deal,
the ramifications of which might take years to unfold.

Most adult children somehow muddle through in the aftermath
of their parents' deaths, watching the orbits of their lives and relationships gradually realign, feeling not so much sadness as out of
joint—there's something different about themselves they can't quite
put their finger on. Rarely do they understand what has happened
to them: *the literal end of childhood*, the effects of which are only
incrementally apparent, but which, taken together, form a compre-
hensible whole.

All of which provides some hints as to why few people talk
about—and hardly anyone has conducted serious research about—
what happens *over time* to the adult children who are left behind.

Passing the Torch

Most books and studies dealing even remotely with the subject of
parental death tend to focus either on grief and mourning, or on the

impact of loss upon young children or widowed partners. But scant information is available about the long-term effects of parental death upon the lives and outlooks of adult daughters and sons.

What makes this hole in the scientific and lay literature so puzzling at this moment in millennial history—when the average age of parental death is around seventy—is that *dying* is very much on people's minds. Now that the 76 million baby boomers—the largest generation ever—have, as of 1994, begun turning fifty and losing their parents in record numbers, mortality has become something of a demographic and marketing bonanza, if not a vogue.

Bookstores and libraries are crowded with volumes about geriatric medicine; the manner of death (including "good" or "assisted"); mourning; the "stages" of grief; and everlasting heavenly and celestial wonders. Which makes it all the more stunning that nearly nothing is written about the following crucial issues:

- The long-term impact of parental loss on this same enormous audience of adult children.

- What it means to be *existentially* "alone," without a parental home base, a mother or father to take you in or bail you out (if only in fantasy), no matter what.

- How the sibling bond fares in the absence of the parental "mortar" or, alternatively, what it's like for only children to have no immediate family left.

- How marriages are tested when a husband or wife of a parentless partner is called upon, however subtly, to provide unconditional (read "parental") love for the partner, and, should the spouse be unable to give it, what happens when one or more children are solicited instead.

- The "developmental push" that often occurs among offspring in the aftermath of parental death, when the maturational "buck" abruptly stops with oneself.

According to an unwritten social contract, when parents die their adult children are expected to honor them, forgive them, or—failing these—to be "over it" and get on with their lives.

Would that it were so straightforward. For a great deal depends on a host of variables: what kinds of people your parents were and became; what kind of person you were and have become; how the relationship to your parents ripened or withered over the years; and what kinds of (or whether) siblings accompanied you along the way.

Much also depends on how the relationship to the surviving parent changed after the first parental death; what adjustments and role shifts occurred in the family after the second parent's death; your age then and now; your gender, marital, and child-rearing status; and the time that has elapsed since the deaths.

Variations on a Theme

Consider two people interviewed for this book—a man and a woman (who do not know each other), each of whose parents were Holocaust survivors.

The man, forty-seven, a fund-raiser for Jewish philanthropies, is happily married and on close terms with his four children, his twin brother, and his frail, widowed father. He has pledged his entire career to the perpetuation of Judaism, making it the organizing principle of his life—a living memorial to his late mother, who died a decade ago.

But in terms of his sense of self as a motherless son, he feels he was "never a child," that he could never be anything but perfectly protective of his parents, who had suffered so greatly in concentration camps. All his decisions have been tethered to an abiding determination to appease his parents' sorrows, to make their lives worth living, and to be seen as a credit to them.

And now, in the interval between his mother's death and his elderly father's, he is beginning to ponder what all this has done to him. He questions whether he has any right even to consider his own losses—the professional and personal choices he dared not make because they might have caused his parents additional agony. He feels that his identity is "on hold"—that it is somehow morally inadmissible to think only, or even primarily, of himself. His greatest fear, he says, is that once his father dies, should he allow himself to weep for his parents and for himself, he will never be able to stop. Yet he knows that that day of reckoning is not far off.

Contrast this man's experience to that of the woman, fifty-six, who is single, childless by choice, has no siblings, and whose parents are both dead. This woman has always been and continues to be resolutely irreligious. When she was a teenager she seldom gave her parents—survivors of Auschwitz—anything *but* trouble, as she attempted to have a semblance of a normal childhood against the backdrop of their devastating wartime traumatization. Five years ago, when her mortally ill father was in his seventies (her mother had died the previous year), and at his repeated pleading, she assisted his suicide—anathema to the tenets of Judaism and in particular to Holocaust survivors.

In terms of how she has changed since then, she believes that her decision not to have children—which her parents had taken as a betrayal—is probably a gift to the next generation. Much of the rage she felt about the damage inflicted upon her parents during the war, particularly in terms of their crushed capacity to nurture her, has dissipated since their deaths. Had her parents not died, she says, she would probably still be caught in the undertow of the Holocaust—reacting to her parents' limitations and unable to claim her own life.

As these two examples demonstrate, individual reactions to parental death can differ widely, despite certain superficial similarities.

But in one respect, adult children who outlive their parents are all the same: They relinquish the single role they have played longer than any other—that of being a son or daughter to a living mother or father. Having viewed themselves, if only in part, for so long through their parents' eyes, they often have trouble viewing themselves as separate and unique, beyond their parents' running commentary.

It is no easy matter to lose one's parental point of reference, to set the "child" role aside and step into a new role—that of "adult orphan." It is one thing to wish your parents were alive or dead; it's quite another to actually *be* and *evolve* without them. This transition takes getting used to, and not everybody handles it seamlessly or well. Indeed, some people don't handle it at all, remaining childlike and immature in their relationships with others—for example, by being overly dependent on their partners or friends for love and approval.

When parents die and the mourning period is long over, one can finish growing up or one can grow old—and these are not the same things. The difference can be found in the degree to which surviving offspring are able, over time, to thoroughly digest and become transformed by this new role. It is a journey that has few guidelines or landmarks, no real road map.

This book seeks to provide that road map.

The Adult Orphan Effect

In the chapters ahead, I intend to explore what happens to grown men and women when first one parent, and then the second parent, dies, and in particular how the offspring—and their attachments to others—are altered by that experience. This is not a book about grief and mourning (or their absence), although these subjects will be examined. Nor is the goal of this book to sanctify or vilify parents.

Rather, this is a book about filial life after parental death, when the "family" you used to call "home" no longer exists.

Methodology

I conducted a survey of ninety-four men and women, ranging in age from twenty-one to eighty-three, from across the country and of various ethnic, educational, and socioeconomic backgrounds. All the respondents experienced the deaths of one or both parents in adulthood—that is, after the age of twenty. The median age of the respondents when their fathers died was thirty-eight; the median age when their mothers died, forty-five; the average length of time between the deaths was seven years. Roughly half (48 percent) still have a living parent; the others are full "orphans."

These respondents generously agreed to fill out an eight-page questionnaire (see Appendix), which posed a number of open-ended questions such as:

"What was the nature of your relationship to your [mother or father] when you were growing up?"

"In what ways did your relationship change in the last years of [his or her] life?"

"If one of your parents is still alive, how has your relationship to him or her changed since the death of your other parent?"

"Looking back on your parent(s)'s death, what, if anything, was left unsaid between you and the parent?"

"In what ways has your relationship with your siblings changed since your parent(s) died—are you closer, more distant, or is the relationship unchanged?"

"If you are an only child, how has your relationship to extended family been affected?"

"How has your marriage or romantic attachment—or the absence of a partner—been affected by your parent(s)'s death?"

"If you have no children, how do you feel about being the last of your line at this stage of your life?"

"In what ways have you and/or your siblings 'stepped into the shoes' of your deceased parent—for example, by giving advice, or maintaining family ties, or keeping traditions?"

Based upon the ninety-four respondents' answers to these and other questions, I interviewed fifty-six people for up to two hours each. I also received completed questionnaires (returned too late for computer tabulation) and lengthy letters from another sixteen people, four of whom I interviewed. In total, I gathered detailed information from 110 men and women whose parents died between one and fifty-seven years ago.

The causes of their parents' deaths included "old age" (extreme elderliness), lengthy diseases, sudden death from illness (such as heart attack), suicide, or homicide. Of the deceased parents, the vast majority died five or more years prior to the respondents' filling out questionnaires; this time factor was important in evaluating the data in terms of "recent" versus "long-range" implications of parental death.

In some cases, two or more siblings from the same family agreed to be interviewed or to fill out questionnaires. In other cases, the respondents were only children. I also interviewed people who had experienced the deaths of a spouse or sibling as well as a parent, and who could contrast the meanings to them of those different "losses." In order to gain a broader perspective on their stories—and for comparative purposes—I talked to six additional people who lost one or both parents in early childhood or adolescence.

In addition, I read numerous books and studies, and interviewed leading researchers and clinicians, about the following topics: parent-child and sibling attachments throughout the lifespan; death and bereavement; suicide; developmental psychology; family dynamics; and wills and estates.

From these interviews and readings, and based primarily on the findings of my survey, I have reached the inescapable conclusion that parental death is a defining event for adult offspring that, with regard to its impact on one's sense of self, often eclipses the variables of marital status, career achievement, being a parent oneself, or the cause and manner of parental death.

To lose one's parents in adulthood is to find oneself at a unique crossroads: a juncture that inspires a reevaluation of one's life, relationships, and choices in ways that simply were not possible before.

Far from being an insignificant event, parental death is *the* milestone—provides *the* indelible line of demarcation—that enables adult offspring to begin to determine whether or not they are, or still must learn how to be, truly grown up.

The Last Growth Spurt

In talking to, or reading the written questionnaire comments of, grown sons and daughters of deceased parents, certain key themes emerged, among them:

A Sense of Relief and Freedom

The most striking finding among my survey respondents was an unexpected feeling of freedom in being able to answer primarily to themselves, rather than to their parents, for their actions, and of their being emboldened by that freedom.

The relief (which for some people was euphoric) of making decisions for the first time in their lives without any thought of parental approval or disapproval was especially compelling. This sense of being "set free" occurred irrespective of the quality of the parent-child relationship or the manner of parental death. To take a dramatic example, several respondents had been members of various Roman Catholic orders, only to emerge from these communities after the deaths of one or both parents to marry and embark on new careers.

A Changed Relationship to the Surviving Parent

Many people remarked that it wasn't until the first parent died that they really got to know the parent who remained. One man, for instance, said that his father was the more charismatic parent who "captured the family agenda," which rendered his more reticent mother all but invisible. Once his father died, however, the mother "came out of her shell" and took center stage in her son's affectionate attentions.

Other people reported that a once-abrasive or even abusive parent became, with the death of the other parent, "softer," more approachable, and in a few cases, even remorseful for his or her hurtful behavior when the respondents were young.

However, in a large minority of cases, the relationship to the surviving parent deteriorated markedly. As one person briskly put it, "The wrong one died." Without the ameliorating presence of the more beloved parent, the negative qualities of the surviving parent either were more obvious to the respondent or became full-blown, in a sense filling up the vacuum of the parent who was "lost."

The Importance of Surrogate Parents

Several respondents made an impassioned point of the enormous influence a deceased surrogate parent had had on their lives. In these cases, a stepparent, or aunt or uncle, or parent-in-law, had spent more time with, or lavished more affection upon, the offspring than had the biological parents. As a result, the surrogate parents were more valued by the respondents, their loss more keenly felt.

Other people said that the need for a "mother" or "father" figure persisted long after their parents' deaths—someone to whom they could turn in times of crisis or triumph, as they once had their parents.

Significant Shifts in Sibling Ties

According to researchers on the sibling bond, the most important predictor of sibling closeness after parental death is the quality of the relationship prior to the death. However, among my respondents, this predictor did not always hold—there were major shifts in their relationships to one or more siblings as a direct consequence of parental death, often regardless of the previous quality of these attachments.

In several instances, connections to siblings that had seemed irredeemably broken were repaired with the deaths of one or both parents. One woman said that her father had always acted as a wedge between her and her sister, playing them off against each other. After the father died, however, the sisters were able to reach an amicable truce specifically *because* the father's divisiveness and manipulation were out of the equation.

In other cases of sibling estrangement, a ne'er-do-well sibling—say, a drug addict or a "family disgrace"—turned over a new leaf. Jolted by a parent's terminal illness, these "bad" siblings returned to the family fold and were of inestimable help to "good" caretaking siblings, which paved the way for their renewed closeness.

However, all was not rosy for other respondents and their siblings; several said that they "drifted away" or became "distant" from one or more of their brothers and sisters. The reason, in most cases: Dormant rivalries or resentments no longer had to be suppressed now that the parental "glue" was gone.

The Final Accounting: Wills and Estates

When it came to the settlement of their deceased parents' affairs, most siblings—even in the event of uneven financial bequests—were loath to raise a ruckus over the division of money or property. In the interests of retaining some sense of family, the majority of respondents were unwilling to make a federal case over who got more or less of anything.

Still, there were alarming, lingering, and painfully raw ruptures on this score among a subset of respondents. A number of people reported that they had had "problems" with siblings (as well as other family members) regarding parental estates—for example, a sibling who absconded with family treasures, or who had persuaded a dying parent to change his or her will to exclude the other siblings from a bequest.

Unearthing Family "Secrets"

A surprising number of people remarked in interviews that a deceased parent had led a "secret" life of which they or their siblings had been unaware prior to the death. Stories of the parents' extra-marital lovers, illegal business dealings, even the respondent's own illegitimacy, emerged, culled by the respondents from conversations with, and letters from, immediate or extended family or the parents' friends or colleagues. The posthumous parents these offspring discovered were not the parents they thought they had known, and this unsettling awareness caused the offspring to rethink what the parents had meant to them.

Interestingly, reactions by the respondents and their siblings to these secrets served either to bring the offspring closer together—confirming various "hunches" each had had about the parents—or, by virtue of whether or not they uniformly "believed" the secrets, to drive them further apart—underscoring their differing filial "loyalties."

Reassessed Intimate Partnerships

Another striking finding was the large number of people who reported that their marriages and partnerships had grown substantially stronger in the aftermath of parental death. This new harmoniousness was not simply an artifact of eradicated "in-law" or "torn loyalties" issues (which in some cases were deathless); nor was it simply that, at this point in many couples' lives, the nest was finally empty. Rather it was that these respondents seemed to make a greater emotional investment in their romantic attachments, investments that were, for the most part, largely rewarded.

But in some cases their marriages and partnerships weakened or were scuttled. Parental death catapulted these offspring into scrutinizing their relationships and seriously considering whether or not they wanted to spend the rest of their lives with their partners—life being, they now realized, astonishingly short.

On a brighter note, other people *got* married as a consequence of their parents' deaths. They felt that they had moved to the head of the developmental class—that they were no longer "kids," which "dating" or "fooling around" represented. They wanted to settle down—to start, and to become part of, a new family to replace the family of their childhoods, and to ensure generational continuity.

Setting New Career Goals

Another strong finding in the survey results was that many people changed careers as a direct result of their parents' deaths. Some people felt that they now had the opportunity to follow their own "dreams," rather than those of their parents for them. Others said their career changes were sparked by a fervent desire to make a lasting mark on or contribution to the world—relative, that is, to their occupations prior to their parents' deaths. Still others were driven to become more financially self-sufficient and professionally focused.

What seemed to motivate most of these career changes was that the respondents no longer were concerned about pleasing or displeasing their parents—the credit, or blame, for their success and failures fell almost entirely on their own shoulders.

Altered Friendships

A significant percentage of people said that their friends were now much "more precious" to them, or that their friendships had become "qualitatively better" since their parents' deaths. For example, several respondents commented that they were drawn to people who also had lost one or both parents. "People who haven't been through it don't know what it's like" was a typical response.

Others talked of friends' becoming their surrogate families or stand-ins for the "best friend" (mother or father) who had died. And several childless respondents said that they had become surrogate "uncles" or "aunts" to the children of their closest friends.

A Different "Legacy" for One's Children

The question I posed that seemed to evoke the most ardent reaction from respondents who are themselves parents had to do with how they wanted to be remembered by their children.

Even among people who had had a reasonably good, or enviably affectionate, attachment to their parents, there was a profound wish to leave a singular legacy. Having received certain blessings from their parents in childhood, decades later the offspring had other blessings they wanted to confer. This was one of the reasons that many of the respondents said their relationships to their children had changed significantly.

Other people, whose children were born after the respondents' parents died, spoke poignantly of the "grandparent gap"—that is, they had missed out on their parents' guidance on child rearing, the sharing of parental joys and sorrows.

Respondents who had had wretched relationships with their deceased parents were particularly intent upon providing an emotional legacy to their children that was the polar opposite of their parents' to them. These respondents were vigilant about being held accountable for their own parenting mistakes. They did not want to repeat history by bequeathing similarly frustrating and painful "loose ends" to their children, and were willing to do whatever was necessary to avoid it.

On Uncharted Territory

As these themes and survey highlights make clear, losing a parent in adulthood is anything but a "minor" event in most people's lives. On the contrary; it changes everything. To rework Sophocles, parental death "teaches the steadiest minds to waver."

This mental "wavering" aptly describes my friend Jessica, mentioned at the beginning of this chapter. A few days after she spent the evening at my house last fall, her mother died painlessly in her sleep. At first, Jessica appeared to be untouched by the event, other than feeling an overwhelming sense of relief; her mother's grueling medical ordeal, and Jessica's draining caretaking of her, were over.

Eight months later, however, Jessica seemed to be on increasingly shaky ground. She recounted for me an experience that neatly summed up the impact her mother's death was having upon her, an impact that was slowly reshaping the contours of Jessica's sense of self and her footing in the world. She said:

> Recently I had a medical scare which turned out to be nothing. I was having blinding headaches, reminiscent of Mother's stroke symptoms, and I raced to my doctor, who ran some tests. On the way home I was terrified, desperate to be comforted. I thought: Who can I talk to about this? The first person I thought of was my mom; I couldn't call her, obviously. Then I thought of my dad, but he's too sick. And never did I so wish I had a sister. So I called my daughter. And as I dialed her number, it struck me that when my mom was dying, I was the "parent" for her, and here I was asking my thirty-year-old child to be my "parent." The point is, all my connections are suddenly blurred, the family roles unclear. It feels so strange to be in this place in my life. It's not just that I miss my mom; it's that I don't really know who I am or where I fit in.

Jessica is finding out for herself what many of my survey respondents already know. In losing their parents and regaining their emotional bearings—and in the reshuffling of the family hierarchy—

adult offspring frequently discover pieces of themselves they hadn't been aware of, hadn't *needed*, before.

The evolution of this self-discovery is set into motion when first one, then the other, parent dies—and the offspring who are left behind are on their own.

LOSING YOUR PARENTS
Finding Your Self

Part One

The Changing of the Guard

CHAPTER
1 Point of Departure: When One Parent Dies

I would think of it later as a movie in my head. It would start with the day my father first got sick, November 15, and end the day he died, Christmas Eve. And in between there's this upsetting but very compelling movie, with my mom falling apart, me taking care of my dad and my kids, my husband consulting all kinds of doctors, my brother and friends and nurses running in and out of the house—and then suddenly, they all go away. That was very disorienting; one day you have a father, and the next day, it's over. In six weeks, we went from my parents being the responsible generation to my husband and me being in charge. And I thought, you know, they die in the end. And you have to figure out a way to make sure that when they die, you're going to be okay.

—Maryanne, forty-two

It has been eight years since Maryanne's vibrant father, a trim, retired military man, died at the age of sixty-seven in her Maryland house. As she begins to tell me about the experience, it's apparent from the rush of color that spreads across her neck that she's ill at ease, as if she were speaking out of turn.

Maryanne had been reluctant to grant me this interview, doing so only at the persistent behest of a mutual friend. "I may not be a good candidate for your project," she had hedged when I called her to arrange an appointment. It wasn't just that she was worried about anonymity, although, being a private sort, that was a concern. Rather, she said, it was that her story was hardly the stuff of high drama, nothing—compared to friends of hers who had endured one tragedy after another—that would leave a gaping wound.

But as we continued to chat, she slowly warmed to the subject. It was dawning on her, now that she thought about it, that her father's dying and death had been a pivotal period—*the* pivotal period—in her life. In finally consenting to talk into my tape recorder about it, she hoped to make greater sense of it to herself—to articulate the amorphous dilemma posed by her father's absence and tack a label to it.

The way Maryanne remembers it, so swift had been her father's decline—and so unforeseen the aftermath—that it was like a hurricane. All she could do was watch it happen, as it ineluctably bore down on the picture-perfect, three-generation family that had defined and sheltered her for so long.

After her father was diagnosed (he had a galloping form of incurable cancer, the doctors said), Maryanne's distraught mother—a well-meaning but high-strung woman in the best of times—was in no shape to nurse her husband by herself at their own house across town. She seemed to be paralyzed. She simply could not cope, neither with the idea of her husband's impending demise nor with the queasy, minute-by-minute details of his disintegration. Maryanne's unmarried younger brother, who lived an hour's drive away, was never one for handholding, especially for sick people.

Thus it fell to Maryanne, the apple of her father's eye, to provide a temporary, ministering harbor—she could not bear for him to end his days in a hospice—as they all rode out the storm together. And when the storm passed, in the weeks and months that followed her father's funeral, the "family" of her childhood and young adulthood would be washed away.

It was this feeling of being set adrift that bewildered her, that she could never have forecast, given her idyllic background. She had been raised, she said, in "a close-knit, loving, typical middle-class family; I have no horror stories from my childhood." Even in her adulthood, as the family expanded to enfold her husband, a successful architect, and three children, they all stayed in close contact, visiting each other weekly and talking on the phone nearly every day.

But looking back now, Maryanne could see that the "ideal" family of those years contained barely visible hairline fractures that would snap when her father was no longer among them.

"My dad was the charismatic key family figure around which we all revolved, especially my mother," Maryanne recalled. "It was clear to everyone that he was the main event. And when he died, that was the defining change in our family." She continued:

> My mother became very depressed and angry because I had something she had lost—a husband and young children, a "family." She also lost her status; she had been an army officer's wife, and now she was a widow with no job or "rank." That's when my relationship to her totally shifted—we weren't really close anymore. Within a year, she sold her house and moved to Arizona. It made me realize that she wasn't really that connected to us—that she could so easily leave us. As for my brother and me, some tensions had built up between us over the years; after my dad died, my brother and I went our separate ways. I thought I was a grownup, but I didn't have a clue—it was like all the rules changed.

At first, Maryanne and her husband and children pulled together, even as her mother withdrew into herself and her separate life three thousand miles away. But as time went on, Maryanne began to take stock of what was to become of herself as a wife, a mother, and as an adult. All outward appearances of stability to the contrary, she felt a nagging sense of uncertainty, a stealthy vulnerability, the way an immigrant feels when uprooted from the "homeland" and set down upon a foreign shore.

Maryanne examined the terrain of her life and did not like what she saw. A college dropout when she married, she was utterly dependent upon her husband, who, despite his lofty professional standing, could, just like *that*, lose everything or—God forbid—up and die on her. Her kids wouldn't be kids forever. She imagined herself one day ending up like her mother, stripped of her pedigree—title, social position, parental indispensibility, family proximity—too defeated to begin all over again.

And so Maryanne made a series of decisions that would shake the foundations of her life. She went into therapy to sift through the pieces of her suddenly compromised self; she enrolled at a local university and got her undergraduate degree; she began to write essays, submitting them to local newspapers. Her articles were repeatedly rejected but ultimately led to a reporting job.

And through it all, her husband wondered what had happened to the thoroughly domesticated woman he thought he had married. Says Maryanne:

My husband and I had had different periods of closeness and distance. But after my father died, I kind of changed the terms under which we had married, and it presented a lot of challenges to our relationship. For a while, I questioned whether we would be enough for each other over the long haul. But to our great credit, we were able to weather it and continue to grow in the same direction. It took a long time to get from that place to this, let me tell you. I'm not sure it would have happened if my father were still alive.

At the end of the interview, Maryanne walked me to the door, making one last pensive reference to the "anonymity thing." Then, with a dismissive wave of her hand, she laughed and said, "Oh, what the hell. I'm still not convinced of the usefulness of my story. But if you think it can help someone, be my guest."

"I May Not Be a Good Candidate for Your Project"

It was a line, variations of which I was to hear again and again: "I don't think I fit into your project" or "My story is so different" or "Everyone loses their parents—what's to discuss?" or "I thought I'd have nothing to say, and here I am, two hours later, going on and on."

There was an air of apology, even embarrassment, behind such comments—a sense that, in their "normal" experience of parental death, or in their "minority view" about it, the offspring were somehow ineligible for, or unworthy of, journalistic inquiry.

It was the very banality of their "losses"—however horrific the specifics of the deaths might have been at the time—that often required considerable persuasion on my part to reassure my study participants of the significance of their experiences.

And time after time, after an initial awkwardness—a kind of conversational speed bump—the stories that poured forth were of a riveting piece: The respondents were fundamentally, in all the inlets of their lives, no longer the people they had been.

But what was it *exactly* that was different about them? What were they now that they had not been before their parents died? Given the hugely varied circumstances of their lives and perceptions, could one even categorize it, give their experience a unifying name?

The Language of "Loss": A Definition of Terms

To my way of thinking, such questions hadn't been adequately addressed in most of the psychological, scientific, and lay literature I read. Only a handful of people had done any work on the lingering impact of parental death on the psyches and decision-making processes of adult offspring. Specifically, there was a stunning dearth of information on *how the identities of adult children change when their parents are gone.*

What I found instead was a surfeit of information about "bereavement," "mourning," and "grief"—some of it laced with absolutes ("shoulds" and "musts") or euphemisms ("lost" or "loved ones")—terms that fell just short of, or very wide of, what I was actually hearing from most of my study participants.

For example, the word *lost,* as defined by Webster's Dictionary, means "no longer possessed" or "ruined or destroyed beyond reach or attainment," or "denied." As I knew from personal experience— and was learning from some respondents—to have no parents in adulthood is not always a "loss" per se. In certain instances, such as the demise of an elderly mother or father after a lengthy, agonizing, incurable illness, it might be a gain.

Then there is the term *loved one,* which, when used to describe the deceased, seems to make a very great assumption in its blanket application to people who might be uniformly *dead* but who might not have been, in life, uniformly loved or lovable.

As for the words *bereavement, mourning,* and *grief,* many learned and highly esteemed investigators and theorists take the position that varying reactions by adult offspring in the aftermath of their parents' deaths can be collapsed into one or another of these terms—a position about which I have reservations. In my view, these terms, when applied to adults whose parents have been dead for several years, are wanting.

Webster's defines *grief* as "deep and poignant distress caused by or as if by bereavement," and *mourning* as "the act of sorrowing." To be sure, such wrenching emotions characterized many of the people I talked to—for some, their sadness continues unabated. There were those, in fact, who had *keened* when their parents died, their mothers and fathers altogether "loved ones," their absence still deeply "mourned," often in "complicated" (read "unresolved") ways.

Nevertheless, and depending upon the source, the use of such terminology seemed on occasion to carry within it a seed of rebuke. If you didn't "mourn" your parents' deaths at a certain time, or in a certain way, or according to a predictable, orderly progression; if you did not feel that in your parents' deaths you had "lost" them; if you didn't miss or think of them as "loved ones" and hadn't felt an ounce of "guilt" after they died; you might be a candidate for all manner of psychological ailments down the road.

In reading this literature, I felt there had to be a less freighted vocabulary with which to describe the *fact* of parental death that would make room for the very mixed bag of feelings and adaptations *long after the fact* that adult offspring often encounter.

There was one term in the literature that accurately describes the changed status of men and women whose parents have died: "adult orphan." Admittedly, this is a term that in itself is charged, and that, upon hearing it, caused some of my respondents to wince. The phrase unavoidably conjures up the image of a geriatric Oliver Twist, draped in rags and wretchedly abandoned to a nineteenth-century workhouse, timorously raising his bowl to plead, "Please, sir, I want some more."

Still, in the context of this book, and in keeping with its true definition, *orphan* pretty much says it. According to *The Compact Edition of the Oxford English Dictionary*, the word means "a fatherless or motherless child"; Webster's defines it as "deprived by death of one or . . . both parents." This is a situation that can happen to anyone at any stage of life—for obvious reasons, I have added the qualifier *adult.* (I have also, in the interests of specificity, further qualified the term by referring to adults who have one living parent as *semi-orphans.*)

Withal, the term "adult orphan" is not one that falls trippingly off the tongue. Nor is it heard in everyday conversation. And one reason it isn't—linguistic hairsplitting aside—may be because the subject of filial life after parental death has many built-in, muzzling prohibitions.

The Last Taboo

Journalist I. F. Stone once wryly observed that "funerals are always occasions for pious lying." Humorists seem to have less difficulty openly discussing the ironies of death than most people, for whom the topic is socially off-putting, to be broached sparingly and only in the most reverential tones. Self-censorship in this regard is particularly true of adult orphans, especially those whose lives without their parents have taken an upturn.

For one thing, it is not regarded as seemly to profit, financially or emotionally, from the deaths of one's parents; nor is it the done thing, biblically speaking, to say bad things about the deceased. No less prohibited is the candid acknowledgment by adult "children" that they were not as grown-up as they had thought—that they had either stumbled *or* soared as a consequence of one or both parents' deaths.

Death itself—especially now, at the birth of the twenty-first century, when the life expectancy of Americans stands at an all-time high of 76.5 years—also appears to be taboo, something that happens to *other* people, under no circumstances calling attention to itself. As social historian Philippe Ariès points out in his book *Western Attitudes Toward Death: From the Middle Ages to the Present*, in the old days, people died out loud—at home, among their families and friends, and then in public, their corpses carried conspicuously and lavishly through the streets. These days, writes Ariès, "death is so frightful that we dare not utter its name." Ideally, it is to occur when one is alone, or among caregiving strangers, and thereafter to be "hushed up."

The "death taboo" is also alive and well in the unlikeliest of places—that is, among many mental health workers and investigators, for whom the topic of adult orphanhood would logically seem to be their professional meat and potatoes. In reality, the matter barely raises a scientific pulse. The first systematic study of the psychodynamic reactions of adult offspring to the deaths of their parents did not see publishing light until 1979. It might be, as Miriam S. Moss and Sidney Z. Moss of the Philadelphia Geriatric Center have written, that the subject is "so painful that we as researchers and clinicians flee from it to protect ourselves, to escape facing our unresolved guilts and frustrations."

All of which gives explanatory muscle to the reluctance of Maryanne, mentioned at the beginning of this chapter, who was in no hurry to be interviewed about her circuitous, misunderstood, but ultimately liberating adaptation to life without her father. Thus, too, the initial hesitation of many other people in my sample. It was as if they considered their "growing" pains to be insignificant, their identity struggles somehow lacking in gravitas.

Whatever the reasons for their hesitation, the fact remained that *none of my respondents had ever been asked about such things before.* Until my questionnaire showed up in their mailboxes, they had never been encouraged, nor felt entitled, even to consider how, or whether, their lives had been changed by their parents' deaths.

There was another term in the literature that squared with the reticence I was observing among my respondents: "disenfranchised grief." This term was coined by psychologist Kenneth J. Doka, Ph.D., professor of gerontology at the College of New Rochelle in New York and past president of the Association for Death Education and Counseling.

As Dr. Doka conceptualizes it, grief is "disenfranchising" when it cannot be freely expressed or when it is not socially sanctioned. This can certainly be the case for many adult orphans who, in the aftermath of their parents' deaths, undergo an identity crisis. Says Dr. Doka,

> If you're ten years old and your forty-year-old mother dies, everyone realizes that this is a terrible problem. But if you're forty years old and your seventy-five-year-old mother dies, nobody seems to realize that that's still a problem. I think the key issue is that whenever a death occurs, families are systems, so it's like pulling a piece out—something's going to happen. And one of the things that's going to happen is that the surviving family member is going to change.

How the offspring changes is the cardinal question. And should the death result in the survivor's unexpected growth—should it happen, as one respondent bluntly put it, "over the parent's dead body"—well, that is not something you shout in a crowded room. Nevertheless, that is often the taboo-riven reality.

Another signal question is how the family *itself* changes, beginning with the offspring's attachment to the remaining parent and, in turn, to siblings, children, and extended kin, like so many pieces in a mobile.

The Past as Prologue

But before delving into the intricacies of these and other changes, it is necessary to set the stage by giving a brief synopsis—a "crash course," if you will—of what leads up to them. Here the discussion will focus on three key issues:

- The quality of the parent-child relationship to begin with.
- How the attachment developed over time, as the child separated from his or her parents and entered adulthood.
- The emotional note on which the connection physically ended—that is, the tenor of the relationship when the parent died.

The Influence of Parents in Childhood

On the subject of the parent-child tie over the life span, a number of towering authorities on human development—such as Sigmund Freud, Carl Jung, Erik Erikson, John Bowlby, and Margaret Mahler—have contributed a number of groundbreaking theories that have changed the way we think about ourselves in relation to our families of origin. I will confine myself for the moment to two of these authorities: Freud and Bowlby.

"Death Wish"

Because of the pioneering nature of Freud's work over one hundred years ago, he is often the starting point in any discussion of how the behavior of parents—and later, their deaths—affects their off-spring.

In brief, Freud believed that parent-child conflict plays a huge role in children's personality development, and that children have an unconscious wish for the death of the same-sex parent. It isn't that children *really* want to put their parents out of commission—rather, they want to reduce parental competition and domination. To that end they engage in a struggle to overthrow the parents by becoming aggressive themselves, unseating one parent and identifying with the other. Hence, life, death, and the mother-father-child triangle are inextricably interwoven in the parent-child bond.

One of Freud's most enduring legacies is the theory that an-guishing childhood experiences, although not necessarily dooming one's fate, go a long way toward impeding "normal" psychological development. Freud reasoned that children, out of love for or fear of their parents, often repress their painful memories of these ex-periences. But the memories do not altogether vanish; rather, they become disguised—out of mind, but not out of sight. They percolate *down here*, in the child's subconsciousness, only to bubble up *over there*, in the child's self-defeating behavior.

The "repetition compulsion," for instance, in which a person unconsciously reenacts distressing childhood events again and again, is an example of Freud's insights about the role of the unconscious in adult life. For example, you said that you would never marry someone like your monosyllabic father, only to find, to your immense surprise, that that's *exactly* what you did. Unconsciously, you might have hoped that this time you could change the outcome—you'd get your spouse, the strong silent type, to actually talk to you.

To take another example, you said that you'd be a better mother to your kids than your unpleasable mother was to you, only to find that whenever they did something vaguely reminiscent of her, you responded to them *exactly* the way you once did toward her—and then some. Maybe you overreacted by becoming enraged over minor infractions, doling out punishments that did not fit the "crimes." Or maybe you went in the opposite direction—in trying desperately to please, and in being terrified of losing your children's love, you were unable to set any limits. Either way, you were behaving like the child you once were.

We unconsciously duplicate the unhappy past, Freud believed, not because we liked it but because it is *familiar*. In transferring our childhood emotions onto our current relationships, we make them recognizable, in which case we can know exactly what to do, even if it isn't all that good for us.

Freud got us thinking about how the unremembered past has a sneaky way of showing up in the present. But he also got us thinking about triangles; in particular, how any two-person relationship in the family always has an influence on a third family member, just as the third member—even in absentia—influences the other two.

For instance, if your sister informs you that your dad is not thrilled about something you've said or done, this is not just between you and your opinionated sister; it's between the two of you *plus* your father. This is an example of what family therapists refer to as "triangulation"—a three-way stretch that has everything to do with how adult children sort out the emotional legacies of their deceased parents and their own torn loyalties.

Survival Mechanisms

Among Freud's loyal opponents is British psychiatrist and psychoanalyst John Bowlby, who advanced the idea that "attachment behavior"—informed both by biology and by childhood experience—explains human interactions throughout life.

Bowlby believes that when parents provide their children with a "secure base" of love and encouragement, the children can confidently go out into the world because they know—and take for granted—that they have a safe place to which they can return in times of trouble. This secure base becomes the model for children's healthy attachments later in life, because the child has "internalized" it and made it his or her own.

However, should this "base" not be so secure—should it, in fact, be highly conditional, riding on the child's unwavering love and obedience—then the child will come up with strategies to reduce the risk of parental rejection or harm.

Contrary to Freudian theory, these strategies, as Bowlby explains them in *Attachment and Loss*, are not necessarily "pathological," nor are they signs of "regression." Rather, they make evolutionary sense: They are resorted to in times of crisis to boost the odds of survival.

If, for example, the parent is weak or overwrought or rejecting or abusive, the child, depending on his or her "disposition," might respond in one of three insecure ways: by being excessively concerned with the welfare of others ("compulsive caregiving"); or by clinging to the parent or being demanding ("anxious and ambivalent" attachment); or by becoming "immune" to loss and "needing" nobody ("independence of affectional ties").

Parental treatment does not just affect the child's behavior; it also affects the child's *thinking*. Bowlby argues that children develop "working models" of their parents and of themselves in relationship to their parents. For instance, "insecurely attached" children learn to distrust their own perceptions and, instead, believe what their *parents* say about them—persuaded, if not totally convinced, that the parents are correct. Any new information about the parents, or about themselves, that does not confirm the original model will be excluded.

Although these behaviors and thought processes can be altered by experiences outside the family, they often persist throughout adulthood *despite* those experiences.

Let's say your relationship to your parent was entangled and you were overly protected or enjoined never to stray far from home. You might, in adulthood, give no thought to your own desires but, rather, constantly tend to others who appear to "need" you.

Perhaps your attachment to your parent was conflicted—part loving, part strained, because the parent was neglectful or hyper-critical. You might, in adulthood, react to lovers or friends the same way you did toward your parent, feeling alternately fearful, angry, or guilty whenever they seem to be pulling away from you.

Or maybe your parent was cold or brutal or unavailable (as in the case of abandonment). You might, in adulthood, have difficulty getting close to anyone—or, having done so, find that even the hint of rejection causes you to feel either imperiled or ready to do combat.

These habits of the heart, Bowlby believed, can be traced back to early childhood family experience, when offspring receive their first lessons in how to survive when the world comes crashing down.

Parallel Lives: The Mutual Influence of Parents and Children

As much as parents wield tremendous power over their children, it must be remembered that so, too, do children wield great power—if only by knowing *precisely* what sensitive buttons to push—over their parents. Offspring are not simply acted upon; they act as well, evoking either parental love or anger. For this reason, parents and children never *entirely* separate—the "cord" between them is never completely severed. To the contrary; parents and their progeny continue to affect one another in a circle of actions and reactions that can reverberate long after the parents die.

In ways, children always need their parents, even into the off-springs' middle age; and many parents, including those in advanced old age, remain supportive of and enormously interested in their children's welfare and survival.

This mutual need was examined by Margaret Hellie Huyck and Susan Frank in a fascinating intergenerational study of adult children and their parents. The most important finding in this study was that *both generations looked to the other for validation*—for the adult children, that they were lovable or admirable or acceptable, and for the parents, that they got reasonably good marks in family matters and that, at the end of the day (or a life), their children appreciated them.

Psychoanalyst Jessica Benjamin expands upon this theme of mutual validation in her book *The Bonds of Love*. She makes the strong case that one cannot fully *be* a whole person without being seen as such by another whole person. "[T]he issue," writes Benjamin, "is not how we become free of the other, but how we actively engage and make ourselves known in relation to the other."

This mutual recognition, or the potential for it, vanishes when a parent dies. The adult child who has never known, or felt known by, the parent might feel at loose ends when this recognition is no longer possible. As one forty-six-year-old woman put it, "I waited, without success, until the end to hear from my father that he valued and loved me. I never told him how much I needed to hear about his feelings, and even if I had told him, I'm not sure he would have understood. Now I'll never know."

The Sequel to Parental Death: On "Losing" and Being "Lost"

The thing about death—any death—is that it's so *final*. Nothing that led up to it can be revoked or altered; there's no going back for a rewrite. Which is not to say that survivors don't try, if only in rueful or baffled hindsight. In answer to the question "Looking back on your parent(s)'s death, what, if anything, was left unsaid between you and the parent?" most of my respondents had reams to report.

Some people wished that their parents had told them more about themselves—what they had hoped to accomplish in their lives, whether or not their dreams had come true, what mistakes they had made along the way that they might have regretted. Others were haunted by the fact that they never said a proper good-bye, and hadn't really expressed to their parents how much they appreciated them.

Still others were frustrated by the reality that neither they, nor their parents, had been willing or able to hash out their differences. And then there were those who remarked that they and their parents had said too much—as one person put it, "Brutal honesty on both sides was the name of the game."

These comments were registered by both men and women, of various ages, whose parents died in various ways—ranging from suicide in their forties to peaceful expiration while asleep in their nineties—and in various decades past, from the 1920s onward. Common to the respondents' histories was the fact that many of them were still working on their relationships with their deceased parents, rooting around for information about who the parents had been and who they themselves once were.

At the heart of this search was the wish to continue a "dialogue" with the parent that had been "derailed" due to the parent's death. According to psychologist Louise J. Kaplan in her book *No Voice Is Ever Wholly Lost*, "However old or young a person is when a parent dies, the response to this traumatic event will always reflect the developmental issues and conflicts the person was struggling to resolve and work through when the calamity struck."

The manner in which adult children adjust in the aftermath of their parents' deaths may turn on how the relationship itself ended—

that is, whether or not the offspring and their parents had made peace with one another, parting on relatively harmonious terms.

Good Endings

It's hard to adjust to doing without a well-thought-of parent, and some people never get used to it. Many of the people I interviewed were made poignantly aware of their parents' absence each time something wonderful—or dreadful—happened to them. They grew wistful at not having one or both parents to witness their joys, such as a professional coup, or a wedding, or the birth of a child; they also wished that they still had their parents to advise them on such personal matters as menopause, or ruinous financial reverses, or the travails of raising troubled (or troubling) children.

Yet these offspring managed to carry on, unparented, with few or no loose ends to mire them in the past or to trip them up in their current relationships to family members and others. Their attachments to their parents had been "secure"—evolving and changing as the parent and child each evolved and changed.

For this reason, their parents' deaths did not shake their sense that they could trust their own instincts and that they could rely on themselves. Like money in the bank, their benevolent parents lived on in their progeny's memories and emotional reserves, upon which they could draw in hard times.

Edgar, fifty-three, is an example of an adult orphan who retains an abiding and altogether realistic picture of his deceased parents, and who counts himself as "one of the lucky ones." He says,

> I spent a lot of years running down blind alleys, trying to figure
> out what I wanted to do with my life. I must have changed careers
> a dozen times. But my parents were always there to encourage me,
> even if they failed at times to give me the criticism I needed. Still,

I never doubted their belief in me, and they never had a problem saying "I'm sorry" when they messed up. Recently, I had a dream about them—in the dream, they walk into my living room, look at me, smile, and say, "You did good." It gives me the courage to figure out where I've screwed up and where I have some lessons to learn. If they were alive today, I'd only have one thing to say to them: "Thank you."

Unhappy Endings

The outlook is murkier, however, for adult offspring whose relationships to their parents ended on a discordant note. These offspring were left with the stark reality of having, to one degree or another, been emotionally orphaned by parental neediness or domination or rejection all along—the parent's death was only the latest punishing example.

In this case, the difficult parent-child relationship could never be discussed, now that the parent was no longer around to answer for his or her behavior. Indeed, several respondents were left all but literally *sputtering* over the fact that a "dialogue" with an offending parent had never gotten off the ground in the first place.

Tom, forty-nine, recalled that his father—a womanizer who could never hold down a job, and who, after Tom's parents' divorce, had been merely a bit player in his children's lives—was only interested in the extent to which his children could support *him* emotionally and financially. This self-absorption would drive his children from him and would remain undimmed to the end of his life, when Tom was thirty-seven.

Tom is remarkably temperate about his childhood and his father's piecemeal presence in it; he has retired just about all of his "issues" with his negligent father. He is even able to give credit to his father for those rare morsels of attention—every couple of months or so—when he would take Tom for an outing and, on occasion, serve him "juice and cookies."

But Tom may never be able to extinguish the rancor he still feels over a single, burning issue: the fact that his father could never talk about anyone's problems but his own, could never stop blaming everyone but himself for his misfortunes. Says Tom,

> I don't forgive my father. I sometimes feel he did his best—but I don't really believe it. Forgiveness is a funny kind of religious word, and I don't hold with it. I think you have to take responsibility for the harm you've done as well as take credit for the good. I would give a lot to have had *one* honest discussion with my father in which he would have helped me to make some sense of his behavior toward me, beyond simply rationalizing.

Unanswered Questions

As Tom's story illustrates, in the absence of an authentic parent-child "dialogue," the relationship may be frozen at the time in the offspring's emotional life when the parent died. The adult child may appear to be a grown-up in other areas of life—for example, in terms of skills or talents—but, when recalling the deceased parent, may still feel like the "kid" he or she was.

Hence, the insistent wish for this "dialogue" might live on, albeit in a different guise, evidence of which may already be in place. That is, *it may be rerouted to the offspring's other attachments*, such as to the surviving parent or to a spouse—or to a therapist—who may be called upon to fill in for the absent parent.

Put another way, the suppressed desire for the impossible—that the parent were still around to provide comfort, or to know better, or to apologize to, or to haul onto the carpet for his or her sins of omission or commission—can spill over into the adult orphan's relationships and expectations. And should these subsequent attachments be threatened by rupture, the new losses may rekindle the unrequited parent-child conversation.

Waiting for the Other Shoe to Drop

The death of one parent puts adult offspring on notice: It provides them with the first inescapable evidence that their literal childhoods are, or soon will be, at an end, which almost always causes the relationship to the remaining parent to change, as shall be demonstrated in the following chapter.

The semi-orphans I talked to seemed to be on a kind of low-level alert; with one "down" and one "to go," their attention with regard to orphanhood had been captured. The surviving mother or father represented the respondents' last opportunity to mend, or come to terms with, the parental link to the past.

This was the beginning of a series of challenges facing these adult children, who were about to discover how much growing up they still had to do—and how, after both parents were gone, their lives, relationships, and identities would be transformed.

2 The Relationship to the Remaining Parent

When my father died I was bereft, but I didn't feel any great guilt or regret. Our connection had been very complete—there was nothing I hadn't said, and I knew I'd been a good daughter to him. If anything, he kind of opened up heaven for me—he made death less frightening. My relationship to my mother, however, is another story—it's just so unresolved. Ever since he died, she's done things to me she never would have dared if he were alive. And I let her get away with it, because she's the only parent I have left. My mother is very much the puppeteer who animates me. What will happen when no one's pulling the strings? When she dies, I think I will be absolutely devastated.

—Alicia, forty

Listening to Alicia—a vibrant, articulate woman of enormous warmth and charm—describe her overwrought relationship with her mother, you would think the two women lived across the street from one another and were constantly in each other's hair. Indeed, when Alicia speaks of her mother, her voice occasionally dips to a whisper, as if the sixty-six-year-old widow were about to appear on her doorstep. But Alicia, who lives in Chicago, sees her Miami-based mother only once or twice a year.

Still, her mother is seldom far from her thoughts. Every time the phone rings, she wonders if it's her mother calling to remind her to send a birthday card to a relative, or to make a withering remark about Alicia's husband or kids, or to crow about her brother, the Wall Street tycoon, the only member of the family with "a real job."

And when her mother *isn't* calling—a sure sign of trouble— Alicia is on the phone herself, calling to find out if she's okay, only to get an earful of self-pity or criticism. It's almost laughable, this love-hate thing that has filled the vacuum left by her father's death eight years ago. And no one knows it better than Alicia herself.

Alicia *gets it*—the clichéd business of mother-daughter tension and widows with too much time on their hands—because she's in the business of "getting it"; she's a psychotherapist. If a client were to walk into her office this minute with a similar scenario, it's likely that Alicia would gently inquire, "Why do you suppose your mother has so much influence over you? What would happen if you set some limits? What's that all about?"

Yet despite all the professional wisdom she has dispensed to and received from clients and colleagues over the years—and notwith- standing her being a "lifer" in therapy herself—she can't keep herself from going off like a rocket every time she talks to, or even thinks about, her mother.

"I *know* what this is about," Alicia says heatedly. "This is payback for the fact that my father and I were kindred spirits, and she felt left out." Alicia pauses to collect herself and then, in calmer tones, continues:

> Maybe I'm overreacting. All I can tell you is that my mother is incredibly brittle and manipulative. When I was a kid, unbe- knownst to my dad, she was physically abusive to me. I learned early on how to ease things, how to placate people—I've been like that all my life. Now my mother is looking to me to nurture her, and God knows I try, with precious little thanks for my efforts. I

think the real issue here is that I've never addressed my anger at my father for leaving me to deal with her. My mother has never been a friend to me. I keep hoping that she'll change, which is ludicrous.

Last-Chance Childhood

As was illustrated in the previous chapter, the deaths of parents alert adult offspring to the sobering prospect of being at, or near, the top of the generational ladder. How the offspring respond to this reality depends, of course, on whether or not both parents are gone.

In some ways, the consequences of having one parent die, compared to having *no* parents left, are very different; it was to determine these differences that my survey sample was almost evenly divided between orphans and semi-orphans. With regard to the respondents' assessments of themselves—that is, the extent to which they had grown in the aftermath—an important consideration was whether or not they still had a living mother or father.

Except in the rarest cases—as, for example, an airplane crash that kills both parents simultaneously—the vast majority of offspring still have one remaining parent when the other parent dies. Thus, their "childhoods" are prolonged, often well into adulthood.

Americans now spend a greater portion of their adult lives knowing, and interacting with, their parents than at any time in history. In 1900, only about 10 percent of middle-aged men and women had a living mother or father; by 1976, that figure had climbed to 47 percent. Today, the number has soared. According to a 1997 national survey conducted for the American Association of Retired Persons, when asked whether or not they had at least one living parent, *64 percent*—a robust majority—of respondents age forty-five to fifty-four said "yes."

Even among Americans who have themselves raised and launched their children, reached the apogees of their careers, are sweating out their own health and worrying about the state of their retirement savings—even among those who are employing hair color unguents and the services of plastic surgeons to disguise their creeping decay—most are still somebody's "child."

The First to Go

One feature of parental death that has withstood demographic change, however, is its gender sequence; historically, men have tended to marry women two or more years their junior, and women have tended to outlive their spouses.

In 1997, 2.3 million Americans died, roughly evenly divided between males and females. But, according to the National Center for Health Statistics, the age-adjusted death rate—meaning the rate of death at certain ages for certain subgroups—was almost twice as high for men as for women. For this reason, people are likely to be younger when their fathers die than when their mothers die.

This demographic pattern was true of my sample as well—most "lost" their fathers first. More important to our purposes here was the *interval between their parents' deaths*, during which the offspring were semi-orphans. Most (82 percent) of the parents were married to one another when the first death occurred (as opposed to being divorced or remarried). For the majority of offspring, it was the widowed mothers who survived, usually without remarrying, for an average of seven more years.

Whichever parent died first, however, the event usually occurred when the offspring were in the throes of solidifying their careers, marrying, and rearing children; meanwhile, the surviving parent was coping with winnowing finances, increasing infirmities, and loneliness. It was inevitable that there would be a collision of intergenerational needs, which would lead to—and compound—changes in the offspring's relationship to the remaining parent.

And change these parent-child relationships did—*in nearly 75 percent of the cases.*

Patterns of Change

In his memoir, *Patrimony*, Philip Roth elegantly, and piercingly, describes the shift in his connection to his father after his mother died in 1981. Roth writes:

> Over and over again [my father] recounted for me the pure pro-saicness of the seconds preceding her extinction, while all the while I was thinking, "What are we going to do with this old guy?" To have ministered to my mother's needs, had she been the elderly survivor of their marriage, would have seemed manageable and natural enough; it was she . . . around whose quietly efficient presence the family had continued to cohere in the decades since my brother and I had left home.

In the eight years between his mother's death and his father's, Roth would come to know the man who had sired him in ways that he had not when his mother's presence, his father's overbearing "stubbornness," and Roth's own inevitable "physical estrangement" stood in the way of father-son intimacy. "It wasn't that I hadn't understood that the connection to him was convoluted and deep," writes Roth. "[W]hat I hadn't known was how deep it could be."

So, too, was it for many of the people in my study sample. I asked the respondents to characterize how their attachments to their surviving parents—whether father or mother—had been affected by the first death. These were the results:

- Nearly half (49 percent) said the relationship had **improved**.
- About a quarter (24 percent) said the relationship was **unchanged**.
- The remaining quarter (24 percent) said the relationship had **deteriorated**.

These "ratings" varied according to the respondents' gender, marital status, and other characteristics. Let us deal first with the general direction of these changes—the "how"—and then take a closer look at the explanations for them—the "why."

Improved Relationships

Of those who said that their connection to the remaining parent became qualitatively better, several remarked that they felt more "protective" of, or "peerlike" toward, the parent.

Those who felt protective said they visited and called the parent more than they had when the other parent was alive. A number of people spoke of "role reversals" with, or becoming "surrogate spouses" to, the parent. These offspring believed it was their obligation to take on a larger portion of responsibility for the parent's well-being.

Other people said they'd developed a greater affinity for the surviving mother or father and had become faster friends. They had gotten to know the parent better, one-on-one, without the distraction—or interference—of the other parent, achieving a camaraderie that had not been possible before. In the last years of the deceased parent's life, the couple had been in or near retirement; consequently (unless they had divorced and not remarried), they were seldom apart. It had been rare for the respondents to be alone for an extended period of time with one or the other parent.

Now, the offspring had the remaining parent more or less all to themselves. And for many respondents, it proved to be an eye-opener.

Janet, forty-six, says that although she always loved and felt close to her mother, she didn't really get to *know* her until after her father died. When Janet and her siblings were growing up, her parents were very old school, never arguing in front of the children, a "united front." There was no question as to which parent was in charge: her father, a man of strong, politically conservative views and, as well, a strict disciplinarian. Janet's soft-spoken mother always dutifully backed him up, appearing to agree with him on all things. But, as Janet was to find out, her mother had a mind of her own. Says Janet,

> My dad's death made it possible for me to differentiate between my parents—I was *flabbergasted* to discover that my mom was much more politically liberal than he was. I began to appreciate how hard it must have been for her to live with his opinions and how dependent she had been on him. She had very little sense of herself—she was almost invisible, even in her own mind—and it took her a long time to figure out who she was. Instead of being "Mommy," she has become a very dear friend to me.

Other respondents, however, said that getting closer to the remaining parent was a matter of the more "difficult" or dreadful parent being out of the picture and that, in any event, the relationship had no place to go *but* up.

For much of his young adulthood, Edward, thirty-nine, was estranged from both his parents, chiefly because his father had been brutal to him in childhood, and his mother had never intervened on his behalf. After his father died three years ago, however, Edward began to consider his mother in a new light, in part because she requested a reconciliation, and in part because his parents were no longer a "package deal."

Edward now believes that his mother was always under his father's thumb—that what once seemed to be her complicity in paternal hostility was in reality a manifestation of her fear of him. Which is not to say that she's a mouse; when accused by Edward of being her husband's "lieutenant," her prickly response was "*All right, so I was a lousy mother.*" But she has been mellowing—admitting, in bits and pieces, that Edward had good reason to dislike his father. Says Edward,

> For the first time, we can actually have something like a real conversation. Recently she said, "Your father was very hard on you." It made me remember that once upon a time, she and I loved each other. Now that he's gone, my attitude is, why not clean up some of the dirt?

Unchanged Relationships

Of those respondents whose connections to the surviving parent remained virtually the same as before the other parent's death, half said they'd always been close to the parent; the other half said they had never been close.

Several people remarked that they felt neutral about the parent, or that they had little in common with him or her. Others said that a sibling had always played a more dominant role in the parent's life. In some cases, the parent was too ill for a change to be affected. And then there were those parents—or their offspring—who didn't want the relationship to change.

Peter, fifty-one, is trying to maintain the parent-child status quo—an affectionate, although hardly cozy, distance from his eighty-one-year-old mother, who lives in another state. He is attentive to her, calling her at least three times a week. But he wants the relationship to remain as it always was—respectful, but by no means intimate.

When Peter was a child, both his parents put in long hours working at the grocery store they owned. His strongest memory of his mother is of the notes she left on the refrigerator instructing him how to heat up meat loaf; she wasn't, he says, a "hands-on parent." However, after Peter's father died four years ago, his mother began turning to him to make decisions for her—such as whether or not she should move closer to Peter and his wife—a role reversal he thinks will benefit neither of them. Says Peter,

> I keep telling her, "Ma, let's get this straight: I'm the son, you're the parent. You tell me what you want to do, and I will help make it happen. But I can't decide for you." It's hard, because she would happily acquiesce to what I want. And all I want is for her to make up her own mind.

Deteriorated Relationships

As for the people who said that their connection to a surviving parent had worsened, I was surprised to learn that many of them had been close to the parent in childhood, and in adulthood had remained reasonably cordial. But with the removal of the other parent, it was as if a dam had burst—hidden reservoirs of hard feelings and insecurites on both sides broke out into the open.

Many respondents said that with the removal of family "glue"— that is, the more beloved parent—the widowed parent had become increasingly demanding or self-pitying. Others remarked that a sibling had become, or was making energetic efforts to become, the parent's favorite child, putting a wedge between the respondent and the parent.

Still others said that they could no longer maintain the "myth" that the deceased parent had been virtuous when, in fact, he or she had been abusive, which put these respondents in the bad graces of the surviving, "mythologizing" parent. And in a few cases, the parent, having remarried, had simply become less available to the respondent.

All but these last two "reasons" for parent-child friction apply to the relationship between Alicia, mentioned at the beginning of this chapter, and her mother, who cannot talk to or be in each other's company without squabbling. Alicia *wishes* her mother would remarry; then she would have things other than her "disappointing daughter" to occupy her time and attention.

Pieces in a Puzzle: The "Whys" of Change

The quality of these parent-child connections was seldom solely a straightforward, cause-effect consequence of the first parent's death. Rather, the bond rose, or fell, or stayed its current course according to certain circumstances surrounding the attachment, and the characteristics of each parent, and each child. The five most important variables determining parent-child closeness or distance were:

- autonomy
- gender
- the presence or absence of siblings
- marital status
- counseling

Autonomy

One of the most important determinants of affection between adult children and their parents is the degree of independence and self-sufficiency that exists on each side of the generational equation. By "autonomy" I don't mean gritty indifference to others. Rather, I mean the ability to rely primarily on oneself for a sense of well-being and for decision making, instead of depending upon others to supply these things.

Obviously, there are times when you *need* your relatives and times when you just want to have them around. Dr. Robert A. Lewis of Purdue University has studied such needs and wants; specifically, he writes of three patterns of family "dependencies":

> **Interdependencies**, where help or solace—say, a loan or a sympathetic ear—is sought, and reciprocated, in times of personal crisis.
> **Survival dependencies**, where ongoing help, such as for infants or the elderly, might be a matter of life or death.
> **Excessive dependencies**, where one member is more demanding than is considered necessary or culturally appropriate.

Of interest here are the "dependencies" between middle-aged progeny and their parents. During this stage, parent-child problems might erupt for the first time, particularly when the parent's spouse dies. The widowed parent, who might have appeared to be self-sufficient prior to the partner's death, might become excessively dependent—for example, by calling upon grown children to provide aid and comfort that might not truly be needed in order to survive.

Maintaining an easygoing, interdependent parent-child relationship in the parents' later years often rests on the ability of *both* generations to feel that they have a degree of choice in asking for, giving, or receiving help in times of trouble. This comfort level often depends upon who's asking and who or what is being asked.

For instance, many parents would rather call upon a friend or sibling for emotional support or practical assistance, thereby side-stepping the slippery matter of "depending" upon their grown progeny, which would upset the parent-child order of things. To have to lean upon the very people whose independence the parents have labored long and hard to secure would violate a central tenet of American parenting: *Do not become a burden to your kids.*

Power Plays

It might be, however, that it is (or was) seldom clear who is the "parent" and who the "child." For some people, generational authority is a confusing proposition, with the child enlisted to prop up the parent in the best and worst of times, relieving the parent of the chore of being in charge of his or her own life.

This role confusion, especially in the aftermath of the first parental death—when there is no spouse to take up the attentional slack—often fuels the deterioration of parent-child relationships. Several respondents hugely resented being asked to "bail out" the very parents who might have bailed out *on* them, emotionally or physically, when they were growing up.

It wasn't just that help was begrudged by the offspring; rather, they felt it was coerced and—adding insult to injury—was seldom appreciated even when provided. For some parents, no matter how much time and effort were given, it was never enough; they wanted more—at great emotional cost to the offspring.

Researchers have found that when relationships between people are healthy and mutual there is no great moral accounting of who "owes" whom. But if the relationship is neither mutual nor reciprocal, and if the help is somehow extorted, the stress of giving can be burdensome indeed.

An extreme example of the toll exacted by this lack of parent-child reciprocity is Matthew, forty-one, whose father is given to bouts of alcoholic rage and threats of suicide (behavior that, Matthew suspects, contributed to his mother's death when Matthew was thirty-seven).

After Matthew's mother died, his father would call him two or three times a week in the middle of the night, threatening to kill himself. Matthew would try to calm him down, often rushing over to his dad's place to take him to a psych ward or rehab. But Matthew finally reached the point when he simply burned out. The night his father called for what seemed like the hundredth time to say "The gun is in my mouth, I'm going to pull the trigger," Matthew found himself wearily replying "If that's what you have to do, I can't stop you."

Despite his father's demands, his refusal to do anything to help himself—and despite Matthew's ability to set certain limits on his father's intrusiveness—Matthew can't bring himself to abandon his father. Says Matthew,

> My wife always asks me, "Why do you keep seeing him?" And I tell her, "I've tried not seeing him. It just doesn't make me feel better." But it has put me in the terrible position of having to say things I never dreamt I'd say to anyone—like "Go ahead, do it"— just to get a night's sleep.

As this story illustrates, some widowed parents simply *can't* (there are those who would say "won't") make an effort to improve their relationships to their children. Having shored up their lives with layer upon layer of defenses, they might not, at this late date, be equal to the task of confronting their roles in the splintered parent-child attachment. Says Roselyn J. Deyo, a social worker at the Montefiore Hospice in Beachwood, Ohio,

> When I do an assessment of patients, I always find out how close the person is to family members. Sometimes you see that nobody's coming to visit, and if that's the case, I ask the patient, "Would you like the relationship to get better?" And sometimes they say "No." Either they don't want it to happen or it's just so long gone that it doesn't happen. Some patients don't want it to get resolved or better—they die angry and isolated. My hospice team always says "Gee, wouldn't it be nice if." And I always have to remind them, "You know, not everyone has to die in a state of psycho-analytic grace."

To be fair, there are those offspring who *also* don't want an improvement in the parent-child tie—a means by which they and their parents might bridge their considerable generational differences. As psychologist Mary Pipher, Ph.D., points out in her book *Another Country: Navigating the Emotional Terrain of Our Elders*, "From both generations I hear stories of conflict, frustration, guilt, and anger. . . . Hurt feelings often come from taking personally problems that are cultural or developmental."

Some of the adult children I interviewed had become so embittered by their parents' demands that they wouldn't consider a reconciliation. Others were wary of developing an appetite for a loving relationship, thereby running the risk of being disappointed, or rejected, anew. Thus while it is true that some parents die with their grudges, it is also true that some offspring live on with their own grudges.

Peaceful Transfer of Power

If, however, the surviving parents are in genuine need of help and have no alternative but to ask their children for it—as, for example, when a parent becomes catastrophically ill and has limited funds, a situation that falls under the heading of "survival dependency"—the relationship might actually warm up. In this case, the offspring might feel a sense of pride in being able to deal with the crisis, in the course of which an honest and more meaningful relationship to the parent might develop.

Crucial to this newfound bond is for the parent to express appreciation for the child's efforts and at the same time respect the child's need to try to maintain a separate life. Studies show that aging parents would *like* to see or hear from their adult offspring more often than they do, but in the interests of preserving the younger generation's autonomy, they do not as a rule *expect* greater contact. And, to keep the intergenerational peace, parents might try to create what Dr. Gunhild O. Hagestad of the College of Human Development at the Pennsylvania State University calls a "demilitarized zone," silently agreeing not to disagree.

Researchers have found, however, that despite these efforts, younger family members tend to have more complaints about their parents, and find them harder to overlook, than the other way around. Put another way, offspring have very long memories and are less inclined to "forgive and forget" than their mothers and fathers.

Paradoxically, parental illness can sometimes be the agent of a cease-fire between the generations. Several respondents told me that they were able to get closer to a surviving parent precisely *because* the parent had been brought low by a sharp decline in health, which, for the first time, put the parent and the child on a more equal footing. Prior to the illness, many of these parents had been either cold or domineering. But after the onset of the illness, the parent became more vulnerable—more human—to the offspring, in some instances undergoing a metamorphosis that wiped away the adult child's hard feelings.

Sylvia, forty-six, whose widowed mother developed Alzheimer's disease four years ago and is now in a nursing home, says that all through her growing-up years her relationship to her narcissistic mother was abysmal. Her mother was "insanely critical," ridiculing her daughter for everything from her offbeat friends to her "beatnik" clothes, saying that Sylvia had ruined her life. But when she got sick, the mother's caustic remarks suddenly ceased; she became loving and witty, and immensely grateful to Sylvia for her attentiveness.

"I fell madly in love with her," says Sylvia. "She didn't care about the past, she was just so happy I was there for her. So even though it has been a great strain on me to make sure she gets the right medical help, and even though she's dying before my eyes, I finally have the mother I always wanted."

Gender

Whether or not the relationship between respondents and their surviving parents got better was not just a function of autonomy; it was also strongly determined by the respondents' gender. For example, 60 percent of the *sons*, compared to 46 percent of the *daughters*, said the connection had improved.

One explanation for this gender divide is that sons tend to demonstrate filial devotion *instrumentally*—for example, by handling the surviving parent's finances, or repairing a household appliance, or making decisions about insurance. With one parent out of the picture, sons are more likely to assume a more active filial role, especially with mothers, having seldom been called upon to do so before. But "active" means just that—actions, usually of a pragmatic sort, rather than loving words.

Daughters, on the other hand, tend to be *affectively* (meaning "emotionally") demonstrative to their parents, and they are more apt to express disappointment if their parents don't meet their psychic needs. Women have traditionally been "kin-keepers"—taking the emotional pulse of the family and staying in closer touch with the senior generation than men. Women also tend to be more easily wounded if this devotion is taken for granted—their thankless lot in life.

Sex differences account not only for adult children's general behavior toward parents but also for parental behavior and how their offspring react to it. I have found in my own previous studies that certain parent-child expectations and tensions are built into gender pairings—that is, in how mothers, or fathers, interact with their sons, or daughters.

Each of these four pairings has certain specific characteristics that can, in the long run, wreak havoc—or create harmony— between adult offspring and their surviving parents.

Fathers and Sons

Notwithstanding the emergence of the so-called "new, nurturant father"—the theory that modern fathers are as loving and attentive to their children as mothers—the reality is that most fathers behave one way toward daughters and another way toward sons. Studies reveal that fathers have historically been (and still tend to be) the parent who has the greater say on what it means to be a "real man." For example, mothers in general don't care what toys their kids play with, so long as they don't trash the house. But many fathers fret if their sons have the same fondness as daughters for playing with dolls.

Most sons are tacitly encouraged by their fathers to be *unlike their mothers*, which is why fathers and sons tend to relate to each other in terms of identification rather than emotional expressiveness—often to the detriment of the father-son bond.

This point was brought home to me repeatedly in the course of conducting research for a book on the father-daughter relationship. The majority of the middle-aged fathers I interviewed lamented that the "language of love" was not among their skills, chiefly because *their* fathers had not taught it to them. Rather, the paternal lesson that took was that boys should not be "sissies." The men felt redundant to their own grown children, of which they were reminded every time the kids called home and asked to speak to "Mom."

These fathers had been trained to believe that the concepts of "sensitivity" and "masculinity" were antithetical; particularly thorny for them was being openly affectionate to men—including their own sons.

Which helps to explain why the men in my parental loss survey were *twice* as likely as the women to say that they became "more distant" from their fathers as the fathers aged; indeed, it was like pulling teeth for sons to get their fathers to say "I love you" or "I'm proud of you." But it was equally daunting for the sons to express warm, fuzzy feelings to their fathers, especially when the fathers became widowers.

For bereaved fathers to remain inconsolable—that is, to fail to be "men about it"—put their sons in the awkward position of attempting to demonstrate tenderness for which the sons had little paternal training. These sons usually turned the "affective" heavy lifting over to the women in their lives—their lovers, wives, sisters, or daughters—who were more emotionally fluent.

Fathers and Daughters

The father-daughter relationship can be even *more* fraught, chiefly because most fathers, perhaps due to an unconscious awareness of the incest taboo, have traditionally left the primary parenting of daughters to mothers. It is with considerable assistance from mothers that this opposite-sex detachment is often solidified. "Maternal gate-keeping," wherein Mom knows best in the one arena in which she has historically been allowed dominion—the nursery—has helped to make many (if not most) fathers a mystery to their daughters.

This is one reason why fathers, far more than mothers, frequently enjoy their daughters' idealized affection—dad as court of filial appeal. It is also one reason why daughters, when they grow up, often have an advantage over their brothers.

To the extent that "Daddy" will reveal *any* parental tenderness, it is likely to be toward a daughter, with whom he is relieved of the onus of being a role model of unsentimental masculinity. And when a father becomes a widower, and if he has both daughters *and* sons, it is usually his daughters to whom he will turn for love and support.

In my survey, of those respondents who said their relationships to their aging fathers had grown closer or mellowed, more women than men reported this closeness.

Mothers and Sons

To say that mothers often have a soft spot for their sons, and get along better with them than with their daughters, is a masterpiece of understatement. This maternal bias has been immortalized in the writings of Sigmund Freud—a firstborn with several younger sisters and a lastborn brother—who wrote: "A man who has been the indisputable favorite of his mother keeps for life the feeling of a con-

queror, that confidence of success that often induces real success."
(A woman I interviewed put the matter more trenchantly: "As far
as my mother is concerned, my brothers can walk on water.")

Mothers simply expect less from their sons than from their
daughters. For a grown son to keep an emotional distance from his
parents by becoming standoffish or aggressive or professionally pre-
occupied—and therefore "not-mommy"—is evidence that he is the
genuine masculine article. And should he take the time to express
concern for his mother, she might interpret this kindness as a *gift*,
rather than a filial duty—relative, it must be restated, to a daughter's
attentiveness. Put another way, for a son to fall short in filial devotion
is unlikely to be taken by his mother as a deliberate betrayal.

For these reasons, there are fewer emotional booby traps in the
mother-son relationship than in that between mothers and daughters, a point underscored by my survey results: A greater proportion
of men than women reported having grown closer to their mothers
toward the end of the mothers' lives.

Mothers and Daughters

That Alicia, mentioned earlier, goes off like a rocket every time she
talks to her widowed mother is pretty much par for the mother-
daughter course. Nearly three times the percentage of daughters in
my sample, as opposed to sons, said that they had become "emotionally distant" or "estranged" from their mothers in their mothers'
final years.

No other parent-child bond is as complicated, tangled, and im-
pervious to change as the mother-daughter attachment. Daughters
are all but *required* to be there for their mothers in ways that sometimes hijack their lives; sons get the cultural equivalent of the Nobel
Prize just for showing up. Most mothers instantly forgive a son for

seldom calling home because, these mothers assert, he's "busy." But it is a stake in the maternal heart for a daughter to stay at an icy remove from her mother.

For one thing, mothers and daughters are practically joined at the emotional hip. Mothers are their daughters' genetic and social role models, their gender partners in such areas as menstruation, childbirth, and menopause. Ambivalence is the name of the mother-daughter game; daughters can separate, but (again, relative to sons) they seldom detach. And since women are encouraged to talk about their feelings more than men, most daughters are anything but shy about their problems with "Mom."

Complicating matters further, it is routine for daughters to keep an eye on their elderly parents; an estimated *78 percent of American caregivers are women.* And, as has been said, mothers generally out-live fathers. Thus, the relationship to a widowed mother might pro-vide more togetherness than a grown daughter can abide.

The women I interviewed were much more voluble when talking about their mothers than when reminiscing about their fathers. Many daughters were saddened by their fathers' deaths, but the lam-entation they felt was only partially because they missed or idealized "Dad"; it was also because the daughters had so much unbuffered contact with their widowed mothers. As one woman hilariously put it,

My mother loved me with all her heart, and she was often a great help to me. But I never knew why she was calling me—it was like, "What? *What now?*" It's not that we couldn't connect; we could connect. But I was always afraid her need would turn into a *suction.* I felt that if I lay down, even for a second, a giant conveyor belt would take me back home.

The Presence or Absence of Siblings

Having (or not having) brothers and sisters is, arguably, *the most important variable* in the degree to which adult children get along with their surviving parents. Notably more respondents who have siblings than only children reported that the parent-child relationship had deteriorated.

Singletons, in contrast, were more than twice as likely as respondents with siblings to report no change in the relationship to a widowed parent. Most only children had never had to share either their parents' attentions or their own guilt or filial "burden." Whereas *people with siblings had a basis for comparison*; they could measure, to the milligram, which of them was, or wasn't, doing his or her "share" of looking out for Mom or Dad.

Sibling Rivalry

Whenever there is a parental death, it puts the offspring in a survival mode during which their best, or worst, behavior could be triggered. At such times, ancient sibling vendettas, which might have been kept under wraps long enough to get through a Christmas dinner or a Bar Mitzvah, can surge into the open as though the emotional brakes had suddenly failed. Parents tend to have a peacekeeping effect on their offspring when the family gathers; but when one parent dies, most sibling bets are off.

Among the study participants who have siblings (87 percent of the total), it sometimes seemed as though they and their brothers and sisters were in a popularity contest, trying to be the child the last parent loved best.

I asked these respondents how great a role they, compared to

their siblings, had played in monitoring the well-being of, or providing assistance for, a remaining parent. Most had done something
to help—phoning or visiting the parent, balancing the parent's
checkbook, offering long-distance moral support to a caregiving sibling, consulting doctors.

However, beneath these differing sibling involvements was a
hidden but usually decisive variable: *the parent's historic or current
favoritism toward one or another of the offspring.*

As researchers on "social comparison" have discovered, if parents
treat all their children equally—whether lovingly or harshly—the
children are apt to be united in sibling solidarity. But if parents lavish
unambiguous preference for one child at the expense of another, the
children will count the ways in which they feel more, or less, loved
by the parents.

Esther, fifty-seven, recalls that when her father died six years
ago, leaving almost no estate, her frail eighty-two-year-old mother
came to live with her because neither Esther nor her younger brother
could afford to pay for a nursing home. Esther does not resent her
mother's presence, because the two women get along fairly well and
because her mother is undemanding.

But Esther *does* resent the fact that her brother lifts not a finger
to help her out. Says Esther,

I am very angry with him because he doesn't stay in touch with
my mother. He hardly ever calls, and I think it makes her feel bad.
I know he's busy—he's got young kids, he's on the road a lot. Plus
he's a male, and sons aren't "supposed" to keep in touch with their
mothers the way daughters do. That's his rationale; it's my
mother's rationale, too—she blames his wife. I don't buy it. I think
his neglect is inexcusable.

If Esther were an only child, none of this sibling relativity would pertain. And had her brother finally come around and done the "right" caregiving thing—had he, in fact, done it even *better* than Esther, thereby outclassing her in filial altruism—that might have posed another kind of sibling problem.

Several respondents could instantly reach the flash point when recalling the years of sacrifice they had put in attending to a widowed parent, only to be eclipsed at the eleventh hour by a previously invisible sibling. In these cases, the absent brother or sister suddenly descended out of the blue to usurp the caregiving role, often shutting out the other siblings from decision making. In the parent's view, the returning child was a rescuing hero. In the siblings' view, this last-ditch reappearance was a knife in the back; overnight, their cumulative sacrifices seemed to count for nothing.

Authorities on the sibling relationship "hear" in such reappearances the cries of an unloved child. Says Karen Gail Lewis, Ed.D., co-editor of *Siblings in Therapy,*

> When a sibling shows up at the last moment, it can look to the other siblings like dirty fighting, but it's really an attempt to make up for past bad blood with the parent. It seems to the others as though this sibling is saying, "To hell with everyone else, I'll be the good one." More often, the sibling is simply trying to make peace with the parent.

Scientific historian Frank J. Sulloway, Ph.D., a research scholar at MIT and author of *Born to Rebel: Birth Order, Family Dynamics, and Creative Lives,* sees these sibling skirmishes in more practical, supply-and-demand terms: They are, he argues, a product of Darwinian survival mechanisms. Sulloway's thesis, based on over twenty years of research, is that parental "resources," such as time, food, and

affection, become increasingly scarce with the birth of each succes-
sive child. Consequently, the greatest predictor of the quality of the
parent-child relationship is the child's *birth rank*. "The story of sibling differences," Sulloway writes, "is the story of . . . parental investment and any perceived biases in it." He goes on to say, "No
social injustice is felt more deeply than that suffered within one's
own family."

My survey data support Sulloway's thesis. Of those people who
grew closer to a surviving parent, *50 percent were firstborns* (compared
to 15 percent of middleborns and 30 percent of last-borns). Of those
who were not close to a surviving parent, *44 percent were lastborns*
(compared to 22 percent of middleborns and 33 percent of firstborns). In other words, the youngest child might feel parentally
shortchanged and as a result might make one final, desperate bid to
feel otherwise. (Middleborns tend to seek attention outside their
families of origin, a subject that will be explored in chapter 4.)

Whatever the reasons for the drive by siblings to be first in the
hearts of their parents—whether psychological or Darwinian—these
rivalries often take on a life of their own long after the parents die.

Marital Status

A statistically significant variable in my survey data was that unmarried respondents were more likely than married respondents to
say that the relationship to a surviving parent had gotten better: 60
percent of the "singles," compared to 43 percent of the "marrieds,"
reported this improvement.

Here the difference could be traced to the greater intergenerational responsibilities of married respondents, who were squeezed on
all sides—that is, by the wants and needs of spouses and children as

well as of ailing parents. Unmarried respondents, especially if they had no children, had fewer sources of family stress.

But unattached respondents *also* had fewer sources of *emotional support*, which may be why the relationship to the remaining parent often loomed in importance.

Erica, forty-three, embodies the grand slam of solitude. An only child, she is divorced, has no offspring, and her father died three years ago. On top of that, she's a freelance illustrator who spends her days alone, and her mother resides on the other side of the country.

Before her father's death, Erica's relationship to her mother was a frosty, on-again, off-again affair. But since his death, the mother-daughter connection has undergone a total conversion. As Erica tearfully explains it,

> My dad's death made me look honestly at what I don't have. I have many friends and I adore them, but we're all in demanding careers and don't see each other very much. So my sense of isolation is profound. I'm so afraid that my mother is going to die, because then I'll be completely alone. She sends me cards, she prays for me, she immediately forgives me when I'm in a bad mood. When she dies, nobody's going to do all that. That kind of love will just cease to exist.

Being single can be an advantage in terms of accepting, or improving, the relationship to the remaining parent. Says Dr. Lewis, "It's possible that unmarried, childless people resolve the parent-child relationship sooner than married people because they feel the lack of family first."

It is worth noting here that the marital status of the *parents* prior to the first parental death can have an impact on the offspring's relationship to the surviving parent. Numerous researchers have found that adult children of separated or divorced parents see their parents less often—up to 36 percent less often, according to one study—than children of intact marriages, because filial ties often unravel as a result of the breakup.

Many children of divorce learn during the crucial growing up years that they must, to one degree or another, fend for themselves— they have found out the hard way that parental commitment to them can be questionable. When one parent takes off, the other is often left on the emotional ropes, and neither has an abundance of energy to devote to the children. Later in life, these children may choose to keep contact with a surviving parent at a minimum—a trend that applied to the children of divorce in my sample as well.

Counseling

The final variable to be considered in adult children's relationships to surviving parents is whether or not the offspring has had any counseling, such as psychotherapy, support groups, or some other form of help.

Of those who reported greater closeness to a surviving parent, 64 percent had received counseling either before or after the first parent's death. Sorting out their emotional conflicts while one parent was still alive seemed to make a difference for offspring in their greater tolerance of, or appreciation for, their parents' foibles and struggles earlier in life.

What was remarkable, and poignant, about these improvements in the parent-child bond was that many semi-orphans—even in their forties, fifties, or sixties—still longed for a rapprochement, hoping that the painful past, which the remaining parent symbolized, would reverse itself. Counseling often cleared up, or reduced, impediments to this goal—or, when the goal turned out to be unattainable, at least made the outcome less ravaging.

Counseling provided another important function—it helped the offspring put aside their feelings so as to obtain from the remaining parent the last eyewitness account of the family's intergenerational history. Several people were able to retire or at least lower the heat on their "issues" in order to set about gathering the parents' memories, impressions, and perceptions while there was still time. These parental testimonies helped the offspring construct at least a working model of their own contexts, which enabled them to better understand what lay ahead for them when the last parent died.

Dress Rehearsal for Orphanhood

All these variables, separately and collectively, have an enormous impact on how adult children weather the *second* parental death. For within these variables are the seeds of the psychological sturdiness, or disarray, that frequently sets in when the offspring become fully orphaned and assess where they stand in the world.

Many of the people I interviewed were extraordinarily evenhanded about the costs and benefits of their relationships to their mothers and fathers. Hence, if they and their siblings were reasonably resilient prior to the parents' deaths, they were very likely to be resilient afterward, and the past would not cast a shadow over their lives.

The litmus test was the degree to which the respondents had resolved their relationships with one or both parents in their own heads. To return to John Bowlby, if they had discovered within themselves, or within their relationships to their siblings, or in their marriages or friendships, a "secure base" to return to in times of trouble, they would be able to live on without any unfinished parent-child-family business.

But if they had *not* found such a safe harbor—which frequently proved to be the case—the death of the second parent had the potential to make this lack of a "secure base" achingly, and unavoidably, apparent.

For these offspring, the painful legacies of their parents' lives served to widen the vacuum left by their deaths. The primary sources were gone, and the offspring were left to sort through, or be trapped within, the boneyards of their memories.

CHAPTER
3 Voices from the Grave: Legacies and Loyalties

Whenever I hear people complain about their parents, I think, You don't know how lucky you are to have them around to complain about. My parents both died when I was in my early twenties, before I got married and had kids. But I have to admit that my life has been simplified by their deaths. I don't have to deal with things like parental control or family feuds; my wife has never had in-law problems. And I can see even more clearly than when they were alive what wonderful role models they were— their essential goodness has been distilled and clarified in my mind. Nothing ever makes up for losing them, but it does provide another dimension—I feel a kinship with them that is beyond being a son. I'm at the top of the ladder. I'm one of them.

—Norman, forty-two

Hearing Norman, a courtly, self-assured, African American businessman, chronicle the bittersweet paradoxes of having no living parents, it is hard not to feel an amalgam of sympathy and envy. On the one hand, getting hammered by the tandem blows of his parents' deaths so early in his young adulthood was a cruel test of his mettle.

On the other hand, to have had so much to lose puts him in the elite company of the doubly blessed. "You can't broadcast the fact that *both* of your parents were perfect, not if you want to have any friends," I tell him, only half in jest.

"I know," he says, chuckling. "I was incredibly fortunate."

Indeed he was, especially in light of his precarious beginnings. Norman was born out of wedlock (he has never met his biological father), and for the first three years of his life, his grandmother looked after him while his mother struggled to support them.

But the year Norman turned three, into his life came the man his mother would marry and with whom she would have two more sons; the man who would anchor the family, protecting and providing for them (he was an electrician) until his death eighteen years later; the man whose last name Norman adopted and whom he calls "Dad."

> When you say the word *father*, he's who I think of. He was very intelligent, very carefully and eloquently spoken, a deep thinker. He was forever attending night school—when he died at sixty-seven, he was enrolled at a community college to study philosophy. He taught us the importance of self-respect and hard work. That's why I took his name—I'm proud to carry it.

His dad's death was sobering, not only because it robbed Norman of his "wise man" just as he was embarking on his first post-college job, but also because soon thereafter his mother developed an incurable illness. One of the last things his father had said to him was, "Watch out for your mom. Keep an eye on the boys." Norman took his dad's bidding to heart. At twenty-one, he became the de facto head of the family—calling his mother every day, taking her to the doctor, bringing in groceries, making sure his athletic brothers hit the books and not just the high school track.

"It was nice," he recalls, "to be so relied upon. I felt I owed it to my mother, knowing what she had gone through as a single mom to take care of me." He continues:

> It made me feel I could handle anything. Most black families are extremely strong, through crisis, through poverty, through hardship. There's a spiritual fortitude that makes up for that—it certainly did for me.

In reminiscing about his parents, Norman measures himself against all that they accomplished and all that they were unable to accomplish. He is stunned by the realization that his monthly salary exceeds his father's peak annual income. He feels a twinge of melancholy at the thought that his parents never met his wife and children—a three-year-old son and a newborn daughter—that they were never grandparents.

And he wishes his mother had told him more about his biological father, information only she could have provided and that she chose to keep to herself. All he has to go on is a name, carefully inscribed by her in the family Bible. Norman tried a couple of times to locate the man, "just to check out the gene pool," and to formulate a picture of what his mother was like before he was born. But the attempt was halfhearted: "I was afraid I'd be disappointed in the guy," he says. "I didn't want to press my luck."

Norman has now spent as much of his life without his parents as he ever did with them. The thing that has sustained him through their twenty-year absence is his unshakable "sense of family"—the silver lining, he says, of their deaths:

> Losing my parents forged a new bond between my siblings and me. There's an unwritten set of laws that governs the way we act, because we're carrying out this legacy of dignity and decency—we

are entrusted with the responsibility to live up to their values. All three of us are high achievers who put our marriages and children first. So even though our parents are gone, they are very much with us.

They are especially with Norman at night, when he tucks his children into bed, gazes into their faces, and thinks, I bet my mother and father did this for me; this is what they felt for me. It is then, he says, that the loving memories wash over him, guiding him, speaking to him. And from these imaginings, Norman gathers strength.

In Memoriam: The Paradoxes of Parental Legacy and "Loss"

As this case history illustrates, parents may die, but their influence does not disappear, even if the deaths occurred decades ago. And that is because "dead" and "gone" are not necessarily the same thing—depending upon how, or whether, the parents are remembered.

For some offspring, powerful memories, both positive and negative, are of inestimable help in alerting them to the complexity of human beings. In remembering parents objectively (if not always flatteringly), we can take their good qualities inside—"internalizing" them, in the psychotherapeutic argot—and prevent their negative qualities from setting up housekeeping in our thinking and behavior.

But for other offspring, memories might be too bruising or too "disloyal" to recall. Instead they might be suppressed, or imprecisely recorded, or "split off" from awareness, or "acted out" (as therapists also put it). In this case, the *failure* to remember objectively can hold the offspring back—"stuck" in their own development.

In his paper "Loss as a Metaphor for Attachment," psychiatrist George E. Vaillant spells out the importance of full recall in adjusting to parental death. "[T]he psychodynamic work of mourning," he writes, "is to remember more than it is to say good-bye."

The influence of parental legacy and the significance of remembering it all—no matter how conflicted, or contradictory, or incongruous the memories turn out to be—cannot be overstated. For only in honest, unsparing recollections of our deceased parents can we get an accurate picture of *ourselves* in relationship to them— and in relationship to our lives without them.

The Many "Voices" of Legacy

Parental legacies, and their effect upon us, are an extraordinarily complex business because they come in many forms. It's like listening to an enormous chorus singing in close harmony—specific melodic lines and individual voices are hard to distinguish from the whole.

In order to understand the intricacies of parental legacy, it is helpful to break down this "chorus" into four distinct, separate parts:

- How memories of the deceased are uniquely recovered and preserved, and the dilemmas these memories may pose.
- The tangibles of parental legacies—that is, the parents' wills and estates, and personal belongings—and what these tangibles might symbolize to their offspring.
- The intangible legacies of emotional inheritance and filial "loyalty"— the parents' beliefs and values, the "lessons" they passed on.
- The "sticking points" in which offspring often get stalled in their development as they attempt to sort out these legacies.

Necessary Losses: Picturing the Deceased

Of all the paradoxes of parental "loss," this may be the most crucial: Parents have to actually die before their children can fully comprehend the *totality* of their influence.

In dying, the deceased become forever fixed, at least physically. Once a person dies, and as the survivors live on, the reality that the person is not coming back begins to sink in and the implications of that fact gradually take shape.

Immediately following a parent's death, offspring might find themselves being ambushed by tears or nightmares or angry recollections, as if caught in a sudden storm. As time goes by, however, these raw emotions, like newly turned earth, can begin to harden into something else—an unsentimental, three-dimensional awareness of what the parent meant to them and who the parent actually was.

The dead do not themselves change; the *living*, and their memories of the dead, do. It is the very immutability of parental death that allows adult children to begin to take their own and their parents' measure in ways they could not before. The dead must be still—as a statue is still—for survivors truly to *see* them.

Marilyn Frankfurt, C.S.W., a psychotherapist and former member of the faculty of the Ackerman Institute for the Family in New York, conceptualizes the deaths of parents in aesthetic as well as psychological terms. She explains:

> As long as a person is alive, she is constantly in flux. But in death, the person can no longer change herself. Death is seen as an event not for the one who has died, but for those who survive and can contemplate the person's life and form a finalizing image of the person. It is not until our parents have died—not until we can

"walk" all the way around them—that we can develop a perspective on them that permits us to begin a transformation. New ideas and feelings can form about our deceased parents and our relationship to them.

It is through this "imaging" that a psychological changing of the guard can begin to take place within the adult child's mind. As the parents' redeeming and unredeeming qualities come into sharper focus, the child can get a better sense of himself or herself apart from the parents—the "me" and "not-me" of one's own identity, of who one is. In this way, little by little, the offspring can say good-bye to the dead.

But if the "imaging" is incomplete—for example, all idealization or all vilification—or does not even *start*, the adult child's self-concept may be compromised and, in a sense, go to pieces. Offspring may simply put off, or avoid altogether, dealing with their conflicting emotions, only to have them pop up in other guises—for example, in their marital rifts, or sibling rivalries, or ruptured friendships—the true origins of these conflicts not readily apparent. In these instances, the parents may haunt various aspects of their children's lives.

Double Exposures

When one utters the words "Rest in peace," it may not be simply the souls of the departed that are of prayerful concern. The peace of mind of the survivors—and their ability to come out of their parents' shadows and conduct their lives on their own terms—may also be at stake.

To "lose" one's parents presents offspring with a number of uncomfortable questions and dichotomies: Whom do you remember—the parents you had, the parents you wish you had, or the parents whose images you have somehow sanitized? Which of your parents' beliefs should you be held to or act upon or disavow? What family myths should you defend—and what are the hazards if you unmask these myths and tell the "real" story? Where do your loyalties lie— with the parents whose voices still buzz in your head, or with yourself and your own "voice"?

What are your obligations to the dead?

Two Down, None to Go

Such questions gnawed at many respondents after the first parental death, and after the second hit them like a ton of bricks. In the interval between the deaths there had been a kind of cushioning limbo during which the offspring could postpone pondering such weighty matters. "Even if one parent is dead," a woman said, "you still have the other to lasso your feelings onto."

But once both parents were deceased, the offspring were left to face—to the extent that they were capable of facing it—the ramifications of being at the top of the generational ladder. Let us consider, then, the emotional contrast between having *one* living parent and having *none*.

In answer to the question "What are your overriding feelings about being an adult orphan?" virtually all the respondents had plenty to say. But their answers varied, depending on whether or not both parents had died. Some examples:

- Of those who reported having been close to one or both parents in childhood, 40 percent were semiorphans, and *60 percent were full orphans.*
- Of those who said they were "still dealing" with feelings of grief or anger, 78 percent were semiorphans and *22 percent were full orphans.*

These results—which will be explored in detail later in this chapter—suggest that, relative to semi-orphans, full orphans regard their parents in an entirely new and more benevolent light, and that the offspring are, as it were, "home free."

However, the data are open to interpretation. In one scenario, full orphans have put some emotional distance between themselves and their parents and have the breathing room to reflect, to form a fairer, more complete point of view.

In another scenario, full orphans have transferred some or all of their unexamined parental "issues" to other areas of their lives, where history might repeat itself—for example, by expecting their siblings, or partners, or children, or friends to love them in ways that their mothers or fathers could, or could not.

Both scenarios—emotional circumspection and emotional transference—were often at work among the men and women I talked to, depending on their individual circumstances and psychological readiness. Many people bounced back and forth between the two as they zigzagged through the process of adjusting to life without their parents.

Those who had completed the "sorting out" process could lay their parents to rest and not carry over their filial expectations or disappointments to other relationships. Those who disavowed or denied their mixed filial feelings were often in for a bumpy ride.

The Parental Vacuum

Wherever they were in this process, however, *all* the respondents were heaved into an unprecedented point in their own evolution: The "child" role, which defined them for so long, was now at an end. There was no living parent to evoke a *reaction*—no parent upon whom they could rely, or whose care they felt obliged to provide, or whose feelings had to be spared, or against whom they had to push to protect themselves, or whose approval or disapproval might be registered at each turn in the filial road.

Susan Battley, Psy.D., a consulting psychologist specializing in life phase transitions at the State University of New York at Stony Brook, has looked at the conflicts many adult orphans encounter. She says:

> The parental generation provides an emotional scaffolding for off-spring, as well as the framework within which to make and to test their own choices. When the older generation is gone, then the question becomes: Which choices will allow adult children to retain control over their own lives? Some people feel that their life choices are really dictated by their parents—the heavy hand of the parents is alive, even if the parents are not. The task is to correct the relationship with the parents in your mind and make peace with the fact that they may have been imperfect. There may be aspects of yourself, and of your parents, that you don't have in common. You learn to accept these differences and move on.

Dead Reckonings

Many respondents were light-years away from this level of acceptance—there had been an interim, transitional task that had to be addressed first: *Where they stood with their parents after both parents died.*

This final accounting could be calculated in two ways. The first was immediate: their parents' financial or other tangible legacies, as spelled out in their wills or by some other means. The second took time, sometimes years, to add up: the "sleeper effect" of emotional legacy.

In these two ways, deceased parents could continue to "speak" to their adult children, and the offspring could "hear" them, for good or for ill.

Financial Legacies:
What Do the Dead "Owe" the Living?

I asked the survey respondents whether they or their siblings (if any) had inherited either money or property from their parents, and if so, whether these endowments had been equally apportioned. Roughly half (52 percent) said that there was nothing to inherit, either because their parents died broke and/or intestate (without a will), or had been "spent down" to qualify them for government benefits, or because a parent or stepparent survived, or for some other reason.

Another 17 percent said their parents' estates had been evenly divided among the respondents and their siblings (or, in the case of only children, passed entirely to them).

But nearly a quarter of the respondents—23 percent—said that the parents' assets or belongings had been *unevenly* divided. Sometimes the lion's share went to a child who had been the parents' caregiver, or was in the greatest need, or was the "favorite." Others had received loans during the parents' lives that were deducted from their share of the estate, thereby evening up the heritable score. In a few cases, either the respondent was cut out of the will or he or she refused a bequest in order to be "free" of the parent.

Interestingly, the vast majority of people did not want to make a federal case over these "inequities": *80 percent* said that they hadn't been "bent out of shape" by the parents' wills and settlement of their estates. In the interests of maintaining some sense of family, or their own integrity, they were willing to let the matter drop—or at least grumble only in private (or in an anonymous interview).

For example, Irene, forty-one, was disinherited by her mother, who bequeathed her house to a distant relative. The way Irene sees it, her mother was attempting to exact "revenge" for the fact that Irene would not allow her strong-willed mother to dominate her. Says Irene,

> My mother was very competitive, a master of mental cruelty. I came to the conclusion early on that I could never do anything right and that where she was concerned, I was an emotional orphan. At eighteen, I left home and only returned for occasional visits, mostly to see my father. After he died, the family kind of collapsed. So when she died and I found out about the house, I said to myself, "She is trying to ruin my life by doing this to me. I will not let my life be ruined. Let it go." Which I have pretty much managed to do.

But then there's that 20 percent who *were* bent out of shape by their parents' wills and the disposition of their belongings. These respondents, whose main beef was that they had received less than a sibling, tended to hang on to their grievances with unflagging tenacity. It was as if, in their protracted bitterness, they were somehow keeping the parents alive.

Cheryl, fifty-eight, whose widowed mother died seven years ago, is not on speaking terms with her older brother, Steven, because Steven was the sole beneficiary of their mother's will. It's not just being denied an inheritance that distresses Cheryl—more painful to her is a sense of having been betrayed by her mother.

In the last years of their mother's life, Steven lived with her, supplying her with the supportiveness that Cheryl, who lived four hundred miles away, could give only on occasional visits. Originally, both Cheryl and Steven were to inherit equally. Cheryl believes that her brother turned their mother against her, persuading her to put all her assets in his name—a rejection that Cheryl can't get out of her mind. She had always been, she says, a "good daughter," priding herself in never asking her mother for a dime, despite the fact that there were many times when she could have used a handout. Her brother, on the other hand, always seemed to be short of cash and made no secret of it; he had but to ask, and his mother would provide.

"My mother left everything to the one who kept crying to her for help," says Cheryl, still visibly shaken by the experience. "How could she not *know* that she was breaking up the family? What could she have been *thinking* when she changed her will?"

What indeed. There is nothing like a will—and seeing its whereases and hereinafters spelled out in black and white ("I leave my daughter nothing because I gave her so much in life," a true example)—to create a Mount Rushmore of filial memories.

The Last Financial Word

Writing a will can be heady stuff, says Jane Bryant Quinn in her book *Making the Most of Your Money*: "You imagine their gratitude, as you assign your jewelry to Barbara and your antique clock to Jeff. You feel like God; you arrange everything."

This godlike arrangement can go way beyond keepsakes. Parents might, in fact, attempt to posthumously control their children's behavior through the employment of "conditional bequests" outlined in their wills (of which the parents, while alive, might have regularly reminded their progeny). For example: You get a slice of the parental pie under the proviso that you not marry until a certain age, or that you abide by the tenets of your parents' religion, or that you enter a particular profession, or that you have nothing to do with certain kin, or that you be at least forty.

Not all of these "conditions," and others similar to them, are unreasonable—in certain instances, they might be for the offspring's own good. To the heirs hobbled by such provisos, however, the parental "message" may be all too clear: a punishing vote of no confidence.

Some observers might sensibly argue that able-bodied offspring who hemorrhage over assets they neither earned nor built should get a life. There are few sights as pathetic as middle-aged progeny engaged in tugs-of-war over chipped tureens; sorrier still is the spectacle of well-heeled "trust fund babies" wrestling in Surrogate Court over unequal zillions. Conventional wisdom dictates that these injured parties would be better served by meditating upon the difference between money and love—between dependence and self-reliance.

But for all that it might be the noble, grown-up thing to say "I didn't earn it, so I'm not entitled," being *singled out* for less can be a bitter pill that settles uneasily on top of the child's lifelong sense of parental injustice.

The Bottom Line

Kenneth J. Doka, Ph.D., an authority on death and dying, has studied how inheritance disagreements can mirror, and magnify, pre-existing parent-child problems. Says Dr. Doka:

> We found that comparatively few families with good relationships prior to the death had feuds about inheritance. Where there was a history of poor relationships, that's when people tended to have the most disputes; some families that argued over very small inheritances essentially lost more in legal fees than they could possibly gain. If there had always been questions of parental favoritism and who's more "responsible" and who's not, those issues may continue to play out after the parents' deaths.

To state the woefully self-evident: It isn't just the money and the "things"; it's the *meaning of the money and the "things."* And regardless of who in the family did or didn't get whatever, the symbolic overtones can reverberate long after the probate checks have cleared.

Emotional Legacies: What Do the Living "Owe" the Dead?

Many offspring manage to get beyond the tangible piece only to become mired in the *emotional* piece—unfinished psychological business with one or both parents. You will recall from previous chapters that some parents and children have great difficulty parting on cordial terms. Nowhere is the effect of such partings more vibrant, if not totemic, than in the respondents' memories of their final encounters with their parents.

The Last Emotional Word

I asked respondents if there had been any "deathbed epiphanies"—that is, whether or not, at the ends of their lives, their parents had any final words to impart that were of comfort to their children (think Debra Winger saying farewell to her children in *Terms of Endearment*). Judging from the answers, it was a question that sometimes touched a nerve.

Brian, sixty-four, longed to hear some soothing valedictory from his taciturn, widowed father before the old man died a dozen years ago; to that end Brian sought the advice of a therapist on how best to broach the subject. The therapist recommended that Brian send his father a letter enumerating the myriad ways he had felt like an "unloved son." Says Brian,

I couldn't bring myself to do it. If I had written such a letter, my father wouldn't have known what the hell I was talking about! He was in his eighties, he didn't have much education, he was on his last legs. What was I going to say to him, "You *idiot*, you *still* don't understand me"?

Perhaps the sweetest parting my respondents reported was the most unexpected: A consistently neglectful or mean-spirited or narcissistic parent did a last-minute, death's door turnabout to set things right.

Greta, forty-six, and her brother hadn't seen much of their alcoholic father since their parents' divorce when Greta was in her twenties (their mother died ten years ago). But shortly before her father died in 1991, he summoned his children for a final visit so that he could beg their forgiveness. Says Greta,

That was his finest hour—up to then, you couldn't have a conversation with the man. Knowing he was going to die focused his mind mightily, I guess, enough to give him one moment of grace. He said, "I'll tell you anything you want to know." I asked him what had happened between him and my mom and why he had dropped out of my life. He had only nice things to say about my mother. He told me how sorry he was for having failed us. He said how much he loved me and how proud he was of me. In the end, he really redeemed himself.

Such deathbed tenderness was not to be for most respondents, either because the parent died in a coma, or because the respondent was not there at the time, or because, given the personalities involved, it was not in the cards.

Judgment Day

It was at this juncture—when the last financial and emotional words had been "spoken" by both parents, and the bodies in question were cold in the ground—that many people began to consider whether or not they had actually "buried" their dead, and to consider, too, the consequences of the deaths.

Returning to the question of the respondents' overall feelings about being "orphaned"—and taking a closer look at their answers—three trends were notable:

Positive Consequences

Many people had few or no "loose ends" with one or both parents, regardless of the quality of the relationships earlier in their lives. Some had incrementally detached from their mothers and fathers right along by inhabiting their own lives and putting their emotional energies into their marriages, or children, or friendships; others had already begun to deal with their unhappy filial experiences prior to the deaths. Either way, the result was that they looked primarily to themselves for definition and found strength in the aftermath of their parents' deaths.

Fifty-one percent of the responses indicated "positive" effects of being "orphaned." For instance, the offspring felt a sense of freedom or relief, of being more "adult." Or they had developed a greater appreciation for the parents, whose best qualities "lived on" in the respondents. Or they were "euphoric" that an abusive parent was gone, as though a great weight had been lifted. Or they were able to see themselves in a kinder light than their parents had seen them. These people appeared to have "buried" their parents, and they stood firmly in the present.

Ambivalent Consequences

Other respondents were in various stages of working through the maze of parental memory and legacy. Many were brokenhearted that the "home" of childhood, or their parents' unconditional love, was gone. Some felt they had lost their best friends—a mother or father to whom they could "say anything." And some had been their parents' caretakers for so long—in one case, twenty years of back-to-back illnesses (Alzheimer's disease and cancer)—that they had virtually no life of their own outside the family and scarcely knew where to start building one for themselves alone.

Twenty-seven percent of the responses reflected these and other intractable feelings of sadness or nostalgia. The offspring appeared to have "buried" their parents in shallow graves, leaving the offspring with one foot in the past, the other a toehold on the present.

Negative Consequences

And then there were those who seemed nowhere near resolving their relationships with the parents of memory. Some remained so bound to the parents that they were pitted against other family members—vigorously defending the parent in the face of a relative's opposing, or more balanced, point of view. Others were so angry with the parents that every new slight, especially from family members, compounded their vexation. Still others were *reeling* because the deaths had been so shattering—for example, suicide or murder—that they were emotionally paralyzed.

Twenty-two percent of the responses revealed ongoing wretchedness in the aftermath of the parents' deaths. These offspring were least able to "bury" their parents. And these were the people most likely to be trapped in the past.

Sticking Points: Roadblocks to the Future

As these data demonstrate (and as will be even more evident in subsequent chapters), for a significant number of people, life without their parents was a tenuous proposition; it was as if they were rudderless and lacked a compass. In terms of whether or not they regained their emotional bearings after being "left" by their parents—that is, how they regrouped in the aftermath—there were certain barriers that sometimes stood in the way. The three most important roadblocks were:

- family myths or secrets
- "special legacies"
- traumatizing death

Family Myths or Secrets

Filial loyalty in the wake of parents' deaths can be a stormy business—*especially* for those who, while the parents lived, had been unable to disengage themselves from their parents' firm grip on them.

Being "true" to deceased mothers and fathers is not just a matter of "honoring" their virtues—sometimes it is a matter of keeping their dysfunctions closeted and honoring the myth instead. One way to render such parents eternally honorable is to take their relentlessly negative view of you as your own, rather than seeing it the other way around—that the parents themselves might have been flawed, and that you are not, all by yourself, what's wrong with this picture.

Susan C. Vaughan, M.D., assistant professor of clinical psychiatry at the New York-Presbyterian Hospital, and author of *The Talking Cure*, explains this mental maneuvering or "defense mechanism":

A lot of people internalize their parents' critical view of them—
it's a way of holding yourself together and defining who you are.
Many people have trouble reassessing and drawing away from the
relationship to the parents, because they're still intensely involved
and heavily conflicted about the relationship. To give their views
up is like admitting you were wrong about them—hence about
yourself—in some fundamental way. A lot of people just don't
have the ego strength to do that.

Let us take a worst-case example to illustrate this mental cover-
up in the service of mythic family harmony and unity: child abuse.
It is not uncommon for offspring of abusers to choose up sides—
the ones who say "it never happened," and the ones who say "it sure
as hell did."

This usually occurs because no adult confirmed the abused child's
experience. For instance, the spouse of the abuser might insist that
the children adhere to the "party line" of denial in order to justify
staying in the marriage. Young children, out of fear of abandonment,
might go along with the ruse and attempt to "forget" the abuse ever
happened.

But let us say that the child grows up and the abuser dies. Is it
safe for the abused child to remember and "tell" his or her secret
then? Maybe not; the other survivors might not be ready to metab-
olize such disquieting news because it would demolish their sense
(however distorted) of "family."

Family therapist Evan Imber-Black, Ph.D., past president of the
American Family Therapy Academy and author of *The Secret Life
of Families*, has examined the effect upon families of "dangerous
secrets" and what can happen, postfuneral, when they explode out
into the open. Says Dr. Imber-Black,

When parents die, very often the cork is out of the bottle. Funerals are notorious for uncovering secrets—people may feel they can say things they sat on for decades. But some families can't make room for different experiences. Once somebody's dead, loyalty issues sink their hooks in—if I don't do it this way, or think this way, I'm being disloyal.

Revealing dark family secrets seldom goes unpunished. Several respondents disclosed their victimization after an abuser died, only to find themselves being cast as the family pariah or traitor. Others were doubly punished, because the first secret flushed out a second—a sibling had known about the abuse and kept silent, either to avoid a similar fate or to hold the family together.

Elizabeth, fifty-three, is still riding out the family aftershocks caused by her disclosure that her deceased father had molested her. Her mother's response had been, "Well, you were always a very flirtatious little girl." When the mother died, Elizabeth learned that her siblings wanted to hear no more on the subject. She recalls:

It became clear that if I wanted to have a family, I was going to have to "get over" my parents' behavior and shut up about it. My brother flat out said, "It happened to you, not to me. This is between you and them—don't ask me to give up my parents by siding with you." Needless to say, my parents' deaths are not a done deal.

"Special Legacies"

For other offspring, their parents' deaths were *also* not a done deal, but for a vastly different reason; they felt obliged to remain faithful to their parents' religious or political beliefs, which beliefs had cost the parents mightily.

An example of this phenomenon is children whose parents suffered horrific persecution, such as in the Holocaust or as political
prisoners in dictatorships. In these cases, the legacy was that but for
the parents' miraculous survival, the children would never have been
born. These offspring gave meaning to their parents' lives and
ideals—to deviate from these ideals was in a way to kill their parents
a second time. By keeping the faith, the offspring could continue to
make their parents' struggles count for something.

Nathan, forty-six, a rabbi, is such a child. His parents managed
to survive two concentration camps during World War II, and for
the remainder of their lives could speak of little else. To his way of
thinking, the greatest legacy of love and hope from his parents was
for them to have children. Because of all that they had endured, he
believes it is his job to bear witness to the Holocaust, to tell his
parents' stories and those of other survivors.

But Nathan has paid a price for his steadfastness to his parents'
memories; in order to keep repeating these stories in all their hideous
detail—in order to be a teacher—he's had to wall himself off emotionally from them. Otherwise, he says, he'd fall apart. "It's only now
that I've started to acknowledge that those walls exist," he says.
"What would happen if I started dismantling them? I almost feel as
if I'd have to go into solitary—I'd have to unwrap those layers very
carefully to see how bad the burns are."

Dr. Susan Battley refers to conflicts such as Nathan's as the
gravitational pull of "special legacies." She has worked with the children of survivors of various atrocities, helping them come to terms
with how much of themselves might have been lost under the cloud
of such atrocities. Says Dr. Battley:

> Parents who have escaped with their lives have this legacy that
> they give to their children around the issues of survival, death, and
> birth. The fact that the parents had been spared meant that the

children were "special"; therefore, the children had an obligation to carry on certain traditions or beliefs, and if they did not, it might mean they were betraying the parents. It's a question of what the children feel they owe their parents.

It's also a question of what the children—and *their* children—feel they can live with. And for some offspring, the obligation can create tensions with the next generation, who might feel far less beholden.

Traumatizing Death

Finally, there were those respondents whose parents died in excruciating ways. I am speaking here of people whose mothers or fathers committed suicide or were murdered. When these parents died, so did a piece of their children, because they had been unable to prevent the deaths and felt in some way responsible for them.

Six percent of the respondents lost their parents to suicide—or, as some of them put it, the parents "chose to be lost," a fine but extraordinarily important distinction.

One such respondent is Laura, forty-two, whose manic-depressive mother asphyxiated herself a few months after Laura fled from home at age twenty-two to escape the wreckage of her mother's illness. For Laura, her mother died many times. The first "deaths" were psychological—when she was growing up, her mother was catatonic for months at a stretch. The final death was self-annihilation. Twenty years later, Laura is trying to emerge from the fugue state in which she has been engulfed ever since. She says:

> When I was a child, I lost the ability to connect with people, because it was the only way I could get away from my mother in my own mind. By the time she died, I was already on automatic

pilot; I went to the funeral, left the same day, and missed only one day of work. No one in the family ever talked about it. I never cried. To this day I haven't cried. All I ever wanted to be able to do was cry.

Paul R. Duberstein, Ph.D., assistant professor of psychiatry and oncology at the University of Rochester School of Medicine, has conducted dozens of "psychological autopsies"—and been involved in hundreds of others—to find out from next of kin what leads up to suicide. As a result, he knows intimately the effects upon family members of such deaths. Says Dr. Duberstein,

> Reactions to suicide are very context dependent, and all survivors are not the same. But death by suicide is one of the most difficult bereavements to get over—I'm not sure that anyone ever gets over it. The thing that most concerns me is the impact on the younger generation. I'm concerned about the modeling, the sort of license it gives. That legacy, that's the scariest thing. It's not just the effect on the next generation, but also the generation after that.

Another "difficult bereavement"—the term does not do justice to the experience—is that of children whose parents have been murdered. They, too, seldom get over it. And the impact of such deaths can also be felt over many generations.

I would be hard-pressed to come up with a more gruesome loss, or more agonizing aftermath, than that which Amy, thirty-six, endured. Her mother was stabbed to death on a Washington, D.C., street. Were it not for Amy's insistence that this case be pursued, combined with the cooperation of a sympathetic homicide dectective, her mother's murderer might still be at large. Amy refused to let up until her mother's killer had been found, arrested, tried, and convicted—a process that chewed up ten long years of her life.

It began with a telephone call from the police informing her about the murder. The timing for such a call could not have been worse; Amy and her mother, who had never gotten along, had been estranged for years. Thus, Amy was not only faced with the viciousness of her mother's death—she had to identify the body—but also with her own remorse for having stayed out of touch. Says Amy,

> Until that trial, my life was a mess. I had done drugs, dropped out of school, been involved with rotten men. The bizarre thing, the great tragedy, is that it took her dying for me to realize how much I wanted her to be proud of me, how much I needed to know more about her. Until that trial, it had never been safe for me to "be" with her. The only way I could get her back was to listen to every bloody detail of the prosecution's case, to see all the lurid crime scene photographs, to look her killer in the eye, day after day after day. That's how I recovered. I was there for my mother, and I was there for me. Now she's really gone. It's like she's been buried, finally.

Since the trial Amy has gone into therapy, gotten a college degree, and embarked on a career as a paralegal. Amy was lucky—lucky, that is, compared to her older sister, who did not attend the trial and who appears to have "resolved" her mother's death by having no contact with the family. Amy is hoping that she and her sister will one day be able to restore their relationship—"My mother would have liked that," she says. But she understands that such a reunion might not be possible for her more fragile sister.

As Amy's story illustrates, homicide can "kill" on many levels—the victim, and the worldview of one or more members of the victim's family. After such a death, it's hard to imagine how it is possible for survivors ever to feel safe in their own skins, or find a kernel of meaning in the death, or begin to have trusting relationships with other people.

But for Amy, if not for her sister, the prosecution of her mother's killer would prove to be the horrible means by which Amy could at last come to know her mother and know herself in relation to her— the only way she could, at last, let her mother go.

Finding Your Own Voice

When parents die, their adult children are vaulted to the top of the family hierarchy, where the acoustics are sometimes imperfect. It is there that they can find their own voices.

The deaths of parents can leave those who live on with many questions, the most important of which revolve around their own survival and identities. With the parental "glue" removed, what lies ahead?

What will become of their relationships to their siblings—do they have any "family" left, and if so, how sturdy, or flimsy, are these ties, and how might they change? Will the parents' deaths impinge upon, or enrich, their relationships to partners or friends, or make more anguishing the lack of such attachments? Will they become better, or worse, parents to their own children than their parents were to them?

Will the offspring now be able to realize their own dreams, rather than their parents' dreams for them? And what kinds of legacies will the adult children erect for younger generations—what kind of mark, what kinds of memories, will they leave behind?

Such questions, which the offspring *themselves* must answer, can lead to their psychological renewal, in the course of which they may find themselves on circuitious and perplexing detours, as we shall see in the following chapters.

To be able to gain, sometimes you have to "lose." For in the losing, you can discover who you are, what you are capable of becoming, how strong it is possible to be. And with these discoveries, adult children can fortify the rest of their unparented lives.

Part Two

Ripple Effects:
The Consequences of
Parental Loss

Realigned Family Ties: Siblings and Only Children

Ever since my dad died, the family has been a shambles. He was the one who kept everybody sane, the peacemaker who stayed in touch, especially after my mom died. The night of his funeral, that's when the family exploded. My sister created an ugly scene, accusing my brother and me of not loving my dad, of not visiting him enough when he got sick—she was out of control. My brother just turned around, got in his car, and left. He was the most sensitive of us and was hardest hit by my father's death. We later found out that my sister took some of Dad's memorabilia without consulting us, which devastated my brother. He and I have gotten much closer since then. But neither of us will ever speak to my sister again.

—Sandra, forty-three

To the outside world, Sandra's family was the stuff of dynastic legend—one for all, circling the wagons in times of crisis or jubilation, assembling for each birthday and wedding and anniversary. Scions of an empire created by ancestral oil speculators, two of the three siblings—Sandra and her sister—worked in the family refinery business. All three of them, and their spouses, lived within driving distance of their parents' Houston estate.

This was a brood of blond, blue-eyed, toothsome perfection,

perpetually tanned from skiing in Switzerland at Christmas and boating in the summer at their parents' Nantucket compound. This was the embodiment of the American Dream.

That dream has turned to ashes. The summer place has been sold, the family firm taken over by the eldest sister and her husband, the siblings scattered to other parts of the country. Not once since their father's funeral six years ago have they been under the same roof, not even for Sandra's fortieth birthday party, nor for her children's high school graduations.

Sandra, the youngest of the three, is still in a state of shock about her demolished roots. It is as if someone set a torch to her history—the multigenerational imperative to stick together, to burnish the family name, its collective luster now reduced to a dark plume of memory. And she is trying to figure out how it could have happened—how a single burst of sibling rage could send it all up in flames.

"I must be the most naive person on the planet," says Sandra, shaking her head. "If anyone had told me this was coming, I would have called the person a liar. But all the signs were there." She continues:

Looking back, I'd say it all started with my mother. She was the most charming person imaginable, but there was a steeliness to her. She continually ridiculed my brother because he didn't go into the family business—he's an artist. She treated my sister with kid gloves, always giving in to her demands. As the lastborn, I was sort of lost in the shuffle. Only once did I complain to my father about my mother's favoritism. He said, "You know how she is—she's very insecure, but she means well. And your sister isn't as smart or as pretty as you. Have a heart." Out of loyalty to him, I didn't make an issue of it. Only now do I realize how much I went along with the Big Lie about blood-is-thicker-than-water. With my dad out of the picture, my sister just blew the family apart. But at least I don't have to pretend I like her anymore.

With her "protector" gone, Sandra has been forced to do a kind of body count, calculating the little family murders that piled up over the years, all covered over in the name of loyalty. But the unexpected payoff of this painful assessment is that she has developed compensatory strengths. The man she married is very like her father—stalwart, understanding. She has adopted her father's peacemaking ways, reaching out to her brother, providing him with affectionate support and encouragement.

There have been other changes. She has used her inheritance to help environmental causes—to the amusement of her brother, on whom the irony is not lost—"cleaning up" after their ancestors. And as a mother, Sandra has become keenly aware of the harm inflicted upon children by parental favoritism, how crucial it is not to sow seeds of their future discontent. But more than anything, Sandra says, her parents' deaths have simply freed her.

Right after my dad died, I said to my husband, "Now we can do whatever we want." I have a new definition of "home": It's wherever my husband and children are. It has been devastating to go through all this, but I have learned where my priorities belong. I'm not pulled in a thousand directions. And that has been an incredible relief.

Succession: The "Family" That Remains

As Sandra's story exemplifies, families are often irrevocably changed when the key players—the parents—are permanently removed. "I used to think the world divided between those who have children and those who don't," observes Blake Morrison in his memoir, *And When Did You Last See Your Father?* "[N]ow I think it divides between those who've lost a parent and those whose parents are still alive."

It's similar to what happens when a British monarch dies and the heirs to the throne move up in rank. At that moment, the kinship that cohered around genetic and emotional proximity to the parents is put to the test: Are the survivors still a "family"? And how will they relate to one another from now on? Few people can answer such questions until it actually happens—filial autonomy by parental attrition.

The most important consequence of the deaths of one's parents is not grief or mourning, which tend to fade over time; rather, it's the ripple effects of their dying. The most emotionally loaded of these "effects" is the connection between siblings—or, in the case of only children, the impact upon them of being generationally stranded.

This chapter will examine what happens to family attachments when there are no parents to hold the survivors together. Here the focus will be on three issues:

- The *economy* of the family hierarchy—the role of birth rank in determining how children compete for their parents' attention and nurturance.
- The *ecology* of family, or "family systems"—that is, how the intergenerational pieces work together, each person affecting all the others and in turn being affected by them.
- How these two concepts, birth order and family systems, played out among the adult children in my survey sample—specifically, the changes in their family connections when the parents were gone.

Birth Rank

Since recorded history began, the subject of birth order, and the sibling rivalry that can ensue from it, has had an almost mystical appeal. In biblical times, Cain slew his younger brother, Abel, in a fit of jealousy; more recently (1959), writer Jack Douglas quipped that his older brother "was an only child."

Despite its fascinating nature, however, any generalizations about birth order and its effect upon personality must be tempered by two caveats. First, the sequence of children's births is but one theme in the filial story, "only a bit-part in the drama of sibling differences," as human development professors Judy Dunn and Robert Plomin put it in *Separate Lives: Why Siblings Are So Different*.

For instance, the timing of your birth might or might not have been exactly auspicious. You might have gotten lucky and been born during high times of marital harmony and robust financial and physical health. Or you might have had the misfortune to arrive in bad times, right after your father lost his job and your mother teetered on the brink of a breakdown.

The other caveat is that "emotionally corrective experiences" outside the family—such as attaining professional prestige—can ameliorate deficits acquired within the family, as will be illustrated in the next four chapters.

Nevertheless, for most of my survey respondents, their relationships to their siblings—in particular, residual reactions to parental favoritism—became *the key family issue* when their parents died. These respondents held extremely strong views about their own sibling experiences, good or bad, and the "rank" order of things. And while these experiences were not conclusive in terms of their later development and choices, they had a great deal to do with the patterns in their attachments outside the family.

For it is *within* the family that children first learn how to get along with people bigger and smaller than they are—where they acquire their preliminary training in how to negotiate conflict and how to shine in other people's eyes.

All this has been scrutinized with scientific precision by Frank J. Sulloway, Ph.D. In his 1997 book, *Born to Rebel,* Sulloway offers a compelling Darwinian explanation for why children raised within the same family are so dissimilar and how these dissimilarities tend to be driven by a single, unchangeable variable: the sequence of their births.

The evolutionary goal of siblings, says Sulloway, is to make sure that they get a chunk of the parental pie—the pieces of which can be sliced only so thin—so that they can survive childhood, go on to reproduce themselves, and keep the gene pool percolating.

Firstborns, Sulloway has found, tend to be "assertive, socially dominant, ambitious, jealous of their status, and defensive." From earliest childhood, they try to avoid conflict with their parents, identifying with the parents and strenuously guarding their own special family standing.

In childhood, firstborns tend to be larger and brighter than laterborns, which, naturally, gives them an edge. They are also more "emotionally intense" and "tough-minded," and don't bounce back from disappointments as rapidly as their junior brethren. Firstborns are born conservatives—they savor the status quo. But should a sibling appear on the scene, firstborns will take on certain parental characteristics in order to stay the number-one child; they often are leaders and high achievers. And if they can hang on to their privileged status for six or more years before being upstaged by another child, says Sulloway, firstborns will be functional "onlies" (singletons will be discussed in a moment).

Nellie, forty-five, a vice president in an insurance agency, epitomizes the tough-minded, emotionally intense firstborn. Says Nellie:

My mother and I had a highly emotional relationship. She was very possessive, but very supportive and proud of me. The only problem was that she wanted to keep me on a short leash. I was having none of it. We had a terrible fight a few years ago which opened the door to her accepting me as an individual owned by no one. After that, we became very close. I was always her favorite, and my younger sister knew it. She was always trying to one-up me—when my mom died, she took everything in the house. There wasn't much. I didn't care. I've tried to patch things up between us, but she isn't interested.

Secondborns are born into an arithmetically more complex family climate—two parents and a mini-parent who can be very bossy. To attract parental attention and to prove that they are worthy of it, secondborns tend to be diplomats, identifying with everybody; they know whom to please (or displease), and how to curry favor. They also know how to make themselves indispensable. They find a skill or talent not already spoken for—a "niche," says Sulloway—and develop it. In this way, they augment family survival and, as a result, their own.

The strategy for secondborns is to be *different* from firstborns, thereby minimizing the likelihood that their parents will compare them unfavorably to the older child, which might have dreadful repercussions (such as reduced parental rations that previously had been earmarked for the firstborn). Opposite-sex siblings have a head start in this "differentness"—they each have their own gender turf, hence are less likely to evoke negative parental comparison, which augurs well for the sibling bond.

But whether of the same sex or the opposite sex, secondborns still face the reality of limited parental resources. A solution to this problem, Sulloway reports, is *diversification*.

To take a simplistic example, let us say that your parents were

NFL fanatics whose idea of blissful family togetherness was an afternoon of touch football. Your gawky eldest sibling, eager to impress your folks, learned how to throw a reasonably decent forward pass—it wobbled, but it got there.

However, you, muscular natural jock that you were, also wanted to impress your parents, but not at the risk of damaging your big sibling, which would have enticed everyone's wrath. Wisely, you became an ace wide receiver who never dropped the ball. *Together* you and your sibling enhanced the family "team," thereby making it plain to your parents that you were both needed—that, indeed, the game couldn't start without you.

Neil, thirty-nine, a computer salesman, is a classic secondborn. He could sell ice to a polar bear, and he's a party animal, a wiseguy who loves nothing better than swapping jokes with his buddies over a beer on his way home from work. Compared to his more buttoned-up older brother, a corporate attorney, Neil is, by his own admission, "outrageous." But he seldom makes a move on important matters without consulting his big brother. Says Neil,

> I have always trusted my brother with all family decisions, such as overseeing our parents' investments and being the executor of their wills. I never questioned his judgment or veracity, and I always believed that I could totally depend on him. I think that's one reason why was I able to separate from my parents relatively early in life—my childhood has been endless, because my big brother watches out for me. Compared to him, I'm a loose cannon. He's the steady one in the family who keeps me in check.

Thirdborns or *lastborn* children often have their work cut out for them. They may be overlooked in the sibling scheme of things, feeling neglected and outgunned, unable to beat the huge odds against becoming either the parental favorite or even the runner-up. (These also-rans, says Sulloway, are often late bloomers; because of their "open[ness] to radical innovations," they are frequently successful at older ages in whatever they choose to do.)

Lastborns are loath to go up against their older siblings, but—to continue the sports analogy—they don't want to be kicked off the field. Thus, they tend to become the family water carriers—dutiful, uncomplaining followers. This was clearly the case with Sandra, mentioned at the beginning of this chapter. As the baby in the family, she was always the most easily led—and, as it turned out, sadly misled.

On the other hand, lastborns, as their parents' parting genetic shots, might have the ultimate Darwinian laugh. They frequently get coddling from everyone—the parents *and* all those mini-parents. Often they are change-of-life children, forestalling empty nest blues; knowing that this child is the end of the filial line, the parents might have a soft spot for the littlest one.

For these reasons, middleborn children may be the true underdogs; they are, says Sulloway, the Darwinian "losers." In the keyboard of family life, they are middle C—neither the favorite nor the baby. Ordinally speaking, they are spectacularly bland. According to Sulloway, parents tend to favor other birth ranks over the one in between—the oldest, because they are likeliest to keep the family going via future reproduction; the youngest, because they are the most vulnerable to illness.

In the sibling race, middleborns can't win. They pose a threat to the firstborn and put him or her in a survival mode; adding salt to the wound, middleborns are *themselves* "displaced" by a younger sibling. As a result, they tend to be more loosely attached to their parents, and often turn to someone outside the immediate family for the approval they can't get within it.

Penny, thirty-nine, is the secondborn and most successful of three children (she is a well-known fashion designer). She is also the most high-strung. Her older sister was her mother's favorite child; her younger brother (the only son), her father's. Thus, Penny, given the supply-and-demand realities, became the apple of her grand-mother's eye. It was the grandmother, also a designer, who taught Penny all she knows about dressmaking. Says Penny,

> From the start, my mother and I were aliens to one another. She went out of her way to let me know that if I wanted affection, I had to go elsewhere because she was tapped out. Short of setting my hair on fire, there was no way I was going to get any positive attention at home. I can remember back in grade school adopting other people's parents, buttering up teachers, trying to be fetching and adorable. But without all those mentors, I would have been finished. I have never thought of my immediate family as reliable or to be counted upon.

Only Children

All predictive bets are emphatically off for the child who has no brothers and sisters; indeed, offspring who have never had to compete for their parents' attention are a special case.

Although psychological theorists often lump singletons together with firstborns, it would be misleading to suppose that they are *the same* as firstborns. As long as there is a sibling—even if that sibling is ten years older or younger—there is still a basis for parental comparison.

This point was poignantly brought home to me by Olivia, forty-nine, who was an only child by default—two previous children were stillborns. Thus she was not simply a singleton; she was a "replacement" child, standing in for two others. Says Olivia,

I've always had totally unrealistic expectations of how wonderful it would be to have a sibling with whom to share the good and bad times. My relationship with my parents was very complicated—they had a lot of expectations of me which I largely didn't meet. When you lose two children, how could the one that's left ever be enough? My mother took it as a personal affront if I didn't do things exactly the way she did. But knowing all that she had been through, I was a very good girl, and did my best to please her. I have always succeeded at whatever I set my mind to. It's just that my opinion of myself has never been as high as other people's of me; I could never make up for my parents' losses.

Researchers have found that only children have certain advantages and disadvantages. The disadvantages are that they are often raised in single-parent homes. Plus, parents of onlies tend to be older when they reproduce than parents with several children, with the result that onlies frequently are "orphaned" earlier than other children. Moreover, singletons have no one to share the onus of being the jewel in the parental crown upon whom all hopes are pinned.

According to Sulloway, onlies have another huge disadvantage: They have *much more conflict* with their parents than do children raised in larger families (siblings dump their filial frustrations on one another rather than risk parental reprisal).

But the advantages of being a singleton are considerable. Relative to parents with several children, parents of only children tend to be well educated with lofty IQs. Consequently, their offspring might be more richly genetically endowed; only children generally have greater verbal and intellectual abilities than people with siblings.

In addition, only children are often extremely self-confident and self-involved—or at least give that appearance. In a review of the psychological literature on only children, Toni Falbo of the University of Texas posited that the higher academic achievements of only children have less to do with their native intelligence than with their internal "locus of control."

To translate this concept into realspeak, only children, because they have their parents' undivided attention, more quickly and consistently pick up on their parents' undiluted approval or disapproval than do children with siblings. Singletons know in unambiguous terms what will please or displease the parent, which gives them a sense of their own agency—that is, their influence upon the parent.

And when only children are distressed, they usually don't have to wait an eternity for an adult to notice and do something about it; they don't have to queue up for solace. Singletons come to expect an immediate response, which can give them a feeling of entitlement. It is precisely because they were attended to quickly in childhood, says Falbo, that only children "acquire a more trusting style of interaction."

But one advantage might rise above all the others; onlies learn early on how to be independent and to do their own "thing," whatever that is. Indeed, it could be argued—and Sulloway does—that the most predictable characteristic of only children is that they are so *unpredictable*. Relative to children with siblings, onlies are more open to experience. And, according to other investigators, onlies are the most consistently emotionally stable across the life span, identifying with both parents and absorbing behavioral aspects of both genders.

Summing Up: The Impact of Parental Favoritism

The bottom Sullowayian line on birth order (the fallout of which, he states, is not set in stone) is this: "A child who cannot count on parental investment must come to terms with this fact of life and consider alternative options"—a polite way of saying, "Your parents liked your siblings *way* better than you. Get over it."

For the respondents in my survey sample, 87 percent of whom have siblings, this was easier said than done. When asked, "Was one of you a parental 'favorite'?" *85 percent of the respondents said yes* (only 11 percent reported that their parents specifically made a point of not "playing favorites").

These responses followed gender lines. Daughters were more likely to say they were their father's "favorite"; sons were more likely to say they had been their mother's "favorite." Among respondents with opposite-sex siblings, sisters tended to agree with these evaluations—that is, they reported that a brother was the mother's favorite.

Of those respondents with only same-sex siblings, birth order, rather than gender, was the key variable in parental favoritism; the firstborn was usually Mom's favorite, the second, Dad's.

All of which begins to explain why, when parents die, offspring within the same family have not "lost" the same parent—they have lost the parent for whose nurturance they jockeyed, each in his or her own specialized way, in order to stay alive.

Birth rank does not, however, occur in a vacuum; it is subject to the emotional tensions that ebb and flow within the family and between the generations. To get a handle on how offspring interact and feel about one another in adulthood, one needs to look at how the original family unit, and each member of it, *collectively* operated—and how family allegiances may be rearranged when the parents are gone.

Family Systems

Birth rank says a lot about how we behave in our families of origin, but, to reiterate, the numbers alone are not the whole story. Rather, children's behavior unfolds within the larger emotional family context.

All families begin with a triangle: mother, father, and child. To understand the dynamics among them, and to clarify what can happen between offspring when parents die, "family systems theory," the brainchild of psychiatrist Murray Bowen, is extremely helpful.

According to Michael E. Kerr, M.D., who explicated Bowen's theory in his book *Family Evaluation*, "The family is a unit because it operates as a system. One person responds to another, who responds to another, who responds to the first, who has already responded to the responses of others to him, etc."

Triangles are the "molecule" of emotional systems, says Dr. Kerr. If a two-person relationship is stable, a third person will be the outsider. But if the connection between the first two heats up and becomes cantankerous, the third person suddenly becomes important, drawn in to "stabilize," or cool down, the relationship, which inevitably leaves one of the first two out. As was mentioned in chapter 1, this is called "triangling" (or "triangulation").

Here's how it works. As Bowen conceptualized it, people *function* in response to the functioning of other people. So let us say that you were the middleborn of three sisters. Let us further suppose that your parents were having rough marital times and your brainy big sister reacted by getting involved with drugs and flunking out of school. You, the conciliatory B-average secondborn, might have seized upon this opportunity to become the filial star—a straight-A know-it-all.

You used to be the family diplomat; with your older sister in reduced circumstances, you got to be the "functional" firstborn, doing your parents proud and becoming a leader to your lackluster younger sister, who, in response, might have emerged from the sibling fog and turned into Ms. Personality. The firstborn was sent to the cellar of parental favoritism, and might even have become the family scapegoat.

Indeed, scapegoating—a time-honored staple of dysfunctional families—is triangling at its most painful. As long as one family member is cast as the ne'er-do-well or oddball, the rest of the family can be united in disapproval. To avoid *becoming* the scapegoat, siblings might be none too eager to help the "bad" child straighten out. The "good" siblings, along with the parents, might pounce upon the scapegoat, making such "triangling" comments as "You're going to give Dad a heart attack if you keep this up"—hardly an incentive for the outnumbered scapegoat to reform.

In fact, the scapegoat might grow so accustomed to being blamed for family strife—it is, after all, a surefire attention-getter and, to boot, a good way to keep unhappily married parents distracted from their connubial angst—that he or she might keep right on drawing fire well into adulthood.

Triangling, says Kerr, not only helps stabilize family functioning or dysfunctioning within the current generation, but in generations preceding (think *Romeo and Juliet*) and those to come. For example, your father hated his father; the message was that you should hate your grandfather, too—and his sisters and his cousins and his aunts and all their progeny.

To take another example, let's say you constantly argued with your mother and she responded by saying, "Thank God my mother isn't alive to see this—it would *kill* her." The message here—and it's a humdinger of "family systems" subtlety, so pay close attention—is that your mother secretly *admired* you, or else why would she underscore your bad behavior by calling in this dead reinforcement? Your mother's hidden agenda might have been that she never had the courage to tell her own mother where to get off; you, the resident rapscallion, were acting out her anger for her. You became the unwitting instrument of her revenge.

In these triangulating ways, family tension does not evaporate—it is passed on to the next generation (how to undo, or prevent, such a fate will be explored in chapters 9 and 10). As Kerr explains it,

> Once the emotional circuitry of a triangle is in place, it usually outlives the people who participate in it. If one member of a triangle dies, another person usually replaces him. The actors come and go, but the play lives on through the generations.

This "circuitry" is often the precursor of deteriorated sibling attachments in the aftermath of parental death. When parents set an example of taking sides or of rejection as solutions to relationship problems, and no one says "Hey, this is between you and them; don't put me in the middle" (which would short out the "circuitry"), these behaviors are presented as viable options for offspring. The result can be found in their ongoing sibling rivalries—a situation that applied to many of the people who participated in my study.

Realigned Sibling Attachments

When siblings are youngsters, they have no choice but to interact and, to one degree or another, be loyal to one another—their survival inside the family, and *as* a family, might depend upon it. But when children are grown and their parents die, there is no logical reason for them to remain loyal.

Indeed, a comparison of the orphans and semi-orphans in my sample makes this case. Of those who reported having always been close to their siblings, 14 percent are full orphans, as compared to 86 percent of the semi-orphans. Of those who said they are not close to their siblings, 68 percent are full orphans, compared to only 32 percent of the semi-orphans.

Clearly, the deaths of both parents marks a turning point in the sibling relationship and can alter how siblings feel about one another. Put another way, with no living parent to color those feelings, the connection takes on a different hue.

Most of the siblings in my sample have stayed in each other's lives to a greater or lesser extent. What usually holds them together is a mixture of affection and collective history and identity—a kind of chromosomal auld lang syne. But their relationships are seldom *exactly* as they were when the parents were alive; only 19 percent said the bond was unchanged. Over half (53 percent) said they've become closer to one or more siblings, and another 23 percent said they've become distant or estranged from one or more siblings.

In other words, *76 percent of these attachments changed.*

Closer Sibships

Sibling rivalries are a tricky business in the aftermath of parental death and can ultimately backfire—especially should there come a time in your life when you're feeling alone and friendless, out of cash, or out of luck, or when you'd like someone to tell you the unvarnished truth (which siblings are only too happy to do). Siblings are a kind of insurance policy; this is one bridge you might not want to burn.

For most of the respondents—even among those who were polar opposites of their siblings—having *no* contact was anathema, and they weren't about to risk it. "People feel embarrassed and uncomfortable about the fallout of family dynamics when parents die," says psychotherapist Dr. Jane Greer, co-author of *Adult Sibling Rivalry*. "They don't want to shake the family tree, or disrupt whatever semblance of family life they have left."

Of those respondents who have grown closer to all their siblings (47 percent of the females and 32 percent of the males) or to at least one (7 percent of the females and 18 percent of the males), a number of reasons were cited. Many people said, "It's just us now." Others said that sibling intimacy had been revived in the course of coordinating their elderly parents' care and, later, their funerals—the most intense time the siblings had spent together since childhood.

Still others said that they had grown closer to a sibling by virtue of maturing, accepting, or making an effort to be more understanding of one another. In many cases, the parents had been an emotional "wedge" between siblings by displaying obvious favoritism; with this barrier gone, the siblings were able to rediscover, even discover, one another.

Rose, forty-two, and Daphne, thirty-nine, exemplify this increased and redefined sibling closeness. The two sisters were born in Belfast, but came to the United States in their twenties. When they were children, the unrest that divided their city was replicated in miniature by the sisters in their own family. Rose, the overprotected "helpless" one (a functional secondborn), and Daphne, the levelheaded "dependable" one (a functional firstborn), were natural enemies and natural allies, a quarrelsome but united front against their hapless parents.

Their father, who died in 1990, had been a man of almost no words; he seemed becalmed, like a sailboat on a windless sea. Their mother, who died in 1986, exuded an air of defeat, her emotional thermostat set at perpetual anxiety. And their daughters, caught in the crossfire of this silent warfare, gave it lusty voice. "My sister and I fought their battles for them," says Daphne, chuckling. "We had some *beauts*. Once, during a tug-of-war, Rose fell and broke her arm. I swear, it was an accident."

These fights didn't cease in Belfast—they were exported across the Atlantic, as the sisters argued over whose turn it was to go back for a visit, with Daphne generally making the trek. The spats continued even after their virtually penniless parents died. Rose, irked by her father's "head in the sand" financial lassitude, refused to help pay for his casket, and Daphne got stuck with the tab.

And then there was the cumbersome business of a deathbed promise extracted from Daphne by her mother, who had said, "Take care of Rose. You're the strong one. You're all each other's got." Daphne can laugh about much of this sibling infighting—*now*. At the time, she says, she was beside herself.

> Right after my father died, things were really raw between Rose and me. Everything that had been potentially contentious between us just came to the fore. I think we were each expecting the other to fulfill the role of the perfect parent. The biggest change in my life since my parents' deaths has been my relationship to my sister. We're still close, but there's less need for it. We don't have that much in common. But we are *powerfully* connected. What's different is that I'm less angry with her for being the first to get the parental goodies. And I'm more accepting of who she is. I cannot imagine not being on speaking terms with her. That to me would be horrific.

Daphne and Rose had two vital elements going for them: For one thing, their parents encouraged their closeness. More important, their childhood roles were no longer required to stabilize the family. They jointly moved up in rank, which freed them to relate *solely* to one another, rather than through the prism of their parents' troubles. In short, they had to rely on themselves for survival; sibling friendship was very much an optional, and welcome, bonus.

Extinguishing childhood roles, says Dr. Greer, is a crucial factor in establishing, or maintaining, sibling harmony in adulthood. She explains,

When you knock out the role distinction, some of the loving feelings between siblings may return. The long-standing resentments between them can dissipate, and the closeness and camaraderie they shared when they were kids can rise to the surface.

Perhaps the most dramatic example of the benefits of eliminating childhood roles is when a scapegoated sibling is drawn back into the family fold. This usually happens because the "outsider" function, which served a steadying purpose when the parents were around, has outlived its usefulness.

Elena, thirty-five, is the lastborn of three children—she has an older sister and a brother, Timothy. Throughout Elena's growing-up years, Timothy was the bane of her existence—a merciless tease and, when he hit his teens, a nasty drunk. "I *hated* him," says Elena. Many of her brother's problems stemmed from the fact that both their parents were alcoholics—her dad drank himself to death.

Four years ago her mother was diagnosed with an illness which, in a matter of three months, ended her life as well. During that three-month period, Elena, who is married and has a young child, and her unmarried brother became fast friends. No one was more surprised by this turnabout than Elena herself.

The one thing we had in common was our love for our mom— we all adored her, except when she was sloshed. When I told Timothy about her diagnosis, he said, "God, you guys are the only family I'll have left." He stopped drinking. He moved in with my mom to take care of her. He was remarkable—really patient, really caring. I was *shocked* by the change in him, because there had been years when we'd never see or hear from him. Now he spontaneously calls or writes a couple of times a month. It's the best thing that came out of my mother's death, a real gift. He wanted us to be a family, and for the first time in maybe ever, we are.

Unchanged Sibships

Of those respondents who reported that their attachments to their siblings remained for the most part unchanged, most had either always been close, or were never close, or felt relatively neutral about their siblings. And they were in no hurry for it to be otherwise; indeed, the older these respondents were, the likelier they were to report this consistency in their sibling relationships.

Birth order was an important variable in this sibling status quo. As was mentioned earlier, middleborns tend to reach outside the family for emotional support and approval. For many middleborns, the sibling connection remained relatively unaltered; they tended to have the same degree of closeness to or distance from their siblings after the parents died as when the parents were alive. They didn't expect much from their siblings, just as they had not from their parents. (The irony is that their siblings might feel altogether otherwise *about* them. Investigators have found that older and younger siblings prefer middleborns to one another—they cite the middle child as the sibling to whom they are "closest.")

Gender was a significant factor in sibling closeness. Numerous respondents reported having always been fond of one or more siblings, with opposite-sex siblings feeling warmer toward one another than same-sex siblings.

In answer to the question "Which sibling(s) were you closest to in childhood and why were you close?" 41 percent of the *females* said "brother" (evenly divided between older and younger brothers), and 27 percent said "sister" (with younger sisters getting the preferential nod). Similarly, 45 percent of *male* respondents preferred their sisters (again, evenly divided between older and younger sisters), while 36 percent preferred their brothers (here, too, younger brothers won out).

As to *why* they were close, the top three reasons cited by *males* were "closeness in age," "similar values and dispositions," and "parents always encouraged the closeness." The top three reasons cited by *females*, however, were that the respondent was the "mother figure," or the brother was "looked up to" by the respondent, or the sibling was closest in age.

Gender was also a key determinant in terms of which siblings maintained contact—that is, who, if anyone, was the "kin-keeper," a job that previously had been the province of their parents. A sister (or sister-in-law), rather than a brother, usually became the new family switchboard.

Several people in my sample—all females—reported that although their sibling ties had relaxed slightly as a result of divergent interests and geographic locations, these ties were for the most part as affectionate as ever. Says Lydia, forty-five, the thirdborn of five children,

> When my mom was alive, she was the one who kept us all up to speed on what the others were doing. After she died, we had to find a way to stay connected. I'd say I'm the one who initiates most of the contacts between us. I feel a strong need to stay tight with my sibs. Even though one of my brothers is on the strange side—he's the oldest hippie alive—I keep in touch, and I bite my tongue when he gets on his anti-capitalist soapbox. It's important to me that we all be there for each other when one of us is in trouble, and we are.

However, for those adult children who never felt affection for a brother or sister—regardless of their birth rank or gender—it was often too late in the sibling game to manufacture it. Many researchers have found that sibling attachments post-parental death are dependent upon the quality of the relationship earlier on. If they were always at odds, these siblings frequently part company for good when their parents die.

Distant or Estranged Sibships

And then there were those respondents who moved off into the family sunset in the aftermath of their parents' deaths—who rarely, or never, saw their siblings and wanted little or nothing to do with them. While these two items—distance and estrangement—share the same statistical category, the reasons ascribed by respondents to this sibling disconnection put them into two distinct camps.

Siblings with diminished contact often simply took separate lifestyle paths. With little in common except their parents, they became more and more dissimilar as they carved out their niches in the world (studies on human development have found that the older siblings get, the less they resemble one another). While bearing each other no ill will, these siblings gradually sank lower on each other's list of priorities.

In some cases, however, one sibling was cast, unbidden, into playing "surrogate parent" to a brother or sister, which undermined their sibship and placed it under greater strain. For example, the very diplomacy and lack of competitiveness that often endear secondborns to their more opinionated older siblings can cause an older sibling to exploit this cordiality when parents die. Here, the older sibling turns to the younger sibling for nurturing that is no longer available from parents.

One woman, the mother of three young children, found that after her mother's death, her unmarried older brother began asking her advice on everything from girlfriends to health matters to cars—guidance he never sought, and would surely have scorned, when their mother was alive. She says,

You know, it's hard enough to grow up when your mom dies. But I feel as if I've become "mommy" to my brother, and it makes me uncomfortable. He's terribly sweet, but I sometimes feel overwhelmed by the responsibility. If I'm the least bit critical, he acts as though he's mortally wounded. I just want the relationship to go back to where it was—two devil-may-care sibs speeding down the freeway in a convertible with the top down and the radio blasting. I keep wanting to tell him, "Damn it, I've got enough kids."

In other instances, a firstborn sibling became a "parental" martinet, doling out unsolicited advice or heaping disapproval upon younger siblings for their behavior and choices. Here, the older sibling usurped family authority, in a sense resigning as a peer. Says Karen Gail Lewis, Ed.D., a psychotherapist who specializes in sibling relationships,

The sibling who takes over has joined the "parent" rank, and the other sibs often get angry, the same way they did in childhood when one of them sided with the parent. It's "You're not my mom" all over again. You violate your sibling norm.

However, sibling *estrangement*, when the gloves come off, is a whole other ball game. Often it is a consequence of rivalries within the family that reached the boiling point when the parents became ill and that continued to erupt after the parents died. Several respondents who had been their parents' caretakers were so beaten up by the experience, and so resentful of the lesser involvement of their siblings, that their attachments to the siblings collapsed under the weight.

Rea Kahn, R.N., M.P.S., who recruits, trains, and supervises family support group leaders for the Alzheimer's Association in New York, has been privy to many such sibling partings. She says,

Some adult children have never completed the separation process with their parents, and a devastating chronic illness can bring old issues to the surface. Siblings often play out their competitiveness by cutting off another sibling, saying that the person didn't do enough to help. And some caregiving children are so depleted when the parent dies—their own health is in terrible shape—it's as if they died too, and they just pull away from the family.

The most unusual example of sibling fractiousness in the aftermath of parental death was recounted by Dr. Greer: A sister and brother, who had always been on extremely cordial terms, got into a battle over their cremated mother's ashes. The brother took the ashes and refused to release them, not even for the mother's memorial service. Says Dr. Greer, "It was a power struggle. The bottom line for this man was, 'I was the most important and closest one to Mom,' and keeping the ashes established that closeness for him."

Most researchers say that bitter sibling estrangements are by-products of their parents' severe personal difficulties early in children's lives. In their book *Of Human Bonding: Parent-Child Relations Across the Life Course*, Alice S. Rossi and Peter H. Rossi observe that a sense of "kinship obligation" is reduced when parents have emotional troubles such as divorce or alcoholism. But when parents are happily married and manifestly loving to their children, in adulthood these children report that they are on good, even affectionate, terms with their siblings, as well as with other family members.

The people I interviewed who did not experience such parental affection—who, in fact, experienced only harshness or neglect—frequently ran as far and as quickly as they could not only from childhood but from all sibling reminders of it.

Natalie, forty-one, is such a person. The firstborn of three children, she was very close to her father until her twin sisters came along five years later and captured the parental focus. Natalie never got along with her mother, who, Natalie is convinced, "despised" her from the beginning.

Because of her independent personality—abetted by her father's early devotion and attentiveness—Natalie struck out on her own at eighteen and saw her parents and siblings only rarely thereafter. When her parents were dying, she returned to say good-bye and, later, to attend their funerals. Since then, she has had almost no contact with her siblings. Says Natalie,

> I was always the family outcast because I wouldn't be my mother's toadie. My dad loved me, but he always said, "She's the boss." My mother used to smack me when I contradicted her, a punishment never inflicted on my sisters. The rule in our family always was, you can't speak to each other; you can only talk through Mom. It was one of these weird families where everybody was pretending to love everybody, but underneath it was never any fun. My sisters have no identity. They bought the party line that our parents were paragons, and they spent their whole lives doing what they were told. I've tried to get them to talk about our problems, but they just stonewall me. "You're the one with the problem," is their answer to everything.

Other respondents, however, were the rejectees—that is, they were cruelly rebuffed by one or more siblings whom they had previously adored. For these people, the rejection was *much more painful* than the deaths of their parents; it was as if they had been abandoned a second time, only this time it was by one of their own—their generational comrade.

Dr. Lewis says that such "cutoffs" are common among siblings raised by dysfunctional parents. "The more abusive the childhood home, the more problems siblings have and the greater the chance that they will deal with it by protecting themselves however they can, either by pulling away or by fighting."

Late-Life Sibling Reconciliation

Not all sibling estrangements, however, are permanent; sometimes they reverse themselves. Adult children who absent themselves from the sibling proceedings may regroup from afar and thereafter reappear on the family scene. As Drs. Helgola G. Ross and Joel I. Milgram, who have studied adult sibling relationships, put it, "[A]voidance may . . . allow siblings to find strengths, even identities, that will allow them at later dates to re-enter relationships that earlier were too dangerous to deal with."

Other studies of adult siblings show that the older siblings are, the closer they become. In one such investigation, Victor G. Cicirelli of Purdue University found that 83 percent of siblings age sixty and over were close or "extremely close," compared to 68 percent of middle-aged respondents. Dr. Cicirelli concluded that sibling closeness late in life is a form of "attachment" behavior that has its antecedents in infancy and can be rekindled as they approach the ends of their own lives; it becomes preposterous to ruminate over who got better toys a lifetime ago.

As all these survey data and case studies illustrate—and as numerous other investigators have found—siblings are each other's most enduring partners in life, even if they don't see one another for long stretches. When parents die, siblings often become each other's reference points.

It is from their brothers and sisters that adult children frequently find greater tacit understanding than with anyone else. With a sibling, one doesn't have to put on one's party manners, or set an example, or *explain* everything. For many siblings, the fact that they were together in the past and are still around to enjoy what's left of the future is sufficient to justify their ongoing connection.

Alone at the Top: Only Children

I have saved for the end of this chapter the discussion of "orphaned" only children because, as in childhood, they remain a special case—and also because small family sizes, particularly one-child families, are becoming increasingly prevalent.

For an adult child to be without either parents *or* siblings is to have all buffers against one's own death removed. Now it's just the survivor and whatever extended kin are out there—aunts and uncles, cousins once or twice removed. Depending upon the tenor of these relationships—and for the most part, in spite of it—being "orphaned" places the only child in unique existential straits.

Thirteen percent of my survey sample were only children, and when it came to their overall response to parental death, they were in a league of their own. They were less likely than others in the sample to have been close to their parents in childhood and more likely in adulthood to have married and reproduced, and to have carried on certain family traditions.

If these singletons had one thing in common, it was that most of them, even the married ones, always felt alone on some fundamental level—now more than ever. Says Anthony, forty-four, a surgeon whose parents died when he was in his late twenties,

> I pretty much gave up on my parents long before they died. They did their best, but they didn't have whatever it takes to be a good parent. My mother never praised my accomplishments, and my dad was disappointed that I didn't become a lawyer. So I never

thought of them as "home." What blew me away when they died was that I was really alone—not only were my parents gone, but I had no siblings. The overwhelming feeling was that I was next on the tarmac. If it weren't for my wife and kids, the sense of isolation would be horrendous.

According to life span developmental psychologists, the largest hurdle for only children when their parents die may be that they seldom were "children" to begin with. Onlies so identify with parents and other adults that their main problem often is learning how to co-exist with their peers.

The singletons I talked to had to bear the burden of being their *parents'* point of reference. Nearly all of them said that one or both parents had always been dependent upon them for love and approval, rather than the other way around, which caused considerable consternation. It is understandable, then, that most of these singletons were relieved by their parents' deaths, however much the deaths might have underscored their sense of vulnerability.

Freedom from responsibility for their parents' well-being was not, however, an unalloyed joy. Having been the suns to their parents' moons, they were having trouble *not* being the center of other people's universes. "I still find myself looking for approval," said a fifty-one-year-old woman, "and I still get furious when I don't get it." To fill this void, several singletons turned to religion or mysticism after their parents died, where they found a new sense of importance and context.

Still, few of these respondents could be characterized as having been crushed when their parents died. In becoming, as one respondent put it, "tough little soldiers" in childhood, they were veterans of self-reliance and of self-definition, eager to claim a stake in their own generation—but rarely being completely sure where they fit in.

On Borrowed Time

Most people, by the time they reach their forties and fifties, begin to take more than a passing interest in their heritage—their parents' histories and those of their parents and grandparents before them—a rough blueprint of their futures. Parental death is a watershed moment for adult children that alerts them to the reality that there might be less time ahead for them than has already passed.

As long as one has kin, one is never entirely marooned in this sobering recognition. "Orphaned" men and women become acutely aware that the future is upon them, and as a result often look to their siblings as a safe harbor to which they can periodically return when they encounter heavy weather.

The sibling connection can serve as a kind of weather vane for life outside the family, the yardstick against which adult children can measure their own losses and gains. If they are fortunate, they and their siblings will help each other along the way. But if their sibling relationships remain unresolved—the unhappy residue of parental favoritism or of ancient, half-remembered vendettas—other relationships, or lack of them, may assume a new urgency.

Either way, parental death can jolt them into reevaluating and rebuilding their lives, often from the ground up, not only with their remaining kin but also with (or without) partners and progeny and friends—and even in their careers.

And for the majority of people in my sample, this is exactly what happened.

CHAPTER
5 Changes of Heart: Effect on Romantic Partnerships

My husband is my true "mother" and "father," and I think I function in some parental way toward him, too. But it took a long time for us to reach this level of closeness. When we were first married, every time we had a disagreement I'd say, "That's it! I'm outta here!" because that's all I heard when I was a kid. He'd always say, "That's not an option." He's stuck with me through all the rough times—I went through hell with my parents, and he was constantly there for me. That's what brings tears to my eyes—not my parents' deaths, but the joy I feel when I think of how he's helped me become the person I always wanted to be.

—Beverly, forty-two

Beverly and her husband, Victor, recently celebrated their twentieth anniversary, a milestone she counts as something of a miracle. Married a scant four months after they met—Beverly, a piano teacher, was twenty-two, and Victor, a surveyor, was twenty-eight—the couple could not have been less alike, given their disparate histories.

When Beverly was growing up, she and her mother were exceptionally close. "My good little helper," her mother said of her willingness to pitch in with the dishes or baby-sit for her younger brother; "such a comfort" for keeping her mother company whenever her hotheaded father blew his stack and stormed out the door. But the year Beverly turned fourteen, her parents divorced and the chemistry between mother and daughter soured; suddenly, *she* was the root of all her mother's problems. Beverly's mother accused her of disloyalty, of being "up to no good" with boyfriends. From then on, Beverly's brother took center stage in her mother's affections.

Victor's childhood, on the other hand, was something out of *Little House on the Prairie*. The youngest of three children, he grew up in a family of stability and unflagging supportiveness; in this family, all the children were their parents' favorites. Victor never doubted that he was loved, and he has nothing but good memories of his boyhood.

Which is one reason why, when they met, Beverly instantly fell in love with him. In Victor, she found not only the man of her dreams but also the *family*—his parents wholeheartedly embraced her and, later, Beverly's and Victor's children. The same could not be said of Beverly's mother, who had disapproved of the match from the start and became increasingly unavailable to Beverly.

It was the contrast between these two families that caused Beverly to return again and again to her mother, entreating her to take a greater interest in her. It was as if she needed permission to enjoy her own husband and children—as if, by having a family of her own, her life had become a repudiation of her mother's, for which Beverly was to be punished. But the more she tried to endear herself, the more her mother found fault.

And then six years ago there came a Passover seder at her mother's house to which Beverly's brother and his wife were invited, but not Beverly and her husband, who were pointedly asked to make other plans. It would be "too much work," her mother said, "to have so many people." Of that day, Beverly recalls,

We stayed home because I was not fit company—I spent the day sobbing because I was so tied up with wanting my mother's approval. And at the end of the day I looked at my wonderful husband and children and I thought, What am I doing? Why am I ruining this day for the people I love most and who love me? And I said, "It's over." From then on, I was in the clear—I quit trying to win my mother back.

Within a year, Beverly's mother was diagnosed with a terminal illness, and Beverly made a last visit to say good-bye, pretending that all was well between them. At her mother's funeral, Beverly shed not a tear—she was all cried out. Her mother had already "died" that spring day when Beverly realized that her allegiance belonged to the family she had, by some uncanny stroke of luck, created for herself.

But her painful connection to her mother was not entirely over. Victor was instrumental in helping Beverly to put her difficult childhood into perspective. With him as a gentle sounding board, she has come to understand that her parents were essentially unhappy people who tried to wrest from their children the devotion they could not summon from one another. She now believes that they did the best they could, under the circumstances, and that, in retrospect, she has far less to be bitter about than they. "They must have done something right," she muses. "How can I hate them when I have so much?"

And that is what Beverly means when she says that Victor is her "true mother and father." It is within her marriage that she has felt free to *be* herself—where she has been able to let her parents go, finish growing up, and finally find a home.

The Sleeper Effect of Parental "Loss": Who Loves You Now?

For most people, any major setback evokes an almost automatic calculation of who truly cares about them and where they might find sanctuary—an awareness of what they do and do not have in the breach. But the death of a parent gives this awareness a decidedly sharper edge.

As was demonstrated in the preceding chapter, when parents die, adult children often turn to their siblings or another relative for solace. But they also scan the wider horizon of their day-to-day lives for someone to fill the void. That person is usually an intimate partner, whether a spouse or a lover. For those who do not have a partner, the void may be more keenly felt, its implications more anguishing.

You will recall from chapter 1 that when people are in great distress, they often revert to what psychiatrist John Bowlby calls "attachment behaviors" to allay feelings of vulnerability or abandonment, attempting to cobble together a "secure base" for sustenance.

For example, they might suddenly feel a desperate need for someone—anyone—to have and to hold, if only to get through the night. Or they might become more unsure of the significant other already in their lives, anxiously clinging to or testing the fidelity of the person. They might become more protective or possessive of a partner, worrying constantly about his or her health. Or they might become more aloof from a partner so as not to become too dependent. All these are routine, and usually subconscious, survival mechanisms, mobilized in periods of crisis.

As the months and years go by, however, and adult children gradually adjust to life without their parents, *something even more profound happens*: They reappraise their private lives in view of the stark reality that they are, now and forever, nobody's "child." As one married respondent, whose father died a year ago, put it, "I feel a bit unmoored in all my relationships. I need to start at ground zero and reevaluate everyone in my life."

The purpose of this chapter is to examine the changes in intimate partnerships, or lack of them, that are a direct result of such reevaluations.

Counting the Ways

In answer to the question "How has your marriage or romantic attachment—or the absence of a partner—been affected by your parents' death?" 39 percent of the respondents said that this area of their lives had *improved*, 17 percent said it had *deteriorated*, and 31 percent said it was *unchanged* (the remainder left the question blank). In other words, slightly over half the sample—*56 percent*—see their private lives in an entirely new fashion.

In talking to these people, I discovered three distinct trends. For example, several people said that they *got* married as a direct result of their parents' deaths. With the senior generation removed, they felt a strong desire to find a suitable mate with whom to form a new family, to replace the one that no longer existed.

The second trend pertained to people who were already married when their parents died. The effect of the deaths took two forms: Some people said that their marriages had gotten stronger; others said that life was too short to remain in marriages that were unsatisfying.

The third trend occurred among people who, at the time of their parents' deaths, were single or divorced and who remained unattached. They had to adjust to the fact that they might spend the rest of their lives not only unparented but unpartnered. For these people, the word *alone* took on new meaning, some seeing it as a blessing, others seeing it as a curse.

Before delving into the details of these three trends, it is important to set the stage by examining the generational differences that form their background.

Our Parents/Ourselves: Differing Views of Love and Marriage

To gauge how profoundly the love lives of adult children can be affected by their parents' deaths, it is necessary to understand the parents' influence in this area while they were alive. For instance, you might have chosen your mate in part because he or she passed parental muster; this was a union your parents could bless, the withholding of which blessing might have put the kibosh on things.

Let us say that your parents were devout Jews. It probably crossed your mind that the person for whom you set your cap better be of the same religion. So you did the "right" thing; you married a Jew, leaving you to suffer the possible negative consequences of your loyalty to their religious beliefs rather than to the dictates of your ecumenical heart.

Parental opinion might also have played a role in staying in a marriage that, in the long dark night of your middle-aged soul, didn't exactly ring your chimes—again, doing the "right" thing for the wrong reasons. You might, for instance, have considered shedding your spouse, but you would have been the first person in your Roman Catholic family ever to do so, and you weren't up to facing your parents' dismay, so you stuck it out.

On the other hand, perhaps you were making a statement by remaining resolutely unattached because your parents kept pressuring you to "settle down," and you were going to show them a thing or two about the meaning of independence—of being able to live without anyone, even if it killed you.

But when parents die, taking their generational mores and matrimonial track records with them, their feelings and opinions about your love life are rendered moot. Now, a world of choice opens up—you can decide for yourself what counts most in affairs of the heart. You can stay with your partner or leave, couple up or swear off romance, repeat your parents' mistakes or conjure up new ones. Either way, Mom and Dad aren't around to weigh in on the subject.

Of course, all this freedom comes at a price: Without your parents to influence you one way or the other, it's on *your* head how your love life turns out. And it is this alarming awareness that can shake adult children to the core, causing them to seriously question their own judgment and reevaluate their romantic choices—to figure out who, if anyone, they really want to come "home" to, and whether or not the person to whom they may be currently attached fills the bill.

Marrying After Parents Die

Logic dictates that such reevaluations would be a piece of cake for adult children who decide to marry after their parents die, because they have only themselves to answer to. But a great deal depends on whether or not their choice of mate is driven by an underlying urgency to fill the parental vacuum.

Numerous psychological pundits, from Freud onward, have theorized that a hallmark of adulthood is the ability to detach from one's parents and reattach to others. But healthy reattachment does not mean forming a tie that is *identical* to the parent-child bond. By reattachment, these theorists are talking about the capacity to love and trust a member of one's own generation, equal to equal, as opposed to a replication of the parent-child connection, in which one person dominates the other.

Many of these same theorists also posit that when people marry, they inevitably bring with them the templates of their relationships to their parents. For example, they might hope to get from a spouse what they could not get from their parents, or they might expect a spouse to love them as unconditionally as their parents once did.

Such hopes and expectations were clearly at work among some of the respondents who said they got married *as a direct consequence* of their parents' deaths—on the rebound, so to speak. For example, Karen and Jack, now in their early forties, had been dating one another when they each experienced the death of a parent (her father, his mother) two decades ago, which jump-started the couple into making their romance legal. Not only did this couple marry within eighteen months of the parents' deaths; so did all their siblings.

"I don't think that's a coincidence," says Karen. "None of us was in any hurry to tie the knot when our parents were alive. I certainly wasn't." She explains,

> I was much closer to my father than my mother—a real "daddy's girl." I find it fascinating that only after my dad died could I feel free to marry—I was afraid my father would get nuts if he had to "give me away" to another man. It's also fascinating to me that my husband popped the question right after his mother died. Our parents' deaths allowed us to switch our loyalties and make families of our own. Our siblings all said the same thing.

But of these siblings, only Karen and Jack are still married; the others have since divorced. What has kept this couple together is that they had known each other for years before they married, they have a great deal in common, and they have grown in the same direction.

Other respondents who married after their parents died approached the matter more temperately, easing rather than plunging into the nuptial waters. In these cases, the urge was not so much to merge as it was to *attach on their own terms*. Many of these people were previously divorced, having married the first time while their parents were alive and with their elders' opinions and values in mind. But after their parents died, these respondents felt emboldened to hold out for someone who came closer to their own romantic ideals.

Joseph, fifty-four, is a case in point. Raised by devoutly Jewish parents, at thirty-nine he married a Jewish woman primarily because he knew that marrying a gentile would have disturbed them, but also because his parents had begun to despair over their son's seeming inability to settle down. "The heat was definitely on," he recalls with a chuckle. "I was gonna get married. The only requirement was that the bride-to-be come from a Jewish family—not exactly a recipe for bliss, if that's all you have going for you. The marriage ended within two years."

Shortly after Joseph's divorce, his father, a spokesperson for Israeli political interests, suffered a fatal heart attack. Five years later, Joseph remarried, this time to a Protestant. Joseph is certain that his father would have admired this woman; she's an historian who specializes in the Middle East. Even so, Joseph doubts that he would have had the guts to marry her while his father was alive. Says Joseph,

> Intellectually, I can tell you that my father loved me utterly; ipso facto, he would have found a way to love my second wife. But in my heart I don't buy it. I wasn't mature enough to deal with disappointing him—marrying out of the faith would have bothered him *a lot*. Had I met my wife before my dad died, I would have

asked her to live with me instead of getting married, and she would have told me to hit the road. After his death, I didn't have to worry about upsetting him—I could marry a non-Jew without feeling guilty.

Not all of the respondents who married after their parents' deaths had such rosy connubial outcomes; several reported having made disastrous mistakes. While parental death was the spark that got these respondents to the altar, it was not the engine that drove their marriages.

A common thread among these respondents was their unhappy childhoods with unhappily married parents. The matches these respondents made were textbook examples of the repetition compulsion—the attempt to rewrite, or to make recognizable, the past by repeating it.

Henry, forty-four, who married soon after his father died eight years ago, is representative of such ill-fated unions. Says Henry,

> When my dad died I figured it was time to grow up, which getting married symbolized. I could not have picked anyone worse for me—my wife was a harridan. After a while, I felt that I was reenacting the worst aspects of my parents' marriage. Needless to say, the marriage didn't last.

Other respondents who also married in haste, only to repent at leisure, ran afoul for the opposite reason: They had been extremely close to a deceased parent and were trying to replace the beloved parent via wedlock. One forty-five-year-old woman says that she married her husband fifteen years ago because he reminded her of her father, who had recently died. To her great sadness, her husband has turned out to be anything *but* her father's clone.

My marriage has been very difficult. My expectation for an all-wise, ever supportive mate was totally unrealistic—I was looking for "dad" in all the wrong places. I need to take my husband for the man he is, not the "father" he isn't; it's still a problem for me.

As these stories illustrate, when adult children marry after their parents die in the hope that their spouses will do double duty—be substitute parents as well as partners—their marriages often suffer. Those who are able to acquire insights on the matter either retire their naive expectations, in which event their marriages become more peerlike, or they cut their losses, part marital company, and determine to grow up on their own.

Changes in Existing Marriages

Respondents who were already married when their parents died faced many of these same issues—the difference, of course, is that they were already in mid-marital stream. Here, the parents had made known their opinions about these marriages, and often were an active presence in the couples' lives. In some cases, the parents had been a steadying influence, serving as de facto marriage counselors by encouraging the couple or sympathetically listening to their woes. In other cases, the parents had been a divisive irritant, intruding upon the couple with an endless barrage of unsolicited advice or "I-told-you-so's." It was inevitable that when these influential parents were permanently removed from the equation, the respondents' marriages would change accordingly.

Investigators have found that when parents die, it is not uncommon for their adult children's marriages—even the best of them—to sustain a heavy hit. In a study of long-term changes in adults' lives in the aftermath of parental death, Joan Delahanty Douglas examined forty adults between age thirty-five and fifty-five, most of whom were married. Over half (57 percent) of the women, and 28 percent of the men, reported that they had experienced a "marital upheaval" within three years of their parents' deaths. Although most of the study participants said that the "upheaval" ultimately resulted in increased closeness in all their connections, including to spouses, for some it was the end of the marital road.

I found similar results among my respondents: Parental death had been the catalyst for changes, both positive and negative, within their marriages.

Improved Marriages

Nearly half—45 percent—of the married respondents, almost evenly divided between males and females, said that they have grown much closer to their spouses. Some of the improvements were a matter of degree; a good marriage simply got better. But other improvements were *major*; a troubled or rote or so-so marriage achieved much greater intimacy and friendship.

Rekindled Love

Of those who said their marriages had improved, most remarked that the deaths of their parents had caused them to reinvest emotionally in their marriages. The energies they had plowed into maintaining ties to their elders, or in worrying about them, or in artfully (or artlessly) dodging their opinions, could now be rerouted into their partnerships.

Some respondents, whose parents had disapproved of their marriages, gained new respect for their spouses because of the spouses' kindnesses to the respondents' ailing parents. Their mates might have failed to pass in-law muster, but they passed *marital muster* by valiantly coming through for the respondents.

This was abundantly the case for Ursula, fifty-two, who refers to her husband, Luke, as "a prince among men." This was a man for whom his in-laws, especially Ursula's mother, had little affection. Yet when her mother was terminally ill, Luke ran her medical records from doctor to doctor, even fed her when she was too ill to do so herself. It is a memory that Ursula will carry with her all her life. She says,

> One reason I married Luke was to have a buffer between my mother and me. I loved my mother, but she had a hard time letting me go. I didn't have what it takes to keep her at arm's length, which being married made easier, and no doubt is why she disliked Luke. He was good to her despite her coldness to him. He would tell you he did not do it for her, and I would believe him. I don't care why he did it, I am just so grateful to him. And it proves how right I was to marry him over my mother's objections.

Other respondents said that the deaths of their parents had made them "wake up" to the importance of their spouses to them and that they became "more reflective" about their marriages. These respondents felt a new sense of responsibility for their own happiness. As one man put it, "When my parents died, my wife and I grew up fast. Until then, we had enjoyed an extended form of childhood—like playing house—because my parents made us feel taken care of. Now, we really take care of each other."

Several people noted that sharing something profound—the deaths of their respective parents—had bound them more tightly to their spouses. Others, whose elderly parents had lived with them, said that with the demise of these parents, the couples reclaimed their privacy and got to know each other all over again. Still others said that they realized they "only had each other," as though huddled in a storm; they were less inclined to take their spouses for granted.

A number of people made the additional, poignant point that only after their parents died were they able to grasp what the parents had *gone through as a couple*; these respondents developed either greater empathy for their parents' marital struggles or greater admiration for the parents' marital triumphs.

Interestingly, most of the people who reported such relatively improved marriages had themselves grown up in reasonably stable homes.

Love Among the Ruins

It was the respondents who had *not* been raised in loving families whose marriages benefited most as a consequence of their parents' deaths. People who had been repeatedly demeaned by their parents—or who were estranged from them—said that the deaths had simply made *everything* better, like a rising tide that lifts all boats. Said one woman, who had had a tempestuous relationship with her parents, "I'm much easier to live with—it's like someone stopping hitting me. I greet each day eagerly, because my parents aren't putting me down anymore. I can breathe more freely."

But there was more to this marital cheeriness than mere relief. Something deeper was unfolding.

As has been mentioned, when couples marry, each person brings something to the party: the lessons in love they learned from their parents. Adult children whose parents set an example of mutual affection and respect have a leg up—they can allow themselves to trust and learn from their spouses. But offspring whose parents were at eternal loggerheads often have farther to go in the trust department; they may be on the lookout for similar behavior in their spouses, which puts a damper on their marital enthusiasm. Yet they, too, can find connubial contentment.

While these offspring might get off to a rocky marital start, over time it is the spouses' *better* natures that overrule the parents' negative ones. Because these offspring receive repeated benevolent feedback from their partners, they can all but literally change their minds about themselves, and their marriages become more compatible.

These were among the conclusions arrived at by Margaret H. Ricks of the University of Massachusetts in an intergenerational study of attachment behavior over the life span. In this study, it was found that for a subsample of women who had been raised in chaotic families, loving marriages provided a safe zone within which they could develop self-regard. These women had remarkably sturdy bonds not only to their husbands but also to their *husbands' families*. The women were able to reframe their parents' treatment of them as defects within the parents, rather than as reactions to defects within the women themselves. Consequently, these women were able to discount their parents' negative views of them and internalize their husbands' positive views instead.

In my sample, however, there were some married women for whom this "internalization" of their husbands' esteem required the deaths of the women's difficult parents to take hold. As long as the parents were alive, the women maintained a kind of siege mentality in all their relationships, as though waiting for a bomb to drop. Although their husbands were unfailingly affectionate, these women couldn't be confident of that affection—couldn't even make room for it—until their parents were out of the picture.

One forty-seven-year-old woman, who has been married for twenty-three years, and whose hostile mother died a decade ago, said that she chose her husband because he was loving, energetic, came from a close-knit family, and shared her interests. But it was the "loving" part that rattled her—that she could not really absorb until her mother was long gone. She says,

> Friends of mine who adored their mothers tell me that their mother's voice is always in their heads, and the voice says, "You're the best." The voice in my head always said, "You stink." Naturally, I brought this into my marriage. I constantly had my emotional bags packed—I was prepared to be abandoned. But after my mother died, it was like the sky began to clear and I could gradually let my guard down. It's been a process, but through the years, my husband has become the only person I have ever let myself totally count on.

Similar marital epiphanies occurred for several men in my survey sample who were also raised in traumatizing circumstances. It was as if, in the aftermath of parental death, they had acquired a new lease on life—and with it an entirely new personality. Where once they might have been pugnacious or withdrawn, now they became the soul of diplomacy. As one man put it, "Watching how my wife lives her life, every day, and the warmth she shows people, has completely changed me. If it weren't for her, I'd still be pissed off at the world."

The prevailing feeling among all the respondents whose marriages improved was that they had achieved more reciprocal and supportive relationships with their spouses. Without the distractions either of well-intentioned parental advice or parental animosity, the couples were able to find in one another a new best friend. And once they reached this degree of intimacy and maturity, there was no going back—they could apply it to all aspects of their lives.

Unchanged Marriages

Of the respondents who reported that their parents' deaths had not affected their marriages, most said that they had long ago relinquished any fantasies about the Hollywood version of "happily ever after." For these respondents, there were no dramatic marital reevaluations or epiphanies postparent. They had either gotten rid of their marital lumps—a smoothing of the rough edges—or gotten used to them.

There were, however, *substantial gender differences* in these neutral assessments. Forty-one percent of the men claimed that the deaths of their parents had no impact on their romantic partnerships. But only 27 percent of the women made the same claim; the rest said that their parents' deaths had greatly affected their intimate attachments.

Sometimes these differences were registered within the same marriage; several couples sent in completed questionnaires, with men reporting "no change" and their wives reporting *many* changes, both good and bad. It was as if they didn't really know each other, could not read the other's signals.

Certainly they had not read each other's questionnaires—with one notable exception. This couple, who after thirty years of marriage are still besotted with each other, made me laugh out loud. Not only had the wife read all her husband's comments, she had *critiqued* them. In answer to the question about parental wills and estates, the husband had tersely written, "no problems." Next to his answer, in gigantic letters, his wife had scrawled, "THIS IS A VERY BIG LIE! BIGGER THAN THE ONE ABOUT HIS 'UN-CHANGED' SIBLING RELATIONSHIPS!" (As to their marriage, he says his parents' deaths had no effect; she says her parents' deaths made her appreciate her husband even more.)

Many of the married men I interviewed said that they had never been particularly close to their parents and were even less so after they got married; hence, the deaths of their parents had left no mark on their marriages. To the extent that they were close to anyone, they added, it was to their wives.

This would have been news to some of their wives, who reported that their husbands weren't given to displays of fondness and—making matters worse—had not been all that sensitive when the women's parents died. Their husbands couldn't seem to identify with or even recognize what these women were going through.

Carla, forty-four, who lives in Michigan, has been married to Ralph, fifty-two, for nearly eleven years. During her mother's final illness in the early 1990s, Carla had to fly to Miami, where her mother resided, with increasing frequency, especially toward the end. Ralph made no secret of his annoyance over Carla's absences, and she felt torn between her "obligations" as a daughter and as a wife.

Since her mother's death, Carla says, her marriage has improved in some ways, but in others it has gotten worse. On the up side, she is surprised at how liberated she feels not to *have* to visit her mother, which gives her more time to devote to her home life. On the downside, she is still simmering over Ralph's lack of supportiveness during the trying months leading up to her mother's demise. Says Carla,

I can't seem to give up my resentment toward him. With my mother gone, I can see more clearly what I'm dealing with in my marriage. Being angry at my husband has given me license to quit knocking myself out trying to please him all the time. I used to be such a nice person! I've become more outspoken and independent—I can stand up to him. My illusions are gone, which I suppose is a good thing.

Such sore marital feelings in the aftermath of parents' deaths often serve to expose marital weaknesses—or fissures—that already existed. In a study called "Marriage as Support or Strain? Marital Quality Following the Death of a Parent," psychologist Debra Umberson of the University of Texas found four "themes" of marital "decline" among male and female respondents: The spouses were unable to provide sufficient "emotional support"; or they were not willing to talk about the death; or they didn't express empathy; or they failed to understand why the respondent did not bounce back quickly from the loss.

Several of my respondents disclosed similar marital disappointments. But in the long term, these disappointments occasionally had the serendipitous effect of allowing the respondents to recognize that their spouses could only be their life's companion, not their "parent." It was this recognition—arrived at, to be sure, the hard way—that forced them to look for *other* sources of self-esteem, such as their careers or educational pursuits or their friendships. The payoff was that they felt better about themselves and found it easier to accept the marriages they had made.

Alas, for some married respondents, the outside support they sought took the unfortunate form of leaning heavily upon their children. Although this often served to maintain the marital status quo, it did so at the expense of the parent-child bond, as will be illustrated in the next chapter.

Deteriorated Marriages

Of those respondents whose marriages had unraveled in the aftermath of parental death, more women than men weighed in with this sorry appraisal.

Some of these respondents said that the absence of their sym-

KVCC KALAMAZOO VALLEY COMMUNITY COLLEGE LIBRARY

pathetic parents had caused their already crumbling marriages to collapse rather than to mend. Without their parents' supportiveness, there was little to hold these couples together.

However, some of these marriages unraveled for another reason: The respondents had impulsively (and imprudently) married at an early age to escape their demanding or dysfunctional parents, a strategy that proved ruinous to their marriages when the parents died. As long as there had been a parent to defend against, these respondents had been able to "make do" with their spouses, who at least offered a semblance of protectiveness from the parents. But once the parents were gone, the respondents had to face the reality of their terrible marital bargains.

The villains were seldom the respondents' spouses, although obviously, poor romantic judgment was a factor. Rather, the primary problem was the respondents' inability to sort out their complex relationships to their parents. They had simply transferred their filial unhappiness from one arena to another. These marriages were the stage upon which unexamined parent-child conflicts played out and where, inevitably, unmet childhood needs remained unassuaged.

Of such unhappy marital transactions, family therapist Evan Imber-Black, Ph.D., says, "A lot of couples therapy turns on helping people to sort out the fact that your husband or wife is not your father or mother, and getting a clearer picture. Losing your parents can bring a lot of these issues to the surface."

Once the "picture" is clear, however, the marital damage already done may be beyond ignoring, and perhaps beyond repair. Valerie, thirty-four, put it in a nutshell: "My mother's death made me wake up and look at my life. My life got better. But my marriage got worse."

Valerie's mother, who suffered from mental illness, committed suicide six years ago. Because of the horrific nature of the death,

Valerie was forced into an unsparing assessment of her own life up to that point—including, and especially, her marriage to an abusive husband. She had blundered into the relationship when she was still caught in the undertow of her difficult childhood, a period in her young adulthood that was marred by addictions to drugs and to domineering men.

Now Valerie realizes that her marriage was but one in a series of misguided attempts to obliterate the past rather than address and deal with its legacy. Having reached this new awareness—this clarified vision—she doesn't want to lose psychological ground by remaining in a relationship that is so harmful to her, and she has filed for divorce. Says Valerie,

My mother's death made me see that I got married for absolutely the wrong reasons. I was depressed for years and didn't know it. When my mother got sick, I thought I had caused it and deserved to be punished for it. Marrying my husband was a form of self-punishment. My mother is dead and I don't have to keep penalizing myself anymore.

If there was one predominant reason for the deterioration of these marriages, it was that they simply could not stand up to the scrutiny the "orphaned" respondents brought to bear on *all* facets of their lives. The marriages they had made were no longer tenable, and they felt that they deserved better. For many of these people, the result was that they summoned the courage to leave their marriages and repair themselves on their own. Only then, they said, would they stand a chance of finding happiness within a healthy attachment. If they didn't succeed, they were prepared to go it alone.

Cut Loose: Reevaluating Singlehood

Respondents who had never married or who were divorced when their parents died, and who remained unattached, faced a different set of adjustments. For example, there were those who had made their parents the center of their lives, without whom they felt dazed—the concept of "reattachment" wasn't something they were ready to consider. But for others, being without either their parents *or* a partner led to their feeling reborn.

Flying Without a Net

Martina, forty, the eldest of three children whose mother died two years ago, is an example of the first scenario. As a child, she was a witness to constant domestic tension. Her father, who had a hair-trigger temper, bullied Martina's mother as well as her brothers—behavior that resulted in the parents' divorce when Martina was nine.

During the years preceding the divorce, and for years afterward, Martina was her mother's safe harbor. "I was absolutely her favorite child, her treasure, her reason for living," says Martina. "I was her best friend, and she was mine."

At the age of twenty-four, Martina became a choreographer and moved out of her mother's house; she also began a ten-year relationship with an alcoholic who bore more than a passing resemblance to her father. Through it all her mother continued to be her closest confidante—they spoke on the phone several times a day and saw each other at least once a week, going out to the movies or to museums or to restaurants.

When her mother was killed in an automobile accident, it set off an earthquake in Martina's life. She broke up with her boyfriend and embarked on the agonizing business of trying to find a place for herself in a world that did not include—was not filled up by—her mother. Says Martina,

> Nothing is the same—now I'm totally alone. My mother loved me no matter what, and that's gone. It's like my childhood has ended and I have to grow up. Losing her has been the biggest turning point of my life, because I hadn't really separated from her. I always realized how attached she was to me. What I didn't realize was how attached I was to her. I have to learn to be by myself before I can even think about having a lover.

In his practice, psychotherapist R. Benyamin Cirlin, C.S.W., executive director of the Center for Loss and Renewal in New York City, has found that the people who seem to have the most trouble adjusting to their parents' deaths are those whose parents were their sole source of unalloyed affection. Says Cirlin,

> Many of the participants in my bereavement groups have been single, never married women in their late forties and fifties. In their parents' later years, these women served as caretakers to their mothers and fathers, and in many instances they found this role to be extremely gratifying. For many of these women this relationship was the only source of love in their lives. When their parent died, the gratifying give and take of deep love and concern vanished in their lives. Their life journey and struggle is to find new sources of love and meaning in a parentless world, whether or not they remain single.

No Strings

Finally we come to those unmarried respondents who found that the deaths of their parents caused them to discover that freedom and privacy, alone and unencumbered, suited them perfectly. Although many of them greatly missed their parents, who had played a huge role in their lives, in time they began to savor the solitary life—the headiness of having no one to report to, of doing as they pleased.

Inez, forty-five, is such a person. She believes that she never *had* to grow up until her parents died a decade ago. "I have led the most selfish of lives," she says. "I am essentially the same individual who dislikes crowds and social engagements as I was when my parents were alive—the only difference is that I have become much more mature and self-sufficient. I really like being alone, something my parents never understood."

In ways, men and woman who are single have an advantage over people who have spouses and children—they often come to terms with their own existential "aloneness" sooner. Some channel their energies into their careers, turning out better work than they ever have. Others have made their friends their new "families." For these people, being single has not been a handicap—rather, it has been a gift for which they never bargained.

Contrary to "attachment" theorists, British psychologist Anthony Storr believes that the capacity to be alone is as important, as "therapeutic," as the ability to form intimate connections—in ways, even more important. In his book *Solitude: A Return to the Self*, he writes,

> If we did not look to marriage as the principal source of happiness, fewer marriages would end in tears. . . . Intimate attachments are *a* hub around which a person's life revolves, not necessarily *the* hub.

A New Kind of Love

The overwhelming lesson to be derived from the stories and experiences of these married and unmarried respondents is twofold: First, the deaths of parents alter who we are now—adults who are defined by what we make of ourselves rather than by those who made us. Second, this redefinition allows us to develop a new kind of love, whether in the company of others or alone.

To be "nobody's child" is to be truly separate in a way that people with living parents are not. This separateness brings us face-to-face with our most basic longings and emotions—throws us back upon our intrinsic natures—making it possible for us to reinvent ourselves.

The result can be an extraordinarily liberating capacity for intimacy *as well as* for solitude. And it is these capacities that pave the way for other changes that enrich the rest of our unparented lives.

Parenthood Reconsidered: On Having, and Not Having, Children

You know, as long as your parents are alive, you think you're still a child in some way, even as an adult. That was certainly true for my husband and me. We had toyed with the idea of having a baby, but hadn't gotten around to actually doing it. Then my mother died, and I suddenly realized I wasn't going to be a sweet young thing forever—that if I was going to have a baby, I'd better hurry. So I got pregnant almost immediately. When my baby was born, I remember sitting in the hospital, sobbing because my mother wasn't there to be with me. She was a tough lady, but this was one time she would have been terrific—she was at her best when she was taking care of people. That really affected me—that I didn't have a mother to take care of me.

—Diane, forty-six

I am sitting with Diane at a trendy Manhattan restaurant, a block from the advertising agency where she works, leaning close so that I can hear her over the deafening lunchtime clatter. She glances at my tape recorder, which I have been inching in her direction, and apologizes for the less-than-ideal interview setting. This was the only time in her busy week that she could arrange to meet. Evenings were out—each night after work she races home to be with her husband and ten-year-old daughter because she doesn't want to miss a minute with them; weekends, too, are cordoned off for family.

Every moment with her daughter is precious to her, she explains—so precious that she kicks herself for having waited so long to become a mother. But she had good reasons to stall. For one thing, she and her husband hadn't really hit their stride as a couple—it had taken a while for their marriage to settle into a kind of rhythm. Then, she wanted to make sure her career had advanced to the point that she could delegate business trips to junior staffers and stay closer to home.

But the *real* reason she waited, she says, was that she wasn't all that confident that she could be a good parent—that she had the right maternal stuff—given her own complicated history.

Diane left home for college at eighteen with the eagerness of a greyhound streaking after a rabbit. Although she adored her gentle father, her connection to her brilliant, beautiful, but vain mother had never really taken hold. Her mother seemed to require constant infusions of reassurance and attention, which Diane struggled to supply. But she was insufficient—too small a portion to satisfy so great a hunger.

In her senior year at college, Diane met Ian, whom she married a year later. Ian was a lot like her father—encouraging her ambitions and listening sympathetically to the saga of her childhood. "He really earned his stripes," says Diane. "He had to go through all the years of hearing me talk about my mother morning, noon, and night. It helped me to get her out of my system, to make her seem less formidable."

By the time Diane reached her mid-thirties, her own emotional house more or less in order, she began to consider her mother in a new light—to see her not as a woman intent upon making her daughter feel inadequate but, rather, as a fascinating, monumentally insecure creature, like a character in a Tennessee Williams play.

Because of these changes within Diane, she decided to visit her mother more frequently. "I was able to deal with her woman-to-woman," she recalls. "It was still dicey between us, but it was nice, because we had finally reached some sort of truce. She was a great wit, and I was able to enjoy her company. And she actually seemed glad to have me around."

It was at this juncture that her mother developed an illness that would end her life in a matter of weeks. Diane raced to be with her, bringing along lipstick and eye shadow because she knew how important it was to her mother to look gorgeous to the end. "The first thing I did when I got there was to put on her makeup for her," Diane recalls. "I said, 'Just because you're dying doesn't mean you have to look wretched.' That made her laugh. All the years of contention between us just melted away."

Diane has strung together these few happy recollections like tiny, bright beads on a necklace so that she can have a mother worth remembering, to sustain her whenever she is feeling forlorn. But every so often the bad memories break through in a rush, reminding her that, however mesmerizing her mother might have been as a personality, she was not exactly a parental paragon, not someone to emulate.

She recounts an experience that illustrates these tandem emotions—the missing, and not missing, her mother. A few weeks prior to our interview, a constellation of events caused Diane to feel that she was coming apart at the seams. She was exhausted from a major project at work; a friend of hers had recently died; and her husband had lost an important client, which would put a serious dent in their budget. One day during this stressful period, as she was driving her daughter on an errand, Diane suddenly burst into tears. She describes what happened next:

My daughter turned to me and said, "What's wrong?" I said, "Oh, sometimes I wish I had a mother." She said, "Don't worry, *I'll* be your mother." It was as if I'd been struck by lightning. I pulled the car over, looked at her, and said, "*No, you won't.* You're the kid and I'm the mother, and don't you forget it. That's what my mother did—she tried to make me her mother!"

Diane chortles as she finishes this story; she is reasonably certain the exchange went flying over her daughter's head. But for Diane, it was a crucial line in the sand. She knows from experience that some people look to their offspring to make up for all that they lacked in their own childhoods, and she is not, she firmly vows, about to become one of those people.

Still, there are times—and there will be more of them, as she enters menopause, sends her daughter off into the world, approaches her own old age—when she wishes that her mother, flawed as she was, were still around to share all Diane's tomorrows. Maybe her mother would have taken pleasure in the landmarks of Diane's grown-up self—in particular, her daughter. Maybe she would have been a fabulous, zany grandmother. Maybe she died too soon.

Or maybe—and this is what Diane has come to believe—her mother died at just the right time. For had she not, Diane is convinced that she would not have had a baby. And had she not had a baby, she never would have known that she could become a different sort of mother—one who never loses sight of who is the adult, and who the child.

Second Acts: The Next Generation

As Diane's story illustrates—and as has been stated repeatedly throughout this book—when parents die, their adult children often find themselves reassessing their entire lives. Nowhere is this reassessment more intense than in deciding whether or not to reproduce—or, having already become a parent, in deciding how good a job one has done of it.

As we saw in the last chapter, it is one thing to have chosen a partner who might or might not be the person with whom you hope to grow old; here, at least, you have some wiggle room—you can elect to part company and either try again or go it alone. In procreating, however, there is no such leverage; this is one attachment from which you cannot, or should not, walk away, especially when the progeny are young.

The decision to reproduce is difficult enough, resting, among other things, upon your own readiness and whether or not there is a partner who would make a suitable co-parent. But actually raising children without your parents to provide emotional ballast, or at least a buffer to your own mortality, can seem like a high-wire act.

Which is one reason why adult offspring whose parents have died tend to contemplate the matter of having and of raising children with a new sense of urgency. Adult children who already have children may ask themselves: How can I provision my offspring, emotionally or otherwise, for their futures? Have I made sufficient peace with my parents to allow my children to be who they are, rather than expecting them to assuage my losses? What kind of example have I set for them, good or bad?

Adult children who do not have offspring may ask themselves: Does it all end with me—all that I have acquired, all that I have learned? Who will remember me after I am gone? Does it *matter* that I be remembered, and if so, is giving birth, or adopting children, the only way for that to be accomplished? Or is there some other way I can put my stamp upon the generations to come?

Such questions, more than any other line of inquiry, touched a nerve among my respondents, causing them to do considerable, often anguishing, soul-searching.

This chapter will explore the results of that soul-searching. First I will discuss the respondents whose children were born either before or after the respondents' parents died, and how their relationships to those offspring have been affected by the deaths. Then I will concentrate on those people who did not and still do not have children, and how they feel about the possibility that they are the last of their generational line.

Parenting Without Parents: When Memory Will Have to Serve

If ever adult children are grateful to have their mothers and fathers around, it's when they have their first baby. There's nothing like bringing a tiny newborn home from the hospital to give you a sense of staggering responsibility, of breathtaking ineptitude.

In raising a child, you need all the help you can get—which is one of the reasons grandparents are so important. Even if your parents aren't up for hands-on involvement—even if they are exemplars of what *not* to do and are the very last people you'd ask for advice—they're still a link to your childhood history, able to provide you with information about yourself that only they know. The craving for such information mounts with every step of your child's development.

For example, a mother or father can remind you, as you tear your hair out about your child's "terrible twos"—or fret about letting your teenager have the keys to the car—that you were once *also* a kid, and you made it through just fine, despite having screwed up royally from time to time. "This too shall pass" is the soothing vote of confidence that has more resonance, carries more weight, coming from parents than from anyone else.

Even if your parents can't find a single good thing to say about you, reminding you instead of the endless grief you caused them and the thanklessness of their sacrifices, they might become wonderful grandparents. Your children are your parents' second chance—their best shot at biological immortality—and many a frayed parent-child tie has been rewoven by the experience. Indeed, the possibility of *not* having access to their grandchildren has inspired more than one tart-tongued grandparent to become a sweet-talking pussycat.

Likewise, more than one frosty filial heart has thawed at the sight of a parent, who once embodied the wrath of God, cuddling with a grandchild. A forty-four-year-old man I interviewed, who had a largely off-again relationship with his "impossible" father, described this very reversal of intergenerational fortune:

> When my son was born, I saw a side to my father I had never known. I wasn't sure how he'd be as a grandfather, but he was amazing. It was really restorative watching him be so loving to my son, because it felt like he was giving love to me. That meant a lot to me. It helped me get rid of most of the anger I had felt toward him.

All these second chances—for your relationship to your parents, and for their potential relationship to your children—vanish when parents die, a point poignantly made by respondents in written questionnaire answers:

"My daughter was born many years after my parents died, but surely I hug her tighter because I don't have them. It is painful to me that my daughter has no grandparents, and that I don't have a mother and father to help me down the circuitous road of parenthood." (female, thirty-nine)

"Not having grandparents for my children has been the worst deprivation caused by my parents' deaths. At this stage of my life, I think about that a great deal, the chance to have had a renewed relationship with my parents through my kids. That's a big loss." (male, forty-five)

With no mother or father to advise you, to calm your anxieties, to be a steadying presence in your children's lives, to chronicle their history and yours, you are left with only memories to drawn upon. It is precisely *because* of this parental vacuum that adult children often become aware, in ways that they had not been before, of the enormous impact they are having upon their own children.

Changing Connections

This was abundantly the case among my respondents who have children—77 percent of the sample—regardless of their children's ages. In answer to the question "How has your relationship to your children changed since the death of your parent(s)?" over half—54 percent—said that the connection had shifted, almost always for the better (in a few cases, it took a nosedive, as shall be seen in a moment). Another 33 percent reported that the relationship was unchanged. The remaining 14 percent said that the question was not germane, either because their children were infants at the time or had not yet been born (although, as can be seen above, these relationships were, in fact, profoundly affected by the absence of grandparents).

There were significant gender and age differences in these evaluations. Women were twice as likely as men—63 percent versus 38 percent—to report changes in their ties to their progeny; the older the women were, the likelier they were to cite them. It was the reverse for men; the older they were, the more they perceived these ties to be "unchanged."

These gender differences can be accounted for, in part, by the fact that historically women have played a greater role than men in childrearing. As is noted by Alice S. Rossi and Peter H. Rossi in their study of parent-child attachments across the life span, children tend to discuss personal matters with their mothers much more than with fathers, a pattern of intimacy that continues into the offsprings' middle age. Thus women are likelier than men to monitor the emotional family climate and to notice changes in it.

Two additional variables colored the respondents' evaluations of their relationships to their children. The first had to do with the respondents' own childhoods. People who had been close to their parents felt more confident about *being* parents and were inclined to report that their relationships to their children were as good as, or better than, ever. People who had *not* been close to their parents, however, reported dramatic changes; their relationships to their children often underwent a complete overhaul.

The other significant variable in the respondents' evaluations of their bonds to their children was whether or not the respondents had siblings. You will recall from chapter 4 that parental investment is correlated to birth order, with onlies, lastborns, and firstborns the "Darwinian winners." Adult children who felt that they were their parents' "favorite" child—or at least were in their very good graces—were more likely to cotton to the idea of reproducing, and to be happy about having done so, than their more conflicted brethren.

The respondents' fertility rates bore out this birth order effect: Singletons were the *most* likely to have children, followed by lastborns, then firstborns; middleborns, the "Darwinian losers," were least likely to have families of their own.

These survey findings are consistent with those unearthed by the Rossis in their intergenerational study. "It is when children have married and are rearing children of their own," the Rossis conclude, "that early family life influences may be demonstrated." Those in the

Rossi study who had loving attachments to their parents tended to form families that were similar to the ones in which they grew up. Whereas those who had thorny relationships to their parents wanted to rewrite the "family" book; they had weak ties to their parents but correspondingly *stronger* commitments to the people they chose to become attached to—which would, of course, include their own children.

Thus, it is not surprising that my respondents whose childhood memories were gloomy were *hypervigilant* about being better parents than their parents had been—they were unusually sensitive to whether or not their children thought well of them.

Whatever their family backgrounds, however, the bottom line for these respondents was that once they were no longer in the "child" role themselves, the quality of their relationships to their children took on greater importance—for many, their self-regard was riding on it.

Strengthened Ties

Of those who said their connections to their children became more meaningful, many remarked that they simply were better parents now than when their own parents were alive. The reflective tone of these respondents' comments was striking: "I'm trying to be different," or "I want my children to know me," or "I'm more patient with them," or "Perfectionism is not so important."

Where once these respondents might have hoped that their children would reflect well upon them, now they were more concerned with how their offspring felt about themselves.

Keeping a Good Thing Going

Respondents who had had enviably close relationships to their parents were eager to secure that closeness in the next generation.

Angela, forty-nine, who has a doctorate in biology, grew up in a huge family—she was the eldest of six children—that was extraordinarily affectionate and close-knit, a pattern she and her husband are replicating with their own children, who range in age from seventeen to twenty-two. As her children enter into adulthood, Angela has gradually shifted gears as a mother, from authority figure to something more peerlike—a friendship similar to the one she enjoyed with her own parents when she became an adult.

For most of her children's lives, Angela worked only part-time in order be available to them. It's a trade-off she never regretted but about which she felt some ambivalence—before, that is, her parents died. Says Angela,

> Like a lot of women of my generation, I was weaned on feminism. I used to think, Here I have this fancy degree, and what have I accomplished with it? But after my parents died, I started to think about all that they achieved with just a high school diploma. They raised six kids who are all college graduates and who have a strong sense of family. I believe that when parents fail their children, future generations suffer. And when parents succeed as parents, future generations thrive. How my parents treated me influences me every day, and I want to have that same influence on my children. So I don't have a big career, my name in the papers. That's not so important to me anymore.

Other respondents who had affectionate relationships with their parents also wanted to replicate the past, but a more up-to-date version of it. In these instances, their parents had been actively involved as grandparents, offering advice with which the respondents did not always agree, sometimes creating tensions between them. But once their parents were gone, the respondents felt less constrained—they could orchestrate their relationships to their children entirely on their own terms. Said a forty-six-year-old mother of two adolescent daughters,

> I feel the loss of daily connection to my mother, because she was a great cheerleader. But I am relieved that her expectations of me are not an issue I have to live with. She came from a much more traditional generation—she didn't really understand today's teenagers. She was sometimes critical of my daughters, and I felt uncomfortable listening to her criticism. Since she died, I have been more open-minded with my kids—I see my maternal role more clearly and feel freer to follow my own instincts.

As these stories demonstrate, some relationships between adult children and their offspring improve simply because there has been a change in emphasis, from overprotectiveness to a more relaxed camaraderie. Studies show, for instance, that parents of young children are expected to act like grown-ups, chiefly by putting a lid on their own impulsiveness. But once their children are older, parents can return to their more spontaneous—more human, even goofy—selves.

The deaths of one's parents can hasten this process. Many life span developmental psychologists have found that stress—including that occasioned by adult orphanhood—is a "life-force dynamic," as University of Texas associate professor David A. Chiriboga, an authority on life transitions, dubs it. He argues that *but* for enormous stress, one might *never* change—including, and especially, with one's own progeny.

For adult children, the world without their parents is not the same world it was, which means, says Chiriboga, that the survivors must "reformulate" themselves. Their offspring frequently are the beneficiaries of this reformulation. When adult children are forced to become self-reliant, they often discover aspects of themselves—

untapped strengths or unrecognized weaknesses—that alter the shape of their parenting goals, in particular, the wisdom they hope to impart to the next generation.

There was one question I posed to all the parents I interviewed that flushed out this new sensibility. The question was "Do you want your children to remember you in the same way that you remember your parents?" For the majority of respondents, even those who admired their parents, the answer was that they did not. Rather, they wanted to have a singular influence, one that reflected their own best efforts, the lessons they themselves had learned through trial and error.

Rewriting History

This was especially true of offspring who had turbulent relationships with their deceased parents. Indeed, the earnestness that these respondents brought to bear upon their parenting role was fueled by painful comparison.

Of those who reported improved relationships to their children, 51 percent had *not* been close to one or both parents—their childhood memories were pocked by parental neglect or abusiveness. "My parents were role models of what not to be," was a typical response.

Many of these respondents expressed a kind of self-consciousness, drawing upon a fantasy of the "perfect" parent to guide them. It was as if they had grown up hearing one language and were raising or interacting with their children in another, making it up as they went along. For these people, childrearing has not been easy—they keep measuring themselves against their own parents, hoping that they have improved on the old model.

Nina, forty-three, is an example of this self-consciousness. When her father died two years ago, they were not on speaking terms—not by her choice but by his. She is, she blushingly admits, a very late bloomer. She didn't move out of her parents' house until she was thirty-two—she simply lacked the confidence. Her father viewed this step as a betrayal; as far as he was concerned, he told her, he no longer had a daughter. He refused to attend her wedding five years ago, and never met her daughter, now age three.

Still, Nina misses her father. Well, perhaps *miss* isn't quite the word for it—it's more like the earth opened up beneath her when he died. "Even though we were estranged," she muses, "I always knew he was there. And now he's not there. It forced me to mature much more than when I had my baby. That was a *big* surprise to me. I thought parenthood makes you an adult, but it doesn't. Being an orphan does."

Nina waited until she was nearly forty to get pregnant because it was only then that she felt she had a fighting chance of being a decent parent. Still, she says, it's a constant struggle—she is heckled by self-doubt.

> I've really had to grow into this role. I was terrified of having kids because, as my father used to say, "They destroy your life." I had a hard time bonding with my daughter. Now I love her desperately. But I still can't relax with her. Every time she exhibits some insecurity, or shows some bizarre behavior, I get nervous, because I'm so afraid she's having the same childhood I had. I work very, very hard to make sure she has a solid ego. It is the driving force of my life that she look back on her childhood fondly.

Several other respondents also remarked that their parents' deaths marked the pivotal point in their own parenting—a kind of before-and-after metamorphosis. Before their parents died, they had seen themselves through the prism of their parents' negative views of them. But after their parents died, they began to see themselves through their *children's* eyes, and the picture they were getting was not always flattering.

Larry, forty-one, the father of two middle schoolers, is an example of this sobering recognition. Both Larry's parents were exceptionally talented, but theirs was a match made in hell, and it ended in divorce when Larry was twenty-four. Larry's father, a "genius" who burned out as a consequence of chronic alcoholism, had always been more childlike than fatherly, an example Larry emphatically did not want to follow.

When his father died six years ago, it was an immense relief to Larry. "I felt raw, but I wasn't sad," he recalls. "Nobody really wants to hear from you that yes, you feel a lot, but no, it's not grief—it's that you're just so damn glad to be rid of the person." But the death had another effect—it made him vividly aware of how crucial it is that his children never think of him as he thinks of his father. To avert that dreadful outcome, he entered psychotherapy. Says Larry,

> Everything I've done as a parent is in response to my father. It wasn't just that I wanted to do the opposite of what he did—it was more that I was scared of parenthood because what I had experienced had been so shattering. But once I got into it, I felt compelled to right the wrong, to not extend the multigenerational train. That's the main reason I started seeing a shrink. My attitudes have changed so radically from what they were six years ago. If I've made any mistakes with my children, at least they're my own, not my father's.

Other respondents, whose children were well into adulthood when their parents died, faced another challenge: How to come to terms with their deceased parents in order to give their children a "home" they would wish to visit, rather than avoid, as the respondents had done.

Doreen, sixty-one, who with her husband has four grown children, worries that she was too strict with them when they were growing up and that they will one day resent her the way she resented her own mother and father. Says Doreen,

> What do children owe their parents? I wrestle with that a lot with my own kids, because I don't want them to feel as guilty and angry as I did. I really think I failed my parents—they expected so much that I could not give. They never saw me in any other context than as their daughter; I was supposed to put them ahead of my own husband and children. After they died, I was determined to be more understanding with my children. I don't ever want them to feel that they failed me. I just want them to like being with me. So I try not to have too many expectations of them.

Her strategy appears to have paid off. "I can't get rid of them!" she announces with a grin. "I spend my life baby-sitting!"

The success of all these relationships between adult children and their offspring can be traced to the respondents' ability to hold themselves accountable for their own childrearing mishaps.

Where Unhappy History Repeats Itself

Alas, such self-appraisals don't always take place, or if they do, it is very late in the game. For a small number of respondents, their connections to their grown children took a downturn after their parents died; in these cases, the respondents' unresolved childhoods came back to haunt them. Having essentially "lost" their parents' goodwill earlier in life, which the actual deaths had simply underscored, they had relied upon their children to supply them with a sense of worth—with heartbreaking repercussions.

These schisms took two forms: Either the respondents transferred their anger toward their deceased parents onto one or more of their children, viewing them as ingrates (or worse); or the respondents transferred their neediness, loving their children to the point of suffocation. Both scenarios—resentment and smothering—were spawned in the same source (the respondents' unfinished business with their deceased parents) and had the same result (their children's withdrawal from them).

The Resentful Parent

Gary, sixty-four, a self-made millionaire, is an example of the first scenario. The father of two grown sons, he had exceptionally high standards for them. They would, he vowed, attend the best schools, join prestigious investment firms, be independently wealthy by the time they reached thirty-five. To that end he pounded into them the importance of being competitive.

Both sons matched their father's expectations—but one of them, Christopher, the firstborn, keeps his father at arm's length. For a long time, Gary regarded Christopher as unappreciative, as failing to pay homage for his many advantages, the glorious dreams Gary had for him that have come true.

But ever since his father's death five years ago, Gary has been considering the possibility that Christopher might have had dreams of his own—becoming a musician, perhaps—that were quashed out of fear. Maybe all Christopher ever really wanted—and Gary's wife has been saying this for *decades*—was for his father to accept him, to love him for who he is. Says Gary,

> God, I wish I'd done things differently. I wasn't interested in whether my kids were happy; I just didn't want them to be dependent on me, the way my father was. He was an immigrant who never made much money and always relied on me to support him financially. I built up my business so that my sons wouldn't feel I

needed them, and I raised them to be that way, too—to depend only on themselves. Well, it worked—they're big shots. But it alienated Christopher. If you ask me now would I want a son who loves me but who's not a huge success, or a son who's a success but angry at me all the time, I'd answer the former. I thought I was making him independent. What I did was push him away.

The Smothering Parent

Clarice, fifty, is an example of the second scenario, wherein parents bind their children to them with hoops of steel, wanting their offspring to love them as they themselves were not loved in childhood. Clarice has a handful of good memories of her childhood—her affectionate father took an interest in her, but only when her domineering mother wasn't looking.

Which is one reason Clarice couldn't *wait* to have a family of her own, as recompense for all that she had missed. She married at twenty-two, and within six years she had three children, two boys and a girl. She took to the task of raising them as if to a religious calling; she would blot out her childhood by swaddling her children in layers of devotion.

But Chloe, the only girl, would get special treatment. Clarice would give her daughter the unwavering affection that she had craved from, but had failed to evoke in, her own mother. In return, Chloe would love Clarice with equal ardor. They would be best friends, forming a mother-daughter bond that would make up for everything.

When Clarice's mother died four years ago, she felt liberated, because now the past could literally be buried. At around the same time, her daughter, then twenty-three, stopped having anything to do with her. The combination of these two experiences—her mother's death and her daughter's retreat—brought Clarice's childhood crashing onto her doorstep. "Losing my mother forced me to recognize that I was never really a mother," she says. "I was trying to make my daughter the mother I never had." She continues,

> I could never do enough for her, and I think it warped her. I never laid down the law—I just adored her. And now she doesn't return my phone calls. This has been the bitterest consequence of my childhood. You thought you'd done it all; you thought you could reverse history. But it wasn't reversible, because my need for her was so great. I'm dying to go see her, but my husband says, "No, don't, you've got to let go," and he's right. For the first time, I'm trying to set some limits. It's the hardest thing I've ever done.

Middle Passage

More painful than being rejected by your parents is being rejected by your children. Parents who have been through it often feel that they have failed in three generations—with their parents, their children, and themselves—and may either blame these fallouts entirely on their children or entirely on themselves. Somewhere between these two extremes is a middle ground in which these parents can begin to figure out how all their good intentions could go so utterly wrong.

In her book *The Bonds of Love*, psychoanalyst Jessica Benjamin argues that the root of such difficulties often lies in the inability of parents to engage in a *mutual* relationship with their children, where each recognizes and is recognized by the other as "different." Instead, writes Benjamin, the emotional boundaries of these parents are virtually nonexistent—they can neither be together with their children nor apart from them without feeling in some way threatened.

Psychiatrist Susan C. Vaughan echoes this theme in her book *The Talking Cure*, which examines how psychotherapy can help people change their minds—or at least their thinking patterns. She makes the compelling case that children form "prototypes," based on their experiences with their parents, that—if left unchallenged—become the basis for their responses to others later in life, including their own offspring.

For instance, if your parents routinely responded to you harshly or coldly when you were a young child—and did not reengage you in an affectionate way—you might, in adulthood, automatically assume that others will treat you harshly or coldly. Alternatively, if your parents never criticized you—but, instead, praised every breath you drew, hung on your every word—in adulthood you might automatically expect others to adore you or forgive you anything. Writes Vaughan,

> Without disapproval, the child cannot be educated about what he should and should not do, and he remains fragile and overly dependent on the praise of others. But without repair, the [child] is left for a protracted time in a state of deflated negative emotion.

Children need both—their parents' criticism and their parents' warmth—in order to be able to take charge of their own feelings. But children who have experienced only parental harshness, or only adoration, might grow up to become parents who allow their children to control their emotions for them, just as their parents once did.

This is what appears to have happened to the respondents who looked to their children to make reparations for the past. However, the deaths of their parents often woke these respondents to the devastating, but necessary, insight that they had simply passed their unfinished childhood business on to their own progeny, like an unopened letter.

For the rejected parents in my sample who had neither separated from their parents *nor separated from their children*, the task before them was to learn how to detach without defecting, how to attach without dissolving. Those who recognized their own complicity in their children's estrangements stopped expecting others to make amends for their childhood miseries and began filling in the holes in their own psyches.

The result was that they were able to draw the line between themselves and the people they love—to recognize their children's integrity as well as their own. And with this recognition, many of them found the opportunity to start over with their offspring—to put the relationship on an entirely new footing.

It's Never Too Late

It is the very fact of parental death that inspires all these courageous self-appraisals. You will recall from an earlier chapter that children's attachment behaviors tend to persist into adulthood, primarily because their parents continue to treat them as they always have. But when parents die, so does the necessity to react to that treatment. Adult children can then change their attachment "styles," as John Bowlby put it, which can lead to a renewal in their relationships to their offspring.

The key to this altered parenting style may be the capacity of adult children to develop an understanding of why their parents might have felt compelled to act in a certain way (a subject I'll explore in detail in chapter 9).

More than any event in adult life, the deaths of one's parents can allow this understanding to take place. Still, for it even to begin, it might be necessary for adult children to go back to square one— to undertake the bruising process of assessing the damage done to them in childhood, which is now revealed in their strained relationships to their own progeny. As psychoanalyst Carl Jung wrote, "It is not . . . a question of the parents committing no faults . . . but of their recognizing them for what they are."

Which brings us to the good news of this awakening: Many of the respondents' seemingly hopeless relationships to their offspring were righted when they became *grandparents*, at which time they were invited back into their children's lives. These respondents leapt at the chance to demonstrate all that they had learned the hard way. Said one sixty-one-year-old woman, who had been on the outs with her daughter until the arrival of grandchildren,

> My daughter routinely compliments me on the changes she's seen in me. I'll make some offhand comment about something, and she'll say, "Gee, it's just remarkable—you never would have reacted that way years ago." We are closer than we have ever been, and there's no question that it's because I am not the person I was. I'm a whole lot easier to be with.

As was mentioned earlier, when people become grandparents, it is often their second shot at parenting. These respondents were able to make up for their parenting mistakes by becoming loving, patient, nonjudgmental grandparents. Consequently, their children could see them as fallible human beings who were capable of change, and could develop new regard for them.

Rethinking Childlessness: When There Is No "Next Generation"

For people who have no children, the deaths of their parents are often more distressing than for those who have offspring, in large part because there is no "family" of their own to help cushion the blow, which leaves them stranded in their own intergenerational history. Indeed, the question I posed in questionnaires, and followed up on in interviews, that provoked more emotional responses than any other was this: "If you have no children, how do you feel about being the last of your line at this stage of your life?"

Sixty-three percent of these men and women reported either that they were "okay" about being childless or were resigned to it, having wrestled with the matter earlier on. The rest were anything *but* "okay." They felt "unsettled" or "horrible"; they had no one to whom they could "pass on" their memories, their wisdom, their possessions; they felt "more alone" than ever.

But it was the childless *women* who made such comments and had such second thoughts more often than the men, for the obvious reason that the female biological clocks were ticking.

The range of female reactions to being childless was shaped by three key variables: age, whether or not they had siblings, and how satisfied they were with other areas of their lives—their worlds beyond "home."

The Age Factor

For the majority of childless women in the sample age forty-five or older, the question about not having offspring struck a chord. "Oh, *that*," some of them joked. "I'm ready emotionally, but it's too late," some of them sighed. "That's the one thing . . ." some of them sobbed, unable to go on.

A number of these women were childless by choice—they grew up in dysfunctional families and were not about to risk having their childhood experiences repeated. They felt unequal to the parenting task, were terrified of it, and were relieved to be spared the possibility of becoming parental failures. They were unmoved by the Darwinian imperative to perpetuate their gene pools. As one woman dryly put it, "Our genetic line was pretty spotty, so this question does not speak to me."

Others, who came of age during feminism and access to birth control, said that they had been driven to succeed in their careers from the moment they graduated from college, and that ambition, rather than baby-making, had captured their agendas—until their parents died.

Louise, forty-six, a divorced radio producer, goes up and down on this topic. Get her on a good day, which is most of the time, and she's *ecstatic* not to have kids. She knows all about the guilt of working outside the home, the anxiety of finding decent child care, the despair of seeing your kid turn into a reprobate, the money involved, because she's seen her friends who have children go through it.

But get her on a bad day, as I did—it was the second anniversary of her mother's death—and she suffers from what she calls "typical baby boom angst." She explains,

> I have always done my own thing. The only problem is I don't have much to show for it. Yes, I'm living this glamorous life, and I'm always doing nice things for myself because I have the financial wherewithal. Still, I've had such a self-centered existence. I saw how much my parents sacrificed for me, and I was never prepared to make the same sacrifices. But now, I look at women I used to make fun of—the ones who stayed home with their kids and baked cookies—and I envy them. I'm obsessed by what's missing in my life, how shallow it's been. This stuff just never occurred to me before my mother died.

Several of the younger married respondents were even less happy about being childless, and Liz, forty-three, is one of them. When she and her husband married in the 1980s, they agreed to wait until their careers were in high gear before starting a family. This decision did not sit well with Liz's parents, who put her feet to the procreative fire—they were eager to become grandparents. Still, having children had seldom been a gleam in Liz's eye. "When I was kid," she quips, "even dressing my dolls was a chore."

All that abruptly changed when Liz's mother died four years ago. It hit her "like a sledgehammer," she says, that she had no child to love as she had been loved by her mother. And so Liz decided to go off birth control. When she told her husband that she wanted to get pregnant, he was not thrilled. Says Liz,

> He admitted to me that he had never wanted children, something he had never told me before. Not having kids has been the worst part of losing my mother. It's not just that no one will ever care about me that much again. It's that now, whatever I do, there's no child to witness it, to carry on the family heritage. I feel so guilty that I didn't give my parents grandchildren, and so angry that my husband was never honest with me. It's made me question my marriage ever since.

Other childless women had married men who had offspring from previous marriages, men who were in no rush to incur any more college tuitions. These women knew going in that motherhood was not in the cards; in fact, it suited them fine. But after their parents died, they began to feel twinges of regret.

Patricia, forty-five, made up her mind in her twenties never to have children, largely because she had seen the toll that raising five children had exacted from her overwhelmed mother. Most of the time, Patricia feels sanguine about her decision. But ever since her parents died, she's had occasional, wistful second thoughts—for instance, when she's setting the table for a dinner party, using the napkins her mother embroidered, the silver that has been in the family for generations, all of which will probably end up in a consignment shop. Says Patricia,

> Looking back, I think that if I had had therapy when I was younger, I probably would have had children. I mean, if ever I was ready to be a mother, it's now. I console myself by saying, "Who the hell would want to bring another person into this shitty world?" All the same, I can understand why fifty-year-old women go from doctor to doctor, trying to have a baby. I think it's crazy. But I can understand it.

So can another woman I interviewed who is married, has suffered several miscarriages, and is beyond childbearing age. Having lost her parents—and with no generational compensation for that loss—she cannot discuss the fact that she has no offspring without weeping. "I know there are iniquities in the world," she says, "and in my saner moments I think: God has a plan." She goes on to say,

> The most devastating aspect of having no kids is that my mother always had somebody there for her, to love her and take care of her—namely me. I look around my life and I realize that other than my husband, I've got no one. Who will be there for me when I get older? Who will I be able to count on?

According to Roselyn J. Deyo, a social worker who runs support groups for bereaved families, such questions often propel childless women—and men—into seeking professional help when their parents die. Says Deyo,

> For adult children who have no children, you get the sense that they're feeling ungrounded. They don't have any ancestors, and

they don't have any descendants. They feel lost and unconnected, with no past and no future. The task for them often is to try to find other relationships. But it may not be a blood relationship.

On the other hand, it *may* be a blood relationship, one they hadn't really paid that much attention to before, one that was right in their own backyards: their *siblings'* children.

The Sibling Factor

One of the most important findings in my survey was that of those who were childless, *nearly all of them had nieces and nephews,* which could be a primary, albeit subliminal, reason why these respondents hadn't reproduced.

Here again, birth rank played an important role. As was mentioned earlier, middleborn respondents, compared to their brothers and sisters, were least likely to have offspring. Having felt lost in the proceedings when they were growing up, most of them had always focused their attentions outside the family. Several wryly commented that whenever they got choked up about having no kids, all they had to do was go over to their brother's or sister's place and hear a bunch of screaming kids to instantly rid them of any regrets.

But they had not jettisoned the urge to nurture. To the contrary: After their parents died, many of these respondents became closely involved with their siblings' children, serving as the new family "switchboard"—the surrogate grandparents. Because they had fewer responsibilities, they frequently had the time, and the income, to help out their extended kin.

Charles Dickens's novels are filled with heirless aunts and uncles whose generosity changed the lives of nieces and nephews. Charles Darwin offers a theory to explain this largesse. If your sibling has already taken care of your family's intergenerational gene pool, you are off the evolutionary hook. Throughout the millennia, says Frank J. Sulloway in his book *Born to Rebel*, laterborns have typically been less inclined to make babies than their older brothers and sisters; hence, they can afford to be, and frequently are, generous.

Another Darwinian principle, in this case explicated by E. O. Wilson in his book *On Human Nature*, makes sense of this altruism. Wilson argues that childlessness can serve an important evolutionary purpose: It enhances the survival of *other people's children*. Wilson uses the example of homosexuals who have no offspring to make this point. "Freed from the special obligations of parental duties," he writes, "they would [be] in a position to operate with special efficiency in assisting close relatives."

But Darwin was very far from the minds of the childless respondents I interviewed. They could think of a thousand reasons to justify being childless. Yet that did not mean they had no desire to make a lasting mark on the next generation. To justify their very existence, these people still had to contend with what was going on in the other areas of their lives.

The World Beyond "Home"

When social worker Roselyn Deyo remarked that childless survivors might have to find other means by which to fill the double void of having neither ancestors nor descendants, she was onto something. The deaths of their parents can spur countless people who have no children (and countless people who do) into putting their procreative energies into *other* aspects of their lives.

R. Benyamin Cirlin, a New York psychotherapist, has helped numerous men and women who have no offspring to find meaning in their lives after their parents die. Cirlin views parental death as the catalyst for a redefinition of oneself and one's goals, which might or *might not* include marriage and children. Says Cirlin,

Many people whose parents have died say to themselves in one way or another, "I have to grow in new ways and move on with my life. I now know in an intimate way that my life is finite. There are many goals and desires that I have yet to fulfill. It is time to reorder my life and priorities." For these people, parental death is not solely a grievous loss but also an opportunity for growth and self-redefinition.

This growth can result in extraordinary creative output. In her book *Bequest & Betrayal: Memoirs of a Parent's Death*, Nancy K. Miller asks: "[W]hat does it mean to think about the death of one's parents when there is no generation to follow? What happens to our legacy if there is no next of kin?" One of the things that can happen, she notes, is the handing down of one's ideas and longings—the heirlooms of the imagination—in the form of art, as Simone de Beauvoir and Philip Roth, both childless, have done in their writings. In this case, the world is their metaphorical next of kin.

But not everyone can be, or even wants to be, a de Beauvoir or a Roth; not everyone has so great a talent, so vast an ambition. There are other ways to make a personal mark on the next generation. As behavioral psychologist Bernice L. Neugarten once noted, "Some of the psychological readjustments of middle age relate not to the creation of biological heirs, but to the creation of social heirs; the need to nurture and to act as a model or mentor to the young. . . ."

For those who decide not to have children—or whose aging bodies or personal circumstances have made that decision for them—they can draw strength from the fact that it is not the act of having children, per se, that leads to immortality. Rather, it is having a positive *influence* upon children—even if they are not your own and even if your name is never on a plaque.

• • •

It has become a cliché to suggest that we ought to leave the world a little better than we found it. Nevertheless, that is the conclusion the majority of my respondents, whether or not they have children, have reached. Most of these men and women are well aware of their own mortality. They have given long, soul-searching thought to the whole matter of having and of rearing children, and of the crucial role that adults play in children's lives. They want to make a difference, if not within their own families, then beyond.

One fifty-year-old childless woman, whose deceased parents were Holocaust survivors and who herself is an only child, expressed that goal with remarkable eloquence. She said:

> For a long time I didn't think I'd ever get over my parents' suffering in the war. Then I didn't think I'd get over their deaths. Then I didn't think I'd get over feeling alone in the world. But in the last few years I've been meditating about all this, and it has opened my heart. Some kind of integration has taken place. I have never been as compassionate as I am now—people have become very, very precious to me. For the first time in my life, I feel that the world is my family. And I want to do whatever I can to make others feel welcome in it.

**Achievement:
Reappraised Careers**

You couldn't ask for a better father than I had. If I have one
regret, it's that he didn't see me finally become responsible.
When he was alive, every decision I made was in the light of how
he would perceive it. He wanted me be an achiever—he always
said, "You're the greatest!" So I had stars in my eyes, but no real
ambition. I wasn't willing to work as hard as he did—if I didn't
have instant success, I'd quit. It took his death for me to finally
settle into work I cared about. I think I was a good son to my
dad. But I still feel some guilt that I didn't make him prouder
of me.

—Leonard, forty-nine

When Leonard's father, Abraham, died in 1986 at the age of
eighty-two, five hundred people showed up for the funeral.
This was a man who had been a very big fish in a very small
pond—he was a Russian immigrant who came to the United States
at the age of fourteen and who went on to become a highly esteemed
translator of Russian literature.

For months after his father's death, Leonard would receive letters
from people who had known and loved his father—people from the
old country who saw Abraham as a kind of hero, the kid who made
good and never forgot his roots. Leonard grew up hearing the lore

about his father's impoverished beginnings—of having to help support his parents, of living in the squalor of New York tenements—but as far as he was concerned, that was ancient history; it had nothing to do with his own life.

Leonard never encountered any of the hardships his father had endured—his dad wanted to make certain his son would have every Yankee advantage. When Leonard wanted a new bike, he got it; when he decided to go to an expensive college, the money was there; when he soured on a job because it just didn't "feel right," well, that was okay too. "Don't worry!" his dad would say. "You'll land somewhere. You're the greatest!"

As Leonard recounts for me the years when he floundered in his career, his voice thickens. He still cannot talk about his broken track record—in particular, his father's ebullient efforts to conceal his disappointment in him—without choking up. "I never had any self-discipline," he says. "I just took it for granted that my dad would work his ass off, would do without—he never owned a house—so that I could have everything. Somehow I took this as permission to coast."

But in the summer of 1984, when Leonard's father began his long medical decline—he would suffer through two agonizing years of cancer—Leonard realized that his seemingly interminable childhood was about to end. Frantic to do something to earn his father's respect while there was still time, at the age of thirty-seven Leonard fell into a position with a market research firm, punching data into computers. "Very entry level," he says. "But at least it was a beginning. I wanted to show my dad that I could stick with something, even if it wasn't glamorous."

By the time his father died, Leonard had been promoted to department head, concentrating on accounts that intrigued him, some of them in areas where he had briefly worked earlier in his checkered career. "It all came together," he recalls. "All the years of drifting paid off in this job, where my experience could count for something."

The job came not a moment too soon, because now he had serious obligations. It was his father's dying wish that Leonard look after his mother and help ease her passage into widowhood. Leonard rose to the occasion, calling her every day, managing her finances, and when she herself became terminally ill in 1990, arranging for her medical care. "That's when I really started maturing," he recalls. "I couldn't drop the ball."

In the interval between his parents' deaths, Leonard met and married a woman who, he says, would have delighted his father because of her levelheadedness and talent—she is a medical illustrator. "She's a workhorse," he says admiringly. "I never saw anyone as focused as she is—except, maybe, my dad." And except, maybe, for Leonard himself, who routinely puts in long hours, playing financial catch-up so he'll have a chance of one day retiring.

Today Leonard and his wife live in a small but charming house in Westchester County, forty-five minutes from his midtown Manhattan office. Each evening when he pulls into his driveway, he gazes at the garden his wife has created, at the sky over the house that in ten years will be paid for, and wishes his father could come back for just one day to witness the man that he has become.

"If you could change anything," I ask him, "what would it be?" He mulls over this question, his mind meandering backward over his life. Finally, he says,

You know, I wouldn't change a thing. It's sad to admit, but I didn't begin to grow up until my parents died. It isn't just that I started working harder; my goals changed. I finally came to the conclusion that I wasn't my dad—being number one isn't as important to me as it was to him. Being a dependable, decent person is what matters to me now. My dad only wanted the best for me, and as far as I'm concerned, that's what I have. I wouldn't trade my life for anyone's.

A Second Flowering

Nowhere is the impact of parental death upon adult children more apparent than in their working lives and career choices—that is, what they do occupationally and why they do it. Just as the orbits of their personal lives are realigned by their parents' absence, so, too, are their worlds beyond the family. This is where their capacity to survive without their parents—to feed and clothe and house themselves, to prove themselves on their own terms—is put to the test.

Examples of the effect of parental death on one's work can be found in any library. Such contemporary authors as Frank McCourt, Susan Cheever, and Rick Bragg have gone public about their deceased parents' sometimes tarnished private lives.

Many of these authors have taken critical heat for revealing secrets about parents who were no longer around to defend themselves. But it is safe to assume that the risk of censure was worth it; now they could tell the truth of their own childhood experiences. This was certainly the case for McCourt, who sat on the manuscript of *Angela's Ashes*—a harrowing account of his father's abandonment of his wife and children—for thirty years, publishing it only after his beloved mother died. The book was McCourt's psychological salvation. "If I hadn't written [it]," he told a reporter, "I would have died howling."

Far from the spotlight, however, in offices and shops and factories across the country, are millions of other people who, in the aftermath of their parents' deaths, *also* reconstructed the scaffolding of their working lives. Where once they might have labored in the shadow of their parents' expectations of them, now they were free to reconsider what the word *achievement* meant to them, and to them alone.

This occupational metamorphosis was one of the most important findings in my study. In answer to the question "Since your parents' deaths, have you made any career changes?" half the respondents said yes. Given the vagaries of the marketplace, this was unsurprising. But of this group, *69 percent* said the changes were a *direct* result of the deaths; they had reappraised their careers from the perspective of their now undeniable mortality and found certain aspects of them to be wanting.

The results of these reappraisals ranged from the philosophic to the practical to the problematic. For example, many people said that their parents' deaths had forced them to "concentrate on" or "examine" what they wanted to do for the rest of their working lives; they felt "more in control" of their destinies; they could pursue their own "dreams" instead of their parents' dreams for them.

Then there were those whose careers veered not because of some ephemeral epiphany but because of the stone-cold bottom line. In some cases, the parents had died virtually penniless, which the respondents viewed as a cautionary tale, impelling them to hunker down in their careers and secure their own financial futures. In other cases, the respondents received a financial bequest that enabled them to go back to school or become entrepreneurs.

But there were those who, after their parents died, simply had no idea *what* they wanted to do. Some had spent years toiling in jobs they loathed in order to please their parents or to live down their parents' low opinions of them; others had scaled back or abandoned their careers in order to take care of their ailing parents. For these people it was as though someone had pulled the plug on their ambitions; they had run out of motivational steam.

This chapter explores these three occupational themes—career redirection, career rejuvenation, and career confusion—in the after-math of parental death. But before going into the details of these themes, it is necessary to lay out the variables that often contoured them.

Different Strokes

Age was not a big factor in the respondents' occupational reapprais-als—people under, or over, fifty-five were equally likely to report changes in their careers. *Marital status* was more significant—single, childless respondents, who had relatively few obligations, cited such changes more frequently than married respondents and/or those who have children.

But three other variables stood out. The first had to do with *gender*. Women were far more likely than men to say that their work goals had been completely revamped. This can be partially explained by the fact that female respondents tended to be more involved with their parents' well-being and care than male respondents; freed of this responsibility, the women were able to focus more closely on their careers.

More important, however, were the traditions with which many of these women had been raised—primarily, the belief that for women, ambition should take a backseat to domesticity—traditions they began to question after their parents died.

In her book *Midlife Women and Death of Mother*, clinical psy-chologist Martha A. Robbins argues that women's "unconscious loy-alty bonds" to their mothers might put a crimp in their own aspirations. In her study Robbins found that many women were more saddened by their mothers' culturally constrained lives than by their actual deaths; at the same time, they were angry that their mothers hadn't somehow managed to surmount those constraints. These two emotions—sorrow and renunciation—allowed the women to "differentiate" from their mothers through "meaningful work."

Such issues were less important to the men in my survey—which is not to suggest that "loyalty bonds" to their parents had not plagued them, as we saw with Leonard at the beginning of this chapter. It's just that, for the most part, the men had always been *expected* to achieve—to be more identified with their work than with their emotions—an imperative that sometimes hobbled them. "Lick the world!" Willy Loman commands his sons in Arthur Miller's classic play *Death of a Salesman*. "You guys together could absolutely lick the civilized world." That's a tough—impossible—mandate to live up to.

The second significant variable with regard to the respondents' altered work goals was whether or not they had *siblings*. Singletons were much more likely than people with siblings—75 percent versus 41 percent—to report "no change" in their careers. The identities and self-esteem of only children appeared to be tied more closely to their partners and children than to their job titles—they were more content with the occupational status quo. Whereas respondents who had brothers and sisters were more likely to carry their childhood rivalries into their work lives, trying to outdo each other in their résumés, an echo of long-standing contests to win their parents' approval.

Numerous investigators have discovered that adult siblings frequently vie for parental favoritism in their careers. In a study of adult brothers and sisters by Helgola G. Ross and Joel I. Milgram of the University of Cincinnati, it was found that the vast majority of study subjects could trace their career rivalries back to childhood, when their parents compared them to their siblings, tagging them with such labels as "stupid" or "intelligent." These rivalries often took on lives of their own after the parents died. "From childhood to old age," Ross and Milgram observe, "achievement is the dimension of rivalry *par excellence.*" (In contrast, when equally favored siblings carve out separate career niches and expertise, they don't try to top each other; rather, they take pleasure in their own, and each other's, attainments.)

Such career contests were common among my respondents who had siblings. They could remember, with stunning clarity, what I came to think of as "the war of the scrapbooks," a typical example of which went like this: The respondent was visiting his or her parents. A neighbor dropped by, and Mom or Dad hauled out the stoutest family scrapbook for public viewing—the one that chronicled, in yellowing newspaper clippings or fading photographs, the kudos piled up by the most "successful" child—who just happened *not* to be the one dutifully visiting. These recollections still caused these respondents—some of them in their fifties, sixties, and seventies, their parents long dead—to seethe.

The third and final important variable, an outgrowth of the one just described, had to do with the respondents' *relationships to the deceased parents.* People who had been close to their parents were likelier than those who felt ambivalent or distant from their parents to report that the deaths had stoked their ambitions. These respondents wanted to begin anew occupationally—some because they wanted their parents to be (posthumously) proud of them, others because they no longer had to be concerned about their parents' possible disappointment in their altered goals. People who had not been close to their parents were more likely to report no change in their careers.

With these variables in mind, let us now turn to how they played out in the respondents' reevaluations of their work.

Career Redirection: A New Beginning

The majority of respondents who embarked on new careers after their parents died were not simply looking for novelty, and did not change direction out of mere boredom. Rather, they were intent upon expressing themselves in ways that reflected the people they had become but without the worry of how their career decisions might have registered with their parents. These career shifts clustered into four patterns:

- Going against their parents' dreams for them.
- Achieving big to compensate for their losses.
- Making creative sense of their unresolved histories.
- Reducing the importance of work in their lives.

Going Against the Grain

The most dramatic example of the first scenario is Rita, forty-nine, who went from being a nun to becoming a guidance counselor—a move, she says, that was triggered by her parents' deaths in the 1980s. She had been considering leaving the convent for some time but knew how disappointed her devoutly religious Catholic parents would have been. "My dad really *grooved* on my being a nun," she says, lapsing into the street-wise jargon of her Boston childhood. "It was a feather in his cap. Plus, it kept me out of trouble."

Rita was the middleborn of three children (she has two brothers) whose formative years were marred by their parents' deeply troubled marriage. Her authoritarian father was often violent toward his sons but never to his daughter, whom he adored; her mother was coiled, cautious—she could not warm up to her own or anybody else's children. "She was a walking anxiety attack," Rita recalls. "I watched her with my nieces. She'd hold a kid on her lap and have a low-grade tremor because she was so ill at ease."

It was in large measure because of the turbulence at home that Rita joined the convent when she was eighteen. The religious life gave her the opportunity to become accustomed to solitude. But it also imbued her with a feeling of welcome—of spiritual and literal sanctuary. Says Rita,

> Being in the convent gave me the chance to escape from a dysfunctional family in a way that would be okay with my parents. I wanted to have an attachment I could be sure of, namely, with God. I was hungering to belong, to gain some kind of acceptance. It was wonderful for me—it gave me tremendous depth I'm not sure I would have gotten had I stayed home. It taught me how to trust. I still have great friends from that time.

Her fourteen years in the convent taught her something else—that she no longer needed to withdraw from the world, that, indeed, she wanted to be part of it. Rita always felt somewhat out of step with the other nuns, and as time went by the religious faith that had initially beckoned began to wane. Thus, when her parents died, she lost the last remaining impediment to her desire to embark on a new life.

Rita thinks of her new career as "an art" that consumes up to ten hours of each weekday. As a guidance counselor, she is able to provide young people with a sense of hope, of their individuality and unique abilities—the very things she seldom received from her parents. (Another benefit to her career change—she fell in love with and married a colleague.)

Other respondents were also motivated to go against the parental grain, but for a different reason. In these cases, the respondents had been reluctant to outdistance their parents when their parents were alive. But after their parents died, they were emboldened to take new occupational risks.

Nola, fifty-four, is an example of this phenomenon. Her parents emigrated from Czechoslovakia to the United States right after World War II. Her father, a university graduate, became a postal worker to provide a steady income for his family. But he was determined that Nola and her brother go to college so they could "amount to something." Nola's education, however, had a chilling effect on her relationship to her mother, who had quit school at sixteen to take care of her own parents. Says Nola,

> My mother brought all the trappings of the old world with her. She felt betrayed because I had really strong opinions and the schooling to back them up. She didn't want to feel inferior to me. She wanted me to be like her—to marry, have kids, and stay home.

Which is precisely what Nola did. She had had career aspirations—her fantasy was to own an antiques store—but did not implement them until her mother was struck down by a fatal heart attack when Nola was forty-five. It was then that she realized that no one would ever thank her for stifling her dreams. She recalls,

> I had a real surge of energy after my mother died. I wanted to do something with my life, not just because she had died, but because there was a kind of vacuum that needed to be filled. I just hitched up my boots and took a business course so I could prove myself in the outside world. That was it. I wanted to prove myself.

Today she manages a consignment shop. "I get to advise people on decorating their houses, and at the same time earn my own money," she says. "It has put my self-esteem over the roof."

Other people said that the deaths of their parents gave them the courage to quit their high-profile jobs and toil in lesser-paying but more psychically rewarding endeavors, a move they wouldn't have dared make while their parents were alive. As one man, who left a thriving Wall Street career to work for an environmental organization, put it, "My dad would have said, 'You're going to give up a six-figure income? Are you *nuts?*' "

Shooting Stars

Then there were the respondents who said that their ambitions didn't get roused—their careers didn't really take off—until their parents died. Prior to the deaths, these respondents had floated from job to job, uncertain which direction to take and not all that concerned about it—they had their whole lives ahead of them. But after the deaths, they realized that if they were going to score, they'd better get hustling. And hustle they did—some to the highest occupational rung.

Dick, forty-one, an attorney at a prestigious Los Angeles law firm, says that in his early twenties he tried a number of careers—he began in accounting, went on to be a travel agent, got "down-sized" and became a sales rep. But when he was twenty-nine, both his parents perished in a plane crash, and the double loss forced him to "grow up" overnight. Motivated by a desire to honor the memory of his father, who had been a country lawyer, he worked his way through law school, graduating at the top of his class. Says Dick,

Losing my parents was the worst thing that had ever happened to me, and it put steel in my backbone. It made me want to move forward in my life and finish out some of the things that my father had started. My dad never got rich, but he loved the work, which was a key element in my deciding to go into the law. Within three years, I got some incredible breaks—a couple of fabulous cases came my way, and I made partner in record time. It was like I was shot from guns. I think my father would have been proud of me.

The connection between adult orphanhood and extraordinary career success has been a source of endless fascination to students of human behavior. In a book titled *Parental Loss and Achievement*, four researchers from different disciplines discovered that the connection was more than mere coincidence.

Psychologist Marvin Eisenstadt, the lead author, conducted a study of eminence, or "genius," in the arts, sciences, politics, and other fields from 500 B.C. through the middle of the twentieth century. Of the 573 "greats" studied, including Sigmund Freud and several British prime ministers, the adult orphanhood rate—meaning the number of achievers who were in their twenties and thirties when their parents died—was remarkably high.

Eisenstadt concluded that for certain gifted people, the crisis presented by their parents' deaths—that the survivors are "alone" in the world—can evoke the will to compensate for their changed circumstances through mastery and high achievement. For such people, hard times can be the catalyst for outstanding success.

This was certainly the case for the men and women in my sample who suddenly caught fire occupationally after their parents' deaths. They felt that they had nothing to lose, and everything to gain, by going for broke.

Making Creative Sense

However, not everyone I talked to who changed careers had their eyes on some glittering prize. Rather, they simply wanted to be heard—to give voice to passions that had been stored up like so many unshed tears.

I am speaking here of the creative respondents whose dreams for the artist's life had been muzzled either by the parental admonition to "get a real job" or by their own timidity, but who now had only themselves to blame if they didn't at least attempt to realize this dream. Some of these people could afford to take the plunge, if only for a time—either they had saved up enough money to justify quitting their jobs or they had built up businesses or practices they could sell, giving them a financial cushion. Others went from full-time positions to part-time jobs, scaling back their expenses so they could work on their art, whether in literature, music, or some other specialty.

These people hoped to eke out a living from their artistry, but that wasn't the point. The point was they had *something to say* that had been denied—something they were trying to get a handle on, to contain and give creative form.

One such respondent, Carole, thirty-six, grew up in the social margins. Her mother was an alcoholic, her father a remote presence, and she never lived anywhere for more than a year. She was always the new kid on the block, a pattern that continued into her restless twenties; she moved from one town to another, one waitressing job to another, one street drug to another, one lover to another.

But when, in Carole's thirtieth year, her mother killed herself, Carole emerged from her psychological fog. She looked at the detritus of her life and saw two options: Either she would pull herself together, or she would follow her mother's suicidal lead. Carole chose the former. She quit drugs, cobbled together the tuition for a writing course, and landed a part-time job in a bookstore. There she earns peanuts by day so she can labor by night on a play about her mother. Says Carole:

> I always wanted to be a writer, but I never tried to produce any-
> thing until she died. I have this obsessive need to tell her story, to
> make sense of it by writing about it. I'm not saying that my suf-

fering and grief are more profound than those of people whose parents died a slow death. But there's something about the suddenness, the shock of suicide that makes people like me a curiosity—everyone wonders how you could survive such a loss. That's what I'm trying to get across in my play, that you can make your survival count for something—that you can overcome anything.

When Less Is More

Then there were those people who, after their parents died, said that the imperative to succeed had lost its allure, and decided to take a less demanding path. Many of these people had been A-type workaholics, rising to every challenge, heeding every opportunity. But now they felt less compelled to keep testing their mettle; with their own mortality in sight, running the extra mile and pushing themselves to exhaustion served no purpose.

Some of these respondents cut back on their working hours— or removed themselves from this or that advisory committee or board of directors—in order to spend more time with their families and friends. Others simply cashed in their chips and took early retirement.

In the latter category is a divorcée in her late fifties who, soon after her mother died three years ago, resigned from her position at a public relations firm, sold her house, and moved to a small cottage near her children and grandchildren. "My dad died of a heart attack in his office when I was in my thirties," she says. "When my mother died, I thought to myself, Hey, I'm next." She continues,

Quitting my job is the smartest thing I ever did. My nest egg isn't enough for me to take vacations in the south of France; I have had my last manicure, my last limo ride. But there is not one thing

I miss from the days when I was in the rat race. If they made me CEO, I wouldn't go back. Life is too short.

Such people, however, were a distinct minority. The vast majority of respondents were still full of projects or still needed to earn a living.

Career Rejuvenation: A Different Emphasis

Changing careers was not the only way that the respondents' work lives were affected by their parents' deaths. For many, their existing careers suited their talents and personalities. But the tenor of their work shifted as a result of rethinking their goals and taking greater responsibility for their economic futures.

Some of these people had entered their parents' professions or gone into the family business—a smart career move if the parents had paved the way, showing them the ropes; a not-so-smart move if they thought they could do a better job running the place. As long as the parents were alive, these respondents felt hamstrung; they didn't want to go head-to-head with their parents occupationally or buck their authority. After the parents died, however, these people could forge ahead, doing business their own way. Said one woman, a graphic artist who had joined her father's printing company, "When he died I hired more people and went after bigger accounts. I think the reason I hadn't done so before was that I didn't want to be better or more accomplished than he was."

Most people, however, had entered careers that were different from their parents', usually with the parents' hearty endorsement. In many cases, the parents had made enormous sacrifices so that their children would have more opportunities for success than they had

had; these offspring had been eager to live up to their parents' expectations of them. The trouble was that they often felt that their
parents were living vicariously *through* them, regarding each pay hike
or plum assignment as a return on the parents' investments rather
than as the reward for the respondents' own hard work.

Bragging Rights

The concept of "ownership"—that is, the capacity to claim success
for oneself rather than simply to reflect glory on one's parents—was
an extremely important factor in these respondents' career reappraisals. Before their parents died, they knew when their parents were
proud of them. But occasionally parental pride had crossed the line
into meddling, or gloating, and the offspring began to wonder whose
success it really was.

Parents seldom make a secret of their feelings about their adult
children's accomplishments; still, the messages they sometimes impart to their offspring can be mixed. In a study called "My Children
and Me: Midlife Evaluations of Grown Children and of Self," psychologist Carol D. Ryff and her colleagues found that how the kids
turned out—that is, how they fared educationally, occupationally,
and personally—was of great importance to the mothers and fathers.
If the kids had solid jobs and were happy, the parents tended to feel
good about themselves. But if the kids were doing *better* than the
parents had at the same age, or appeared to be more well-adjusted,
some parents were vulnerable to feelings of envy and self-doubt.

From this study it can be inferred that most parents want their
children to do well—but not *so* well that it makes the parents feel
lousy about themselves in comparison. It is just this comparison that
many of my respondents had picked up on intuitively when their
parents were alive—the respondents tended to edit themselves when
talking about their work. They'd tell their mothers and fathers just

enough good news so that they wouldn't worry, but not so much that the parents would either feel outclassed or take undue credit for it.

Once the parents were gone, however, these respondents felt they had a firmer footing in their careers—they could surge ahead in their work and take greater pride in it because now their turf was entirely their own.

Willa, forty-six, an advertising executive, embodies this shift in attitude. Willa's mother, who had been a restaurant cashier, rarely took an interest in the quality or nature of Willa's work—she was more concerned with whether or not Willa was making a living and staying in her bosses' good graces; at least, that's what she told Willa.

What she told the neighbors and anyone else who would listen was something else. Every promotion Willa received was instantly broadcast to the Brooklyn neighborhood where her parents lived and to members of the extended family, news of which would get back to Willa via the family grapevine. Thus, Willa was never certain which maternal verdict was real—the one implying that Willa might screw up or the one making it sound as if she were in line for a Pulitzer Prize. Consequently, she gave her mother as little information about her work as possible, which sometimes created friction between them.

Since her mother's death five years ago, however, Willa has come to think of her mother's mixed messages about her work differently. She explains,

> There were years when I didn't tell my mother about my achievements because she'd embellish or diminish them in ways I didn't want to hear—they irritated me. But now, whenever I do good work, I think about the praise she gave me when I was a little kid, doing something that pleased her. I can remember coming home from kindergarten with a picture I'd painted, and she would be

thrilled. She'd say, "Oh, isn't that *wonderful.*" That's the voice I hear in my head now. I draw on that early feedback, that pat on the head for something mundane—not what she said when I was adult, doing work she didn't understand and couldn't relate to.

Answering the Critics

In other cases, however, "ownership" of their career achievements was not the issue; disownership of their parents' limited, or nonexistent, faith in them was. Many of these respondents had been compared unfavorably by their parents to their more measurably successful siblings; the comparison still stung.

Several of these respondents were slow starters; once they zeroed in on what they wanted to do, they were, in fact, consumed by their work, eventually earning respectable incomes or garnering professional prestige. But they were haunted by a sense that their success wasn't enough, that they had to do *more*, do *better*. They were so afraid of failure, so worried about being outgunned by their siblings, that they couldn't take pleasure in their attainments.

After their parents were gone, however, these respondents could ease up on themselves and begin to count their occupational blessings. The work itself hadn't changed all that much—it's just that now there wasn't so much *riding on it*. The parental heat was off.

Stan, forty-eight, a sociologist, recalls that his parents—who never went to college and were wiped out in the Depression—always compared him to his brother, a venture capitalist. Although Stan won a number of academic honors, they were from organizations his parents had never heard of; they weren't all that impressed. But when his brother was the subject of a magazine cover story or earned a million-dollar bonus, *that* was his parents' idea of a real "success story."

It has been a decade since Stan's parents died, and in that time he has gradually shed both his envy for his brother and his sense of injustice over his parents' differential regard. He says,

> It took me a long time to get over how little my accomplishments meant to my parents. Every time they'd call me to tell me about my brother's latest deal, I wanted to scream, "Look what I did!" They were in awe of his material success, which made me feel like chopped liver. After they died, I decided to just measure myself against myself. Perhaps if I had gotten some recognition from my parents, my brother's success wouldn't have stuck in my craw. But I also think that my parents were just too limited to see things any other way. I know what my achievements mean, even if they just couldn't.

Getting a Grip

Some respondents, however, had an altogether different problem. Their parents had gone overboard with their encouragement and financial generosity, to the extent that the respondents had not learned to stand on their own and become entirely self-reliant.

For Aaron, a thirty-nine-year-old theatrical lighting director, his father's death had the effect of puncturing his immature belief that he would always be rescued, that he could chase his dreams wherever they took him. His father, an insurance broker, had always bank-rolled Aaron's show business ambitions and was willing to subsidize his peripatetic work life by supporting him between theatrical gigs. But after his father died, Aaron realized that the occupational buck stopped with him—he had to earn a lot more money, and on a steady basis. Today he works full-time for a production house. Says Aaron,

> I made some risky career choices in my life that I couldn't have made if my dad hadn't been there to back me up. I didn't want to

end up like him, spending thirty years in a drudge job. I always wanted to do something wild and wacky, and I think that's why I turned my back on security—I saw what a dull life my father led because of his fear of not having a regular paycheck. So I jumped off a lot of cliffs professionally, and I didn't have to suffer the consequences. Well, my backup is gone, and I've had to become accountable. In that way, I've turned into my father; I'm working for the paycheck. It's about time.

Career Confusion: Now What?

Finally, we come to those respondents who, after their parents' deaths, were occupationally stymied. If these people had one thing in common—and they had several—it was that they had never left home emotionally. They had been so bound up either in their parents' negative views of them or in their parents' dependence upon them, that the deaths left these respondents with no idea of what to do next.

Rebels Without a Cause

Some respondents said they had spent their entire careers hounded by their parents' constant denigration, funneling all their anger into their work as if to say, "I'll show *you*." But once their parents died, they lost their momentum. Without their parents' hostility to fuel them, they had nothing to defend against, nothing to want.

Deborah, forty-three, a divorced documentary filmmaker, is an example of this phenomenon. She "made a career," she says, of her parents, especially her mother, who treated her brutally when she was a child. Soon after graduating from college, she landed a job at a television network and plowed all her energies into films about domestic violence. Her outraged occupational zeal seemed boundless—she couldn't get enough of the horrors of other people's lives.

When, three years ago, her parents died within months of one another, Deborah's creativity seemed to dry up. After two decades in the documentary business, she no longer had anything she was *burning* to say—she was suffering from the equivalent of writer's block.

> My parents were my reverse muse—everything that happened to me as a kid found its way into my work. I wanted to find out what makes people do such things to children. But since they died, I've lost my appetite for the tragic, my taste for the darker impulse. My problem is that I have no idea what I want to do; it's as if someone turned out the lights.

Hostages of Misfortune

Other people who were at loose ends occupationally said they had spent a huge chunk of their adult lives serving as their aging parents' caregivers, taking jobs rather than building careers. These people drew enormous satisfaction from being so necessary to their parents, from performing their roles so selflessly. But once their parents died, they were left with the unsettling feeling that life had passed them by and that they had outlived their usefulness.

Thelma, fifty-nine, a lab technician who has never married, is an example of this increasingly common scenario. The elder of two siblings, her parents developed chronic illnesses when she was in her early forties. As the shy, obedient firstborn daughter, she felt it was her obligation to take care of them, a mission she accepted willingly. She moved in with her parents, working by day at a nearby doctor's office and spending the rest of her time cooking and cleaning, giving her parents their medications and, as their illnesses worsened, emptying their bedpans.

As recompense for her ministrations (and with her sibling's blessing) Thelma's parents promised her that she'd inherit their house after they died. This arrangement would consume the next fifteen years of her life and all but devour her identity; only now does she realize how much it cost her.

> I think a part of me never wanted to leave home. As much as they needed me, I needed them, too. I always wanted security, and taking care of my parents gave me that. I had a roof over my head, I could save my money, and I *belonged* somewhere. When they died, all of a sudden I lost my function. I felt very alone and frightened. I was angry that my parents had never encouraged me to strive, angry that I had never accomplished anything. Here I was, middle-aged, on my own for the first time in my life with nothing to show for it. My whole world just collapsed.

Outside Reinforcements

Psychiatrist George E. Vaillant must have had people like Deborah and Thelma in mind when he wrote his illuminating book *The Wisdom of the Ego*, in which he describes such occupational stagnation and offers an intriguing explanation for it. Drawing on data from longitudinal studies of human development, he argues that a midlife work renaissance turns on the ability to relinquish one's anger and find a benevolent source of inspiration.

The men and women in Vaillant's research samples who failed to achieve what he calls "career consolidation"—which he defines as becoming less self-absorbed and making a contribution to society— were those who were either "explosive" or who smouldered within, their anger unexpressed. As a consequence, these people had failed to attract mentors.

"To grow," Vaillant writes, "we need to feel enriched by those we have loved." If we have internalized only our parents' criticism—or their neediness—and have not formed lasting relationships outside the family, the deaths of those parents can lead to feelings of hollowness and despair. But if, as Vaillant suggests, we can find people who believe in us, we can internalize *their* voices instead and be motivated to discover and hone our strengths.

Mentors come in a variety of forms. Several of the people I interviewed whose careers had stalled sought the services of professional counselors in order to breathe new life into their existing work or to summon the self-confidence to find jobs in which they felt valued and valuable. Others were inspired by younger colleagues or co-workers, whose energies, warmth, and respectfulness made them feel revitalized. Still others sought the career advice and encouragement of their grown children.

Being mentored in these and other ways did not necessarily lead to financial riches, but it did lead to *a new sense of purpose*. And it had an unexpected side effect; it impelled several respondents to be of use in a way that had never occurred to them before—that is, by becoming mentors themselves.

A number of middle-aged men and women in my sample who had been dispirited by their lackluster track records, or who felt that they had lost their spark, repaired their morale by focusing on the younger generation. Whether they were still on the job or in retirement, they found that in guiding or advising others, they gained a new lease on life.

Expanding Horizons

As all these stories illustrate, the deaths of one's parents often lead to the revival of deferred dreams, or the birth of new ones, by virtue of the painful recognition that there is no remaining buffer to one's own mortality.

With very few exceptions, the people I talked to had fervently wanted their parents to think highly of their work efforts, whether it resulted in an A on a report card when they were in school or a job promotion when they were grown. And although parental esteem was by no means their only career motivation, it was the one continuous yardstick against which they had measured themselves from infancy onward.

Once their parents were gone, however, these adult children had to re-orient themselves and reconsider their achievements. They had to became their own muses, had to steer themselves by some inner star. The very fact of the parental void in their lives proved to be the source of an exhilarating sense of their own agency.

Arriving at this psychological destination was seldom easy, and there were those who didn't make it, who were still marooned in the past. But for those who were able to become invested in the future, the gratification they gained from their self-reliant industry was an unexpected joy.

In his book *Solitude: A Return to the Self*, Anthony Storr argues that work is at least as important as, and in some ways *more* important than, interpersonal relationships. "Even those who have the happiest relationships with others," he writes, "need something other than those relationships to complete their fulfillment."

When our connections to others define our identities or limit our aspirations, we run the risk of never discovering our full potential—of never uncovering our unique capabilities. The deaths of one's parents can allow this potential to be realized. For it is then that we can expand our horizons and set new courses for ourselves, spurred by the bracing knowledge that time is of the essence.

I would like to end this chapter by quoting from a letter I received that exemplifies this feeling of renewal, this quiet pride in the self. It comes from a woman who had been devoted to her parents, but who not did truly come into her own until after they died. She writes:

> My one great sadness is that my parents did not see me live up to their faith in me. I was the problem child, the brilliant lost child, and they followed my career with interest and exasperation, because I was constantly switching jobs. They did their best to steer me through all my bad times—they were my rock. I had to be deprived of that to take charge of my own life. After they died, I used my inheritance to buy a small inn, which produces enough income for me to survive. I finally made a life for myself, and I am astonished by that accomplishment. It has been many years since my parents died, and every day I think of them—they always said I was a late bloomer. In this, as in so many things, they were right. But I had to lose them to find this out for myself.

CHAPTER 8 Friendships Reassessed

When my mother died, I couldn't think of one person I could ask to come be with me, to hold my hand. It scared the hell out of me, because it made me realize that I didn't have anyone to depend on. I was always doing favors for other people, but I was afraid to let them in close, to show them my underbelly. My mother's death made me see that I wasn't really connected to people, and I had no one to blame but myself. It was a wake-up call—it totally changed my attitude about friendship.

—Zoe, forty-five

If you took a map of the world and threw a dart at it, chances are it would land in the vicinity of one of Zoe's chums. A divorced Washington, D.C., lobbyist, Zoe attracts people the way flowers attract butterflies. Should you need a car mechanic in Australia or a dentist in Zambia, she knows somebody who knows somebody who can do the job. A "people collector," she calls herself, pointing proudly to her bulging Rolodex.

But who among her zillion buddies does she call "friend"? Who really *knows* her—knows about the abortion in the seventies, the debts that keep her awake nights, the breast cancer scare? "A lot more people than before my mother died," she says. "I didn't have too many close friendships back then because I never put in the time. I took most of my friends for granted."

For most of her life, Zoe was always the queen of the prom, the most popular girl in school or at the office, the hub of her social set. An only child, she knew how to make herself irresistible to people, but her friendships were only skin-deep. Self-reliance was imperative; she had to be in control.

Zoe didn't need a best friend because she already had one—her mother. "She always said, 'Don't trust anybody,'" says Zoe, "and I didn't. She was the only person I was able to confide in. Most of my friendships were pretty one-sided, with me in the driver's seat. I was happiest dispensing wisdom to other people, helping them out when they were in a jam—that way, everyone owed me. But I was determined not to be beholden to anyone."

Her discipline and self-containment were the making of her career, but they were anathema to intimate comradeship. Zoe was so busy acquiring contacts—being, as she puts it, "winsome and adorable, tossing my hair"—that the fact that she had no close friends barely registered.

It was only when her mother was gone that she began to realize that the facade she presented was not an accurate reflection of who she truly was. Outside, she was the image of charismatic perfection; inside, she was a basket case. Says Zoe,

> Losing my mother gave me the guts to risk revealing my weaknesses. I had to be without her to understand that if I wanted to have any real friends, I was going to have to start opening up. So I've been letting people see my vulnerabilities, allowing them to take care of me for a change. It has made all the difference in my relationships. The ones who have hung in with me have become my lifeline—because of them I am much more compassionate, not so cavalier. Without my friends, I would fall off the planet.

Among Friends

Of all the dilemmas facing adult children when their parents die, few are as painful as the discovery of who is, and who is not, a true friend. The parents might have been ill for years, or they might have died suddenly. Whenever it happens, that's when we need our closest friends—the people whose tender mercies help to make this rite of passage endurable. Just as we would be there for them, so, too, do we wish them to be there for us.

And when they are not, it can be devastating. Some friends are rattled by the unruly emotions that parental death evokes, and simply disappear. Others manage to say precisely the wrong thing to minimize their own discomfort—as in, "He [she] wouldn't want you to be sad." When friends make no effort to understand what we are going through, or impose their feelings on us, they are not likely to remain in our affections, which might cause us to question why we chose them in the first place.

When parents die, we do, indeed, find out who our comrades are. Seldom anticipated, however, is how our friendships are affected *over time* by the deaths of our parents—that is, whom we choose to have, and to keep, as friends. In the same way that we reassess our relationships to siblings, partners, and children, so, too, do we scrutinize our ties to—and our feelings about—our friends.

This was one of the bigger surprises in my research. In answer to the question "In what ways, if any, have your friendships changed since your parents died?" over *half* (53 percent) of the respondents said that these connections had intensified. For example, many people said their friends became "more precious" to them—that they devoted more time and attention to their friendships than ever before.

Others remarked that they were much more particular about

whom they called "friend"; they had thinned out the ranks of their friendships, concentrating only on those people who added meaning to their lives, and eliminating the rest.

Still others commented that they were drawn to people who had also lost one or both parents, as though they had a special bond—a kind of emotional shorthand—because of their shared experience. There was among this group a quality often found in soldiers returning from war, a sense that they knew something about life, and death, that only another "orphan" could begin to understand.

And then there were those who said that they had turned to friends to fill in as surrogate parents or siblings. The family as they had known it (or as they had wished it to be) was gone, and they had found replacements, people who had become their new "families."

Dividing Lines

These reassessments varied along certain demographic lines. Women were nearly twice as likely as men—60 percent versus 37 percent—to report changes in their friendships. So, too, were people without progeny; 73 percent of those who were childless, compared to 47 percent of people who had offspring, said their friends had become indispensable to them. Age and marital status were also significant variables—compared to older, married respondents, singles and people under age fifty-five were more likely to say that they had put more energy into their friendships. (Interestingly, whether or not the respondents had siblings or had been close to their parents were not conclusive factors in these friendship reappraisals, for reasons that will be explained later.)

Of those who reported "no change" in their friendships, it is possible either that their taste in friends had always been good or that their friends were less central to their well-being than, say, their families or careers. Whichever, their friendships remained pretty much the same after their parents died as before—no better, no worse.

It is to the people whose friendships *had* changed that this chapter is addressed. Most of these men and women had always had good friends. But the tenor of their relationships had shifted, for one overriding reason: The deaths of their parents had left a vacuum in their lives, suddenly elevating the significance, even urgency, of friendship to them. It was inevitable, then, that these attachments would undergo a metamorphosis.

What Are Friends For?

To understand the role that friendship plays in our lives after parents die, it's important to understand what it means to us in the first place. From childhood onward, friends are the barometer of our likability, even lovability, in the world beyond home. We are not talking here about acquaintances—the people with whom we play softball or who are in our car pool, whose proximity to us is organized around certain activities. We are talking about *soulmates*, the people who, in fair weather or foul, are privy to a side of us no one else sees and whose company we crave on a regular basis.

Of all our bonds, friendship is unique in terms of its influence upon us. For one thing, countless investigators have found that peers outside the family help us separate from home and provide a niche for us in the real world. *Who* we choose as friends has a lot to do with temperament—we select those people with whom we can be ourselves, and we avoid those with whom we are ill at ease. For this reason, we are often more comfortable with friends than we are with family.

Another reason for the significance of friendship is that the relationship has few strings attached, which allows us to reveal aspects of ourselves that we would not dare expose to relatives or partners. It is precisely *because* the relationship is voluntary—unbounded by the rules and obligations inherent in marital and family ties—that we permit friends to see us at our most vulnerable and to pass judgment upon us. In fact, it is through their unvarnished honesty that we consolidate our identities. Friends confirm the best in us, but also the worst, by giving us information about ourselves that we would not tolerate hearing from anyone else.

Celia, forty-six, a journalist, says that when she began her writing career, each time she got a rejection slip she would take to her bed. One day she was unloading (not for the first time) about all this to her best friend, who is an editor, hoping to be bucked up and comforted. Instead, her exasperated friend blurted, "You're a dilettante! You expect this to be easy? If you want to be a writer, you've got to toughen up!" Says Celia,

> I was so hurt I thought I would die. If my mother had said that,
> I wouldn't have taken it seriously, because she never worked a day
> in her life. Hearing it from my best friend was a major reality
> check, a kick in the pants. She did me a favor.

There are a number of reasons why the opinions of close friends carry so much weight. According to UCLA psychologist Shelley E. Taylor's book *Positive Illusions*, not only do we invite our friends to be candid, we *count* on it—unctuousness gives them no credibility. When friends criticize us, on some level we usually agree with them; for this reason we are motivated to listen carefully to their negative opinions and, if they ring a familiar chord, to mend our offending ways.

Another explanation for the influence of our friends' opinions is that we choose as close friends people who are similar to us but not *identical.* In his studies, psychologist Abraham Tesser has found that in order for friends to remain friends, *they cannot be rivals*—they each must have their own strong suit and allow the other to excel at something different and admirable. For example, Celia, the journalist described above, is an extremely gifted writer; her best friend is an extremely gifted editor. Both value the other's expertise, but they don't compete on the same playing field.

Such differences between friends help them broaden each other's horizons and viewpoints, a kind of cross-pollination. This mutual enhancement was the single most important finding in a 1992 reader survey about female friendship conducted by *New Woman* magazine. Of the 4,000-plus respondents, *86 percent* said that their best friends had helped them grow—a statistic that held true across the age and marital spectrum.

The final advantage of close friendship is this: As a rule, we don't share the same address, let alone the same bed, which gives the relationship some breathing room. Says Karen Gail Lewis, Ed.D., who has studied female friendship,

> With best friends you don't have struggles around money, or sex, or who's going to clean the toilet bowl. You can tell your best friends anything because they aren't your whole life—you have much less to lose by being honest.

For all these reasons, close friends enrich and mirror us in ways that family members and romantic partners cannot, bringing out our best, and worst, on relatively neutral, mutual territory.

So far so good. But what happens when these carefully crafted friendships are tested by the deaths of our parents? More important, what happens to our entire approach to friendship? What makes it even more necessary to our welfare than it was when our parents were alive?

After the Fall: Survival of the Friendliest

These are among the questions that psychologists Stevan E. Hobfoll and Joseph P. Stokes addressed in an examination of "social support," which they define as the people in our lives who provide loving aid and a feeling of belonging. The researchers contend that when we are threatened with loss, we invest in "other resources" in order to reduce the risk of future losses. The value of such support is that *"it extends the self and what the self can achieve alone."* In other words, forming closer friendships actually helps us to survive.

Key to the effectiveness of social support is the perceived motive behind it. If it has strings attached—as, for example, a relative who might be acting out of a sense of obligation—we aren't likely to be perked up by such "helpfulness." But if the support is seen as altruistic—remember, friends don't *have* to be nice to us—then we are enormously buoyed by that help, which encourages us to return the favor.

How men and women whose parents have died go about getting social support, however, is very different. Studies show that men are less likely than women to ask for, and to receive, emotional buttressing from friends when they suffer a major loss. Men might occasionally unburden themselves to one or two buddies, but in general they find greater comfort in the relative impersonality of groups. As they age, men increasingly prize friendship, but they have a hard time *saying so*; to the extent that they show any vulnerability, it's usually to their families.

Women, on the other hand, tend to be more "expressive" in their friendships when they suffer a loss. They'll call up not just one female friend but several, and say to each one, "I'm falling apart here—I could use a hug." Women get greater emotional support from intimate friends because they simply have more of them—and because they ask for it.

All of which begins to explain why, in the aftermath of our parents' deaths, our friendships change. *How* they change, on the other hand, depends on who's talking. To return to the friendship reappraisals outlined earlier, these changes cluster into four areas:

- Placing a greater value on friends.
- Being more selective in choosing friends.
- Feeling an affinity for other "orphans."
- Finding surrogate families.

Deepened Friendships

The concept of "connection" resonated with many of the people I interviewed—they were acutely aware of the impermanence of things, of time not being entirely on their side. This sense of fragility inspired them to work harder at their friendships, to cherish those who care about them, and to nurture these relationships.

Ariel, forty-four, says that until her mother died five years ago, she had numerous acquaintances but no one outside the family to whom she felt genuinely bonded. When she was feeling blue or out of sorts, sometimes she'd talk to her mother (*but not in too much detail, because her mother would get upset*). Or she'd talk to her sister (*but not too candidly, because her sister would find a way to use it against her*). Or she'd talk to her husband (*but not too often, because he'd try to fix her problem instead of just listening*).

After her mother died, however, Ariel realized that family wasn't enough; she had to find some confidantes. To that end she began spending more time with her female friends, delving into deeply personal matters that previously she had kept to herself. To her astonishment, her friends responded wholeheartedly, giving her a feeling of acceptance and understanding that she'd never experienced before. She explains,

> I find it easier to connect to people than I ever have. To have intimate friendships with women I don't share a history with has been exhilarating. In some ways, it's as if we've always known each other. I never knew that you could have a very deep relationship with someone you haven't known your whole life. My friends are vital to me—they're the best thing to come out of my mother's death.

Glenda, fifty-one, an unmarried attorney, had a different problem; she could connect, all right—it's just that her range of friends was confined to people she met through her law firm. Until her mother died, Glenda's only friends were professional colleagues— she had never been able to carve out the time to form attachments that were not, one way or another, work related. But after her mother died, she realized that she had allowed her career to hijack her personal life, such as it was, and to dictate the terms of her endearments. Says Glenda,

> The friends I had from the office were tricky, because we didn't all have the same philosophies. I'm much bigger on pro bono work than most of them are, and I was making too many compromises in my friendships just so I'd have some kind of social life. It was like being stuck in a bad marriage. Since my mother died, I've cut back on my case load for the sole purpose of making room for people outside the business who are more on my wavelength, people I really respect.

The women I interviewed who wanted to form more intimate connections seemed to have little difficulty finding people to befriend. For the men, it was, on the whole, another story.

Many of the men I talked to either acknowledged the importance of friendship to their well-being or had it pointed out to them (usually by their beleaguered wives, who were tired of serving as their sole source of affection). For these men, reaching out to other men had been an acquired skill.

Rick, fifty-eight, says that since his father died three years ago, his male friendships have grown "stronger and more meaningful," but only because he's made it his business to become more emotionally accessible. "Up to that point, my relationships to men were the pits," he recalls. "I was always busy hustling a buck, and afraid that men would think I was weak if I showed any sensitivity. When my dad died, it was like a truck rolled over me—I was pretty shaken up. A friend suggested I join a men's group, and I decided to give it a shot."

Among the "issues" Rick and his men's group friends talk about is the fact that men don't talk about their issues. They don't discuss their fear of death, their career failures, their terror of ending up broke, because it isn't "manly." And they don't pay attention, not to their wives or their kids or even each other. Says Rick,

> In the group we get into really emotional stuff—we don't get into pissing matches, the way most men do. We trust each other—the things that come out are astonishing, feelings we've never expressed before. We've taught each other how to listen. I'm much better at communicating now, more reachable. These guys give me the respect and validation and feedback that I don't get anywhere else.

Of all the men I talked to, Noah, thirty-seven, was remarkable in the number of male friends with whom he could be affectionate, one-on-one. A man of enormous warmth and candor, Noah has always had dozens of pals, so many that he and his wife are booked weeks in advance for social engagements. But it wasn't until his father died two years ago that he realized who his real friends were and how much they meant to him.

Noah found himself rereading the letters he got and marveling at who took the trouble—and who didn't—to offer words of condolence. From then on, he went out of his way to make more time for the people who came through for him. Says Noah,

> Losing my dad made me feel older and less protected, and my closest friends understood that—they said, "Your parachute is gone." I was surprised at the goodness in people, whether it was a little note or someone just embracing me or friends coming out of the woodwork. But there were friends who didn't call who I expected to hear from, and that had a *big* effect on me. These were people I had bent over backwards to help when their parents died, and who just disappeared when it was my turn. It made me really appreciate the ones who stuck by me.

It was clear from these women and men that their friends are dearer to them now than before their parents died, and that in ways their friendships outweigh their other bonds, providing a safety valve for them. Says Anna Beth Benningfield, Ph.D., president of the American Association for Marriage and Family Therapy, "I tell my clients all the time, 'It's very possible to live a long and happy life without marriage, but I don't think it's possible to do that without good friends.' "

Fewer but Better Friends

A significant number of respondents said that after their parents died they looked around at their social circle and concluded that life was too short to squander it on people who were not "best friend" material. Prior to their parents' deaths, their friendships resembled dating—having a full dance card, as it were.

But once their parents were gone, these respondents became much more particular in their choice of friends. This was made apparent by three expressions that cropped up repeatedly on questionnaires: "no tolerance for superficiality"; "no patience for people who play games"; and "no time for bullshit."

Several respondents said that they had terminated friendships with people they'd known since childhood, people whose pretensions or bigotries they could no longer stomach in the name of sentimentality. They discovered that shared history was not enough to sustain these connections; they had to share the same ethics. Others said they had rekindled friendships with people they hadn't seen in *years*—a grade school classmate, a buddy from the old neighborhood—people who knew them when, before life raked them over the coals.

For these respondents, it was as if they were getting back to basics; it wasn't the number of friends that mattered but, rather, the quality. They discarded friends who left them feeling depleted or used, and invested more time in a core group of friends who made their lives richer, more textured.

Eric, forty-four, says that throughout his childhood and for much of his adulthood he was "Mr. Boy Scout." The firstborn of three children, Eric was the man to call if his mother wanted company, or if his father needed extracting from the corner pub, or if one or another of his siblings was short of cash. But since his parents died in the early 1990s, he has said good-bye to this need to take care of everyone, this compulsion to be loved.

> I've always said yes to people, but in my newfound place in my head, I've learned to say no. I've reexamined everything in my life, including my friends; my standards have gone way up. I want more from people, and in fairness, the reason I never got it was because I kept myself hidden behind this altar boy persona. Now I'm much more up-front. Some of my friends have responded really well to the changes in me—there's much more intimacy between us. The friends who didn't respond well I can live without.

Being "more up-front" was a leitmotiv among the women I interviewed who said that they, too, pared down their social set after their parents died. For these women, forthrightness was a new and heady characteristic, a departure from their previous tendencies to do more giving than receiving. These women had been raised to be placators, to put their own needs last—somewhere after the needs of their parents, spouses, in-laws, children, the dog.

So it had been in their friendships. If a friend was out of sorts, these women would apologize, even if they hadn't done anything wrong; if a friend was in trouble, they'd put their lives on hold and rush to help; if a friend was rude or thoughtless, they'd make excuses. But after their parents died, it was as if they'd been released from servitude—suddenly, these women found their tongues.

Maria, forty-three, is by her own admission a "recovering wimp." The secondborn of five children—she has an older brother—her parents were well-meaning but on stress overload, stretched to the limit by too many obligations and too little income. Thus it fell to Maria, the eldest daughter, to become her mother's champion and her younger siblings' mini-mother, a solicitousness she extended to her many friends, who had but to ask and she was there. All that changed when her mother died four years ago. Says Maria,

> I always thought if you just gave enough love, sooner or later you'd get it back. Well, I decided that with some of my friends, there wasn't a hell of a lot of reciprocity. Recently I worked up the nerve to tell a friend that I felt shortchanged because I did all the initiating, that she wasn't doing her share in maintaining the relationship. She was stunned—she'd never seen this side of me. To her great credit, she really heard me. She's become a much better friend.

What had changed for these men and women was that they were no longer attempting to win popularity contests—they wanted more honesty and acceptance, more *substance*, in their friendships. And if they weren't going to get it, they'd rather be by themselves.

Partners in "Loss"

Then there were the respondents who were drawn to people who also were motherless or fatherless. The vast majority of these respondents had been devoted to their parents; facing life without them was an adjustment that only their friends who had weathered similar losses could comprehend. It was as though they spoke a special language, the way twins sometimes do—they could immediately understand, and be understood by, fellow "orphans."

Greg, thirty-five, refers to this phenomenon as "being a member of a club I never wanted to join." Even his wife, whose parents are still alive, cannot fully appreciate how his life—his entire outlook—was blindsided by his father's death three years ago. "My dad was my role model, the person I admired more than anyone," says Greg. "His death rocked my worldview. I'm still not over it—I don't think

I'll ever get over it. That's why my friends who have also lost their parents are so important to me." He continues,

> I was the first of my friends to lose a parent, and for a while, it was a lonely time for me. Some of it was just grief, I suppose. But it's more than that—it's that your life is never the same again. Last year one of my college roommates called to tell me his dad had died. He said, "I wish I had known what you were going through—I would have called you more often. I never knew it was like this." I said, "That's exactly right. You've gone through it, and now you know. It changes everything." I can talk to him about things that no one else wants to hear—like how long have I got, what happens to my kids when I go, how my wife gets spooked whenever the subject of death comes up.

Suzanne, forty, was extremely close to her mother, who died fifteen years ago, and she, too, is not "over it." Suzanne adores her husband and children, but they don't know what she knows—that nothing ever replaces the parent without whose benevolent guidance life seems like one long experiment. Only her friends who have loved, and lost, a parent "get it."

Neither Greg nor Suzanne sought professional help after the parent died—to the extent that anyone could soften the blow, it was these treasured friends. It wasn't just that misery loves company—it was that they now had something fundamental in common.

According to University of California psychologist Karen Rook, an authority on friendship and social support, a crucial element in friendship is not only the sharing of beliefs but also the sharing of experience—that friends be in "synch" in terms of what is happening, and has happened, in their lives.

There are times—and the deaths of one's parents is such a time—when only a close friend who has been over the same terrain will do. For the men and women I interviewed who were comforted by such friends, the operative word was *empathy*. The people dearest to them had felt similar doubts and fears, had been tempered by similar fires. These friends had sustained them during one of the most painful transitions of their lives, a kindness that was never to be forgotten.

The Kinship of Choice

I have saved for the end of this chapter the respondents who said that after their parents died their friends had become their "families." Of the four friendship patterns, these bonds tended to be both the most joyous and the most painful.

In her book *Families*, Jane Howard draws a distinction between blood kin and close friends. Family is the clan we are born into, hence they are not of our choosing. A "friend of the heart," on the other hand, is the kin we choose for ourselves—a person who, Howard writes, "perceives me as one of the better versions of myself, who has troubled to map the oddities of my mind's geography, as I have his." This distinction is significant, and the failure to recognize it can be the undoing of friendship.

The people I interviewed who described their friends as their "families" fell into two categories. One group had formed what I refer to as *healing kinships*: Their closest friends were either extensions of the families in which the respondents had grown up or improved renditions of them. These healthy friendships were based on mutual respect and steadfastness.

The other group had formed what I call *destructive kinships*: These people were excessively, sometimes fiercely, dependent upon their friends, expecting them to be all that their parents or siblings had not been. These unhealthy friendships were based on the respondents' deeply ingrained insecurities.

Healing Kinships

"My friends *are* my family" was a remark I heard again and again from respondents. But most of them made a point of saying that these comradeships were not the *same* as blood ties, even though, in ways, they echoed them.

For instance, a number of people said their passage into orphanhood had been immeasurably eased by friends who were considerably older than they were—people who could serve as surrogate parents, counseling and mentoring them, as their mothers or fathers had done.

Emma was twenty-five when her mother died, a loss that was devastating to her because their relationship had finally reached the friendship stage—two grown women, albeit at different life stages, who could relate to one another as wives and mothers. "I had just had my first child," Emma, now forty-five, recalls, "and I was really looking forward to all the years when my mother could advise me and take pleasure in being a grandmother."

But Emma had an enormous advantage—her mother's best friend, Sally, who lived next door, had been a fixture in the family for decades. "When my mother was dying," says Emma, "she asked Sally to look out for me, and she did." It was Sally who taught Emma how to cook elaborate meals, who came to the hospital when Emma's next two children were born, who was "home base" for Thanksgiving and other holidays. "I have always gotten nurturing from the Sallys of the world," Emma observes. "There have always been one or two older women to turn to when I needed them."

Malcolm, fifty, also managed to find surrogate parents. The

hardest part of losing his father, he says, was watching this once-robust, powerful man slowly shrink into a helpless invalid. Nearly as difficult, Malcolm adds, was losing his father's unalloyed adoration. "I'm pretty much ready to be an adult now. But I still find myself looking for father figures."

Malcolm, who is divorced, has three mentors—men who are ten or more years his senior—with whom he has dinner twice a month. It would be misleading to say that these men have replaced his father. But there's no question that they supply him with much of the intellectual stimulation, support, and warmth that his father formerly provided. "I'm an only child," he says, "always lapping up the attention of older adults."

Other people said that their closest friends had become surrogate siblings, stand-ins for the blood siblings whose lives and interests had diverged over time. "She is my chosen sister," says Renée, thirty-nine, of her friend, Pamela, forty-one. "We often joke that we were separated at birth. We have the same sensibilities—it's uncanny."

When Renée and Pamela met five years ago, there was an instant chemistry between them. Both women are charming, verbally nimble, and ambitious. And both possess a wicked sense of humor, poking fun at themselves for knowing how to work a room, for being shameless extroverts who flatter everyone but each other. Says Renée,

The night my mom died last year, one of the first people I called was Pamela. I asked her to come to the funeral and sit with my family because I felt she was more of a kindred spirit than any of my relatives. I adore my brother, but we have almost nothing in common. We have very different takes on the kind of person my mother was—I saw my mother as limited; he saw her as perfect—and it's hard to talk to him about that because it pushes too many buttons. But Pamela understands *exactly* how mixed my feelings were about my mother, and she never judges me for them. She can read my mind.

In these joyous friendships (a subject I'll return to in chapter 10), none of the power imbalances or hidden agendas that often prevail in families existed. Instead there was an equality and interdependence that seemed to ride on the fact that they were *not* bound by blood—they were bound by choice.

Destructive Kinships

There were, however, others who, because of their difficult histories, experienced a high turnover rate among their friends after their parents died. In some cases, the respondents had leaned too heavily on their friends, which caused the relationships to buckle. In other cases, the respondents were willing to do anything to avoid being abandoned by their friends, only to find themselves picked clean.

Nicola, fifty-three, ruefully recalls the times after her mother's death when she became furious at friends who, in her then estimation, "constantly let me down." She seemed to have a bottomless appetite for reassurance. Somewhere in her mind she imagined that a true friend would be unflaggingly loyal to her, no matter how grim her mood or how often she lashed out—that a true friend would love her as her irritable mother had not. Only when she began to tally her former friends was Nicola able to see that she had simply asked too much.

> I used to think that my friends were disappointing, when, in fact, it was often the reverse. I feel terrible about the good friends I laced into because I thought they weren't paying enough attention to me. This has been the toughest lesson in my life. It took me a long time to have healthy friendships—I have to remind myself constantly that my friends have lives of their own.

Dana, thirty-nine, went to the opposite extreme after her mother died—her neediness seemed to bring out the beast in her friends. For most of her life, the women she was attracted to bore a striking resemblance to her mother—demanding, imperious—and she let them take advantage of her because she was desperate to be loved. This unhappy tendency only worsened when her mother was gone. Says Dana,

> I had a genius for attracting the wrong kinds of friends, people who were hostile and rejecting. I was repeating my childhood over and over, trying to tame some kind of tiger. Even now I have to watch myself, because I'm still drawn to powerful women. It took me forever to stop being so anxious with everyone, so eager to please. That's been the hardest part, not letting people walk all over me.

For people like Nicola and Dana, it wasn't simply their parents' deaths that evoked this hypersensitivity in their friendships. Rather, it was that they hadn't been securely attached to their parents in the first place and had never worked through their relationships to them.

Psychoanalyst John Bowlby would describe the friendships of such people as "anxious and ambivalent." In his research, he has found that people who quickly reject or cling to their friends often were ignored or denigrated in childhood by their parents in response to the children's need for love and attention. Such children, Bowlby writes in *Attachment and Loss*, "increase their demands for attention [and] refuse to be left alone."

And when they grow up, they might behave toward their friends as they once did toward their parents, angrily or hungrily attempting to wrest the nurturing that was denied them in childhood. Where such people go awry is in confusing their friends with their families—that is, in hoping that their friends will provide the perfect, unconditional affection that their parents were unable to supply.

Fortunately, this destructive friendship pattern was relatively rare (and, as shall be demonstrated in the next chapter, is eminently reversible). Most people had outgrown their *need*, if not their desire, for perfect parents. In their closest friends they found the best that family can offer—sympathy, understanding, a sense of welcome—with none of the complications.

The Company We Keep

It has become commonplace for social critics to decry the dissolution of families, to denounce the ease with which parents split up and remarry, leaving their children to wonder what the word *family* really means.

But seldom in the chorus of punditry do we hear anyone say that were it not for our friends, our families might be in worse shape than they are, and that we ought to take our friendships as seriously as we do our blood kin.

The majority of people I interviewed take their friends with exactly this seriousness. They have discovered that without at least one honest friend—a person who, out of love rather than obligation, shares their greatest triumphs and setbacks—life would be cheerless, at times unbearable. It is the friends who have weathered their storms with them who will become their extended families in the years ahead.

In her book *Pleasures of a Tangled Life*, Jan Morris has this to say about these enduring bonds:

Friendship is a complementary quality, filling in gaps, patching cracks, soothing the orgiastic and jollying along the sluggish. . . .

The best of all friendships are the ones that have ripened, over the long years, out of youth's carnality—keeping, when the blood grows colder, the fires of love alive.

When parents die, we find out how *essential* our closest friends are. Just knowing that they are there—and that we have earned their devotion and trust—anchors us in our own generation and gives us the strength to carry on.

Part Three

The Reconfigured Self

CHAPTER
9 Unfinished Business: Coming to Terms with the Past

Every once in a while there are people who come into your life who are powerhouses—they're so full of energy that whether you love 'em or hate 'em, you react to them. My mother was that kind of person—demanding, narcissistic, a presence. To realize that her life was at an end was very, very hard for me, because our relationship wasn't tied up with a pretty pink ribbon—there were a lot of loose ends between us. It took me a long time to recognize that beneath all the bluster, she really loved me. Now I see her as a phenomenal human being who happened to be a not-great mother. I miss her terribly. Of course, you're hearing years of therapy talking here.

—Beth, fifty-two

There are two sides to every parent-child story, and Beth is able to tell me both of them—her mother's and her own—with uncommon equanimity. To be sure, her mother could be exasperating, but she could also be endlessly entertaining and admirably gutsy. So, too, could Beth, by virtue of her almost eerie calm and unflappability, her sheer stubbornness, get a rise out of her tightly wound mother.

Beth tells me all this from the serene distance of "years of ther-

apy" and seasoning—it's been a decade since her mother died. But
the death of her mother was by no means a clean break—the most
civilized conversation Beth ever had with her mother was in Beth's
own head, and that only recently.

The hardest part of adjusting to life without one's parents is not
simply their actual deaths and the sadness that might ensue; it's the
"loose ends" of which Beth speaks.

There are, of course, many adult children who don't have such
loose ends—whose affectionate attachments to their parents echo in
the offspring's sturdy relationships and sense of self. Then there are
those who, having settled their differences with their parents prior
to the parents' deaths, have few feelings of guilt or incompletion.
And there are those who, through the "corrective emotional experiences" of loving marriages or friendships, managed to put their
difficult or negligent parents into perspective, shrinking them to human scale.

But there are also people whose ambivalent or fearful or angry
relationships to their deceased parents live on in the offspring's splintered relationships to siblings, or partners, or children, or friends—
even in their career decisions. These people have *not* sorted out their
conflicts with their parents but, rather, have simply transferred them,
unexamined, to other areas of their lives.

This chapter is addressed to such men and women—in particular, it examines what can be done about the unfinished parent-child
business that can linger long after one's parents are gone.

Organizing Principles: Self-Repair in the Aftermath

When parents die, they take their histories and explanations for their sometimes baffling behavior with them. Whatever happened between them and their grown progeny cannot be undone; whatever was said or unsaid cannot be changed. It is left to us, the living, to incorporate these realities into our identities, to sift through our parents' legacies to us, and to chart a path to the future that is not hampered by the past. It is left to us, the living, to recognize the extent to which we might be "stuck" in our development, to fill in the gaps of our childhood experiences, and to complete the job of growing up.

For some survivors, such tasks are easier said than done. And that is because what we actually think and feel about our parents after they die often contradicts, or is at serious odds with, what we frequently are told we *ought* to think and feel. For this reason, a set of organizing principles—a way to begin thinking about our unfinished business with our parents—is useful.

Mourning Versus Adaptation

As was discussed in chapter 1, much of the literature on bereavement is built on the assumptions that to be able to let go of important people in our lives and to "recover" from their deaths, we "must" mourn, must do "grief work" in a certain orderly, predictable, and timely fashion. The failure to do so, according to this line of thinking, could result in "abnormal" or "pathological" outcomes.

In an illuminating article entitled "The Myths of Coping with Loss," Camille B. Wortman and Roxane Cohen Silver beg to differ with such assumptions. Drawing on rigorous, well-balanced studies, the researchers have found that although many people do indeed experience profound sorrow, even prolonged despair, after a major loss, this reaction is by no means true of everyone. Most people do not become clinically depressed—they bounce back more quickly than is generally supposed.

Nor is the lack of grief necessarily a symptom of "complicated" or "disordered mourning," or an indication that grief has simply been denied or postponed. To the contrary, the absence of grief might be a sign of strength. Certain people are naturally resilient—the fact that they aren't broken doesn't mean that they require fixing or that they are psychological accidents waiting to happen.

On the other hand, say Wortman and Silver, there are some people who, after the death of a major figure in their lives, do not fully "recover," and whom time does not altogether heal. This is especially true in the event of a traumatizing loss—as, for example, sudden, violent death in an automobile wreck or in wartime (or, one might add, via suicide or murder). These survivors might, to one degree or another, remain in a state of distress many years after the fact. They might never "get over it," might never find a scintilla of meaning in the deaths, might never reach a true "state of resolution." The expectation that they "must" do so can serve only to make them feel worse.

Perhaps the most important conclusion reached by Drs. Wortman and Silver is this: "[O]utsiders may minimize the length of time a loss will affect an individual . . . because they may be unaware that, in addition to the loss itself, the individual must also contend with the simultaneous destruction of future hopes and plans. . . ."

I have gone into some detail about the Wortman-Silver paper because it confirms what I found in my own study. Adults react to the deaths of their parents in a variety of ways that might not conform to the received wisdom about "bereavement" but that may, instead, be perfectly normal aspects of adjustment and regeneration. This distinction between mourning and adaptation is crucial in understanding, and respecting, how individuals regroup after their parents are gone.

No Help Required

In answer to the question "When your parents died, did you seek help from therapy, a support group, pastoral counseling, or from another source?" roughly half (48 percent) of the respondents reported that they had not felt the need for it.

Many people said that their parents "lived on" in their memories; in this sense, they had not "lost" their parents, hence were not undone by their deaths. Others said that, prior to the deaths, they had gradually transferred their primary allegiances to their partners or children; they were saddened by the deaths of their parents but not devastated. Still others said that their elderly parents had been so sick for so long that their deaths came as a relief.

Then there were those who remarked that they felt "liberated" or "euphoric" after their parents died, and that there had been "nothing to lose" because the relationship had been unremittingly painful. These people, many of whom had had therapy while the parents were alive, learned to keep their lack of grief to themselves. As one man put it, "If I say, 'There was nothing to mourn,' the response usually is 'Oh, you can't mean that.'"

Help Wanted

However, a substantial number of respondents—49 percent of the sample—said that they had, in fact, had trouble putting their parents' deaths behind them and had reached out for guidance in doing so.

Why these people wanted help was the cardinal question. Only 20 percent said that they required assistance in "working through" their "grief" or in finding "comfort and solace." The *predominant* reasons people sought help were to "become more objective" about their parents, to "gain insights" both about the parents and their relationships to them, to "resolve" their "traumatic childhoods," to learn to "give up" their anger toward their parents, and to "redefine" themselves and their ties to others "postparent."

In talking to these men and women, it was impossible not to conclude that what they most needed over the long haul was not succor, as such, but, rather, advice on how to claim the future for themselves on their own terms. They had to examine the extent to which their ambivalent or nonexistent connections to their parents had colored all their relationships—especially, the costs of their unfinished parent-child business to those relationships.

Most of all, *they had to form an accurate portrait of their parents in their heads*—an honest assessment of their parents' good sides and bad, their intrinsic gifts and limitations. In knowing and remembering their mothers and fathers objectively, they could achieve a more realistic view of themselves. Only then were they able to retire their defenses against the past and fully inhabit their own lives.

These are not "grief" issues; they are *identity* issues that involve coming to grips with the awareness that whatever we might have wished our deceased parents could have given us we must now supply for ourselves, or learn to live without, or simply outgrow. These issues cluster into four themes:

- *Separating:* figuring out where our parents end and we begin.
- *Reframing:* considering our parents from the point of view of *their* histories, rather than our own.

- *Accepting:* making peace with the fact that some childhood wounds may never heal.
- *Compensating:* finding a "secure base" within oneself.

Our Parents/Ourselves: Drawing the Line

The deaths of parents can leave adult children with the uneasy feeling that they are constellations of their parents' dreams and disappointments, rather than their own separate, unique selves.

It has been twenty-two years since Abigail, fifty-one, buried her mother, and in that time Abigail has married, produced three self-confident children, and built a thriving career and a circle of devoted friends. Still, even after all this time, even in the ripeness of middle age, she rarely makes a decision that does not first pass through the prism of the memory of her zealously loving, irritatingly opinionated mother. Says Abigail, only half in jest,

> I am very much like my mother, very correct, ever the lady. And when I'm not like her—when I do something that's totally alien to what she would have done—I always wonder if I'm doing it just to *gripe* her. Is there any way you ever get away from your parents? When do you get to say, *"Enough already with the parents! Now I'm just me and I'm going to do what I want"?*

A number of respondents had pondered such questions at length. Many people were acutely, sometimes agonizingly, aware of the ways they did and didn't resemble their parents. Those who admired their mothers and fathers were on the whole pleased to be compared favorably to them; those who had stormy relationships with their parents were not thrilled if someone pointed out a remarkable family resemblance. Whether they had been on good terms with their parents or bad, however, the point is that many of these respondents were having trouble distinguishing where their parents ended and they began.

Dr. Evan Imber-Black, a family therapist, has found in her own practice that adult children who have not examined their parents' influence upon them might do one of two things: Either they become mirror images of their parents or they do everything in their power to be *different from* their parents—somewhere in the proceedings, these offspring often lose themselves. She explains,

> It's the old cliché: You told yourself you weren't going to do or say what your parents did, only to find yourself doing and saying the exact same things. Unless you take the opportunity to ask yourself how you want to be like your parents and how you don't, you may not be able to experiment, to be open to new experiences, to find out who you are.

We do, indeed, often bear more than a passing resemblance to our parents. The trick is to parse the ways in which their influence controls us and what role our own personalities play in all this. Put another way, the task is to understand how much of our identities is the product of our parents' nurturing (or lack of it) and how much is the result of our inherent natures.

In the last decade, a great deal has been written about the extent to which genes govern our behavior and override environmental factors. Certainly, when it comes to temperament, there's a huge body of scientific evidence pointing to genetic inheritance. For example, some children are born shy and others are born show-offs, traits that exhibit few signs of fatigue over the life span.

Nevertheless, people do not develop in a vacuum. The influence of parents makes an enormous impact on our cognition and behavior—even on how our brains are wired—with long-range repercussions in our relationships and decision making. We cannot change our genes. But we *can* change how we think about our parents and about our separate selves. There are many ways this line between self and other can be determined, two of which will be explored here: psychotherapy, and self-help or support groups.

Psychotherapy

Numerous scientific investigators and mental health clinicians have discovered that how we relate to the world is established in infancy and early childhood. Based on thousands of interactions with our parents (or parent figures), we begin to perceive others, and ourselves, through the lenses of those early experiences.

According to Susan C. Vaughan, M.D., assistant professor of clinical psychiatry at the New York-Presbyterian Hospital who has studied the workings of the brain, these perceptions, or "prototypes," persist well into adulthood, including after our parents die, when our memories of them are rekindled (if only subconsciously) in times of stress.

For example, if your parents were basically decent, stable, and affectionate, and were attuned to your needs, you can evoke loving memories of them whenever you are feeling anxious or depressed, and find comfort in those memories. "I never had the feeling of being an orphan," a seventy-year-old woman told me. "In some ways I still feel my parents inside me, the way they loved life, they way they loved me. When I'm down in the dumps, I talk to them. It always makes me feel better."

But let us suppose that you were frequently neglected or excessively punished by your parents, or that they were unable to intuit your needs, and there was no one to whom you could turn for sympathy and understanding. In times of stress, you might evoke your parents' damaging view of you, believing that you deserve to be ignored or mistreated. Or you might split off any inkling of your distressing or "disloyal" feelings by assigning them to a partner, or friend, reacting to the person as you once did toward your parents. Whichever, the internalized, punitive parent doesn't go away.

Unless, of course, you have the willingness to *retool your thinking patterns*, an aspiration that often is triggered by the deaths of parents. Says Dr. Vaughan,

> When parents are alive, there's still the hope that they could potentially change. But when parents die, the buck stops with you. That's definitely a time when many people seek psychotherapy, especially if their parents were remote or abusive. They want to change this negative, internalized view of themselves.

This process usually begins with the insight that perhaps we could use some emotional surgery. But insight isn't enough to alter our ingrained responses and behavior; for that, we might need the help of a skilled therapist or psychoanalyst to challenge our perceptions and offer an alternative point of view, one that comes closer to who we intrinsically are.

Changing our minds takes time and practice. As has been said, countless parent-child interactions are woven into our prototypes of our parents and of ourselves; repeated interactions with a mental health professional can unravel these prototypes one strand at a time. In telling a therapist the same stories, over and over, and hearing that person, over and over, suggest a kinder, more reasoned way of thinking, we gradually internalize the therapist's better opinion of us. In this way, our previously negative images of ourselves are replaced by an inner cheerleader—the connections between the neurons in our brains can be literally "rewired."

What's fascinating about the therapeutic process is that as our feelings about ourselves become more benevolent, our views of our parents become less harsh, their hold on us less tenacious, because our perceptions have changed. "Five years into treatment," says Dr. Vaughan, "the same mother or father who was once described as critical or intrusive starts to sound very different, even though none of that early life experience has changed."

A forty-four-year-old woman I interviewed says that therapy gave her an entirely new outlook on her deceased father and her relationship to him. "When he died, I was angry that my childhood was over, that my family was over," she recalls. "Therapy helped me not to be angry anymore and to see my father as less saintlike. I was a typical daddy's girl, a role he did nothing to discourage. Had he lived, I would still be his adoring daughter, expecting to be protected. I've developed a much stronger sense of myself apart from him."

Therapy served a different function for a fifty-three-year-old man whose father routinely denigrated him. "It's only now that I can acknowledge the ways I resemble my father without having a heart attack," he jokes. "I share his gift for gab, his sense of humor—he did have some redeeming qualities. Before I started counseling, I couldn't cut him any slack. The suggestion that I had anything in common with him used to send me up the wall, because I was terrified of turning into him."

But therapy is not the only means by which this separation process can take place, nor, depending on the person, is it necessarily the most appropriate one. While a therapist might be exceedingly sympathetic and have impeccable training, one-on-one therapy will have a different focus from that of a group of peers who have experienced similar losses.

Support or Self-Help Groups

That's where support groups of like-minded others are of inestimable value. Because you have been over the same calamitous terrain—for example, the death of a parent as a result of grinding illness or suicide—you can identify with other people's pain, and they yours, serving as mutual reality checks. Just hearing other people's stories, without ever opening your mouth, helps to jog recollections and feelings about your own background. More important, knowing that someone has overcome the same difficulties helps you believe that you, too, will overcome.

Rea Kahn, who supervises support groups for the Alzheimer's Association in New York, has specialized in group therapy for twenty-five years. In that time she has seen adult children of dying or deceased parents undergo enormous psychological growth within the shelter of collective experience. Says Ms. Kahn,

> People often become more open to the possibility of changing their lives. If they survived this terrible experience, it gives them the hope that perhaps other relationships can be worked through as well. Being in the group helps people to suspend judgment by listening to different points of view. They get comfort and support and a safe place to express their emotions. If they can do it in the group, they can be trained to experience it outside the group, too.

This is what happened to Ruth, fifty-six, mentioned in the Introduction, who is the only child of concentration camp survivors. Until they died, she always felt that her pain was their peril—that she dared not complain to them, lest they be sent into an emotional tailspin. Says Ruth,

I often thought of myself as my parents' oppressor—it was quite clear to me that just by being human, I had the capacity to "kill" them. I was so identified with their suffering that I was sabotaging my own life. I didn't think I had a right to be happy.

Had it not been for her participation in two support groups—one for the offspring of Holocaust survivors, another for the adult children of cancer victims—Ruth is convinced she would have had a nervous breakdown. "Therapy didn't work for me, because my story was so unusual," she says. "But the groups blew my mind. Hearing what other people have gone through made me realize I wasn't the only one."

In the years since her parents died, Ruth has been able to recognize the extent to which she lived in reaction to them, trying to compensate for their losses rather than confronting her own. In separating her experiences from theirs, she has come to see the ways in which she is similar to her parents and the areas in which she can permit herself to be different. Like her father, she is imaginative; like her mother, she is extremely intelligent. Unlike them, she is sensitive, unconventional, willing to take risks. "I'm so open now," she says. "It's like I've been let out of a cage."

Reframing: Understanding Where Our Parents Came From

Separating from the parents of memory makes it possible for us to take the next step—to put our feelings about our parents aside and begin to see *their* worlds through *their* eyes. Comprehending what shaped our parents allows us to understand their motivations and unanswered prayers—to make some sense of who they were and why they behaved as they did. This process, mentioned in chapter 1, is called "reframing," a family therapy term for gaining a perspective that is outside our previous frame of reference.

"I often recommend that adult children try to put themselves in their parents' places," says Dr. Imber-Black. She continues,

> It's essential to look at what was happening in your parents' lives when you were born and were growing up. Use your imagination: What would it have been like walking around on this earth forty or fifty years ago with different social constraints and rules? You can talk to people who knew them to get different pieces of the parents, which gives you a fuller picture, less black and white.

Paulette, fifty-three, a novelist, exemplifies the reframing process. She says that since her parents died she has come to know them in a way she never did—never dared—when they were alive. "I was so intent on getting out of that family, and just putting some space between them and me," she recalls, "that I couldn't make room for anything else."

Paulette's father died when she was twenty. "I was not bereft," she says. "We never really had a bond—he was cold, he was mean, he was irresponsible. There wasn't anything to grieve for." Her connection to her mother, who was by turns hostile and generous, was only marginally better. Even when Paulette became an adult and her mother a widow, the relationship between them was fraught; her mother became increasingly anxious and emotionally dependent on her. "I felt so responsible for her," says Paulette. "The older and sicker she got, the guiltier I felt that I couldn't make things better for her. We spent a lot of time together, but we were never close. She didn't have a clue about who I was. And I didn't have a clue who she was, either."

After her mother died four years ago, Paulette began compiling a kind of posthumous dossier—reading old letters, leafing through family albums, talking to assorted relatives—that might explain her mother's perplexing, sometimes frightening, behavior. The facts she has culled about her mother's background are these: She was only seventeen when her mother died; her father was domineering, pressing her into service as surrogate mother to her younger siblings; she married to escape her family, a union that was no better than the family from which she had fled.

With the advantage of informed hindsight—all of which has found its way into her novels—Paulette now has this to say about her mother:

> Basically, she had a terrible life—a hard childhood, a loveless marriage, a lonely widowhood. I have given this a great deal of thought, and what I've come up with is that she endured so much unhappiness, and was so angry, that it was impossible for her to do better as a mother. She was trapped. I don't think it was anything I did as a child that made her the way she was, I think it was just her awful circumstances. The great tragedy of my mother is that she never got what she wanted.

Paulette has reached this compassionate conclusion, she says, primarily because she is a writer. For her, being heard and being understood—the very commodities that were in short supply when she was a child—have been the driving forces of her life. "Like most authors," she says with a wry smile, "my work is my therapy. Everything is grist for my mill."

Revising History

One need not be a published author, however, or even have any literary gifts, for writing to be of enormous therapeutic usefulness in reframing one's childhood experience. As Nancy K. Miller, professor of English at City University of New York, pithily observes in her book *Bequest & Betrayal: Memoirs of a Parent's Death,*

> Realization entails understanding our parents' own unfinished business with their mothers and fathers: seeing it *as theirs,* finding the language in which to name it, and moving on. These acts of revision mean trying to imagine your parent as a person with whom you can deal.

In an article titled "Creating a Participant Text," family therapists Peggy Penn and Marilyn Frankfurt describe a method they have devised to help people "imagine" their parents, and rearrange their feelings about them, by committing their memories to paper. Clients are encouraged to set down both sides of a dialogue with their parents and bring this written dialogue into a therapy session, where it can be elaborated upon and rewritten.

For example, a son might write a letter to his dead father, and then, pretending to be his father, compose a reply. The son would then read these letters to the therapist, who would comment on them, offering another way of looking at things—another "voice." These letters can be revised as new thoughts and new impressions come to mind. Through the written word, and the therapist's reaction to it, the son can go back and forth in time, understanding his father and himself from the perspectives of both generations.

The value of such an exercise was brought home to me by the number of respondents who attached letters to their questionnaires saying how much putting their memories on paper allowed them to clarify their thoughts and feelings. The act of writing brief biographies of their parents and of their relationships to them—and knowing that their words would be read by an appreciative journalist—seemed to be therapeutic. Nothing in their histories had changed; writing about the past in a structured way, however, helped them to reconsider it. As one woman wrote, "Thank you for asking me to fill out your questionnaire. It gave me the chance to reassess yet again my relationship to my parents, and to clear out the cobwebs."

Accepting: Learning to Live with the Unfixable

Perhaps the most troubling aspect of growing up after our parents die is making peace with the fact that some psychic wounds might be irreparable. To ignore this reality is to overlook an indelible part of our characters, an integral piece of who we were and have become. Says Dr. Vaughan,

> There are always things that you wish had been different or that you didn't get from your parents, and the hope of ever getting it— from them, at least—dies with them. It's a huge developmental step to lose your parents, and I'm not sure that some people ever get over it. We've been overly sold a psychological bill of goods that tells us that anything and everything can be resolved. I think once those feelings are there, they're there.

The paradox of this painful awareness is that it is the cornerstone of what it means to be an adult: Having the ability to tolerate ambiguity and to surrender childish expectations.

As was mentioned earlier in this chapter, some people never

completely recover from their childhoods, never reach anything remotely resembling "closure" with their deceased parents. Several men
and women who participated in my study had sustained emotional
injuries that were so deep that the scars could never be erased, as
these questionnaire responses illustrate:

"I think I functioned as an orphan long before my parents died
because they were never there for me anyway. The sadness had more
to do with my life with them as a child, not their deaths per se. I
had to accept as an adult what I found pretty devastating as a kid—a
lack of support and love from them. I'm philosophical, but it cost
me." (female, fifty-four)

"My father and I were estranged when he died. His death did
not diminish the pain that he had rejected me. Therapy has helped
me to look at myself and know that I am a good person, despite my
parents' messages to me. But I don't think I'll ever recover completely." (male, forty-four)

"My siblings and I grew up with a combination of freedom and
precarious neglect, knowing that if the house caught fire, no adults
would save us—we would have to save ourselves. This has left me
with a feeling of impermanence. I don't think you ever get over what
you didn't get in childhood; you just go on." (female, forty)

To imagine that people who were physically or emotionally bat-
tered by their parents could ever "get over it," or that they should
automatically absolve their parents, is to dismiss both the harm done
to them and the strengths they have developed despite that treatment. Says Susan Battley, Psy.D., who is a clinical associate professor
and consulting psychologist at the State University of New York at
Stony Brook,

> To say "You must forgive" is coercive and I think does people a
> disservice. There are some things that, frankly, are unforgivable.
> The idea that you'll be free if you take certain steps is demeaning

and counterproductive. These people have damaged souls, and some of them may never recover. The challenge is to get them unstuck, to do some reparative work. For many people, it's just so painful and so beyond their capacities, that they simply can't. To blame these people for not getting better shows a lack of appreciation for the damage that was done to them.

In talking to people who had endured difficult (in some cases, harrowing) childhoods—and who had undergone the painstaking business of emotional triage—what came through in their recollections was not self-pity. Rather it was their sense of wonder that they turned out as well as they had—their amazement that, despite their obstacles, they were still standing.

Many of these people said that facing the facts of their childhood deprivations forced them to become more resilient and at the same time more compassionate. Indeed, the recognition that some damage might never be repaired was the wellspring for their remarkable growth and awareness in *other* areas of their lives—in particular, the determination never to inflict on others the harm that had been done to them.

Tanya, forty-eight, says that the death of her sexually abusive father did nothing to eradicate the psychological consequences of that abuse. To this day she still has difficulty with trust and intimacy. Every time she has intercourse with her husband, she cannot wall off the dreadful memories that are the residue of her father's devastating "love."

For years, she went from therapist to therapist, trying to "fix" the problem that ailed her, feeling inadequate because she couldn't "get over" her father's treatment of her. No matter how much information about him she unearthed, no matter how willing she was to "break through" her "resistance and denial," she couldn't forget her father's exploitation.

But then she had the good fortune to find a therapist who told her that some wounds never heal, they can only be accommodated. Says Tanya,

> That was a major turning point in my life, just hearing that it is normal to feel the way I do. It took all the pressure off me to keep trying to repair what was essentially my *father's* problem. I cannot express what a relief it was to quit thinking I was a therapeutic failure and to start thinking that I was, all in all, remarkably hardy. From then on, I started getting stronger in other ways.

With the encouragement of her therapist, Tanya went to graduate school and became a social worker who has made it her mission to identify and to get treatment for abused children and their parents. And while she would hardly recommend it, she believes that her experience with her father pushed her to the brink, where she found the will, and the way, *never* to lose sight of what happened to her but, instead, to draw on the memories to help others.

Compensating: Becoming Our Own "Secure Base"

"In the end," observes psychologist Anthony Storr, "one has to make sense of one's own life, however influential guidance from mentors may have been."

The people I interviewed who made the most progress in the aftermath of their parents' deaths were those who had the wisdom to recognize that whatever they did or didn't get from their parents now was moot; they were on their own nickel. A fifty-four-year-old woman whose parents have been dead for a decade put it this way:

> I've been thinking a lot about what it means to be a grown-up. It's hard to face the reality of who I am, as opposed to my ideal self. My ideal self is a wise and wonderful wife and mother. But my imperfect self still has a sense of entitlement because of what I didn't get growing up—things that a child has a right to expect, but an adult does not. I can no longer expect to be taken care of or loved unconditionally. The real challenge is accepting my limitations and making the most of what I have. It's a constant struggle, but I'm making progress.

Many researchers have found that people in midlife are better equipped to take stock of their lives when their parents die because they feel more vulnerable, more open to change, than at other stages of life. According to Carl Jung, these are the years of the "greatest unfolding," when the "real motivations are sought and real discoveries are made." These epiphanies, he goes on to say, "are gained only through the severest shocks." Offspring can then recognize and lay claim to those parts of themselves that had to be denied in order to find parental favor, and look inside themselves for "self-hood."

In their longitudinal studies of children and their parents, Mary Main and Nancy Kaplan have found that the most important characteristic of "very secure parents" is their ability to remember and easily talk about their connections to their own parents, both the good and the bad. Integrating both positive and negative childhood experiences enables people to stop blaming their parents and, instead, become responsible for their own happiness.

This sense of responsibility makes it possible for adult children to negotiate the transition to adult orphanhood and to carve out a future of purpose and emotional fulfillment on their own terms. Says Dr. Vaughan,

> Once parents are gone, adult children often find that they actually have the capabilities to turn their lives around. In some ways it matters less whether you had great parents or horrible parents; the point is to be able to understand what really happened, to tell a story that adds up, even if it was an ugly story, and to move on.

From a Distance

As long as we are alive, nobody's story is ever over; there are always new lessons to be learned, old habits to be relinquished, growth to be added on. The journey toward this self-discovery often begins when our parents are gone. With nothing left from the previous generation to lose, to defend, or to defend against, we can open up new frontiers in our lives.

More than anything else I have been impressed by the extent to which the men and women who participated in my study have found a measure of ease and self-acceptance that did not take root until their parents died. Knowing that they are the agents of their own destinies, that they are accountable for their own behavior, ended up being the catalyst for extraordinary change.

In reexamining their histories, and in understanding where they came from, they began to see their own outlines, silhouetted against the memories of their deceased parents. And while many of these respondents still had unfinished business with their parents, the majority took enormous pride in being able to survive, even to prevail, without them. This awareness enabled them to alter and enrich their other relationships—including those to their siblings, as we shall see in the next chapter—and to reconfigure their expectations of themselves.

It is possible to accomplish much of this maturity while one's parents are alive. But after they die, it becomes *necessary*. A forty-four-year-old woman I interviewed, whose mother died three years ago, might well have been speaking for the entire sample when she said:

> The adjustment to life without my mother continues, and probably always will; a day does not go by that I do not think of her and wish I could talk to her. But losing her deepened me. The surface things are less important. I am more aware than I have ever been of needing to be a nurturing, loving mother to myself. No one can do this for me.

CHAPTER 10 A New Sense of Family

When my parents were alive, my sister and I saw each other maybe once a year, at Thanksgiving—we weren't at all close, because we had our own separate lives. But after they died, she and I made a conscious effort to keep the relationship going, to try to understand one another better. It's incredibly important to me to have a sense of family. That's why I started having Thanksgiving at my house, and every year the party gets bigger. My sister comes, my in-laws, my children and their kids. But I always include close friends. This is my family now.

—Leslie, fifty-one

ome. Family. These are two of the most powerful words in any language, never more so than after our parents are gone. That's when the words take on new resonance, new connotations, new layers of meaning. Where once the parents embodied "home" and "family," now you and whomever you deeply love—your partner or children or cherished friends—are "family." And "home" is wherever you live.

Still, the concept of family seems somehow incomplete if it does not include at least one blood relative from the *original* family—some biological link to one's past. Most adult children yearn for a sense of emotional and historical place, a feeling of belonging and of continuity. That's why they usually stay in touch with their siblings, assembling for life cycle events and holidays such as weddings or Christmas or Passover—rituals that bind and celebrate the family from generation to generation.

Let us suppose, however, that you have lost contact with one or more siblings or are not on speaking terms, either by your choice or theirs. How do these sibling schisms affect your sense of family?

Consider two other scenarios. What if you are an only child? Alternatively, what if you have no children? With no blood ties to the past, or none to the future, how do you keep from feeling generationally unmoored—lost, as it were, in time? What does "family" mean to you now?

Such issues are the focus of this chapter. At the end of my questionnaire, I asked: "In what ways have you and/or your siblings 'stepped into the shoes' of your deceased parents—for example, by giving advice, or maintaining family ties, or keeping traditions such as holiday meals?"

Roughly half the respondents (48 percent) said either that they served as the family "switchboard," or that a brother or sister was "home base," or that they all "shared" various kin-keeping roles equally. These people were actively involved with their siblings and other relatives, taking enormous pleasure in upholding family traditions, whether by swapping recipes that had been handed down for generations or by making it their business to be together for special occasions.

However, the other half of the sample reported that they did not make an effort to be with one or more of their siblings or had not followed their parents' traditions. In some cases, geographic distance or chronic infirmities or advanced age precluded family gatherings; in other cases, there was no family-of-origin left. But the primary reasons these respondents cited for not maintaining ties to their original families were that they had "little in common" with or were "estranged" from them, or that their parents hadn't "encouraged closeness" or "fostered traditions." To the extent that these respondents observed any traditions—either their own or someone else's—it was with partners, or children, or friends.

As these responses make clear, when parents die, their adult children redefine what "family" means to them. The purpose of this chapter is to explore that redefinition by concentrating on three patterns:

- How people who are estranged from their siblings either repair those bonds or adjust to the fact that the estrangement might be permanent.
- How people who are on reasonably good terms with their kin enfold them into their separate lives, reconstituting their sense of family.
- How people who have little or no contact with their original families—or who have no living relatives—reinvent a sense of family with those they love.

Mending Fences: Making Peace with Sibling Differences

You will recall from an earlier chapter that nearly a quarter of the people who participated in my study became more distant from, or had severed relations with, one or more siblings after their parents died. But other respondents, who had been on the outs with their siblings for years, were inspired by their parents' deaths to mend these attachments.

Which begs the question: Why should siblings who never got along with each other, or who have nothing in common, even bother trying to repair their relationship? What is to be gained by attempting to revive the connection? Why risk stirring up trouble? Here's why:

Because siblings are the only eyewitnesses left to our childhoods and to our growing up—they have known us from the start.

Because siblings, having carved out separate family niches, can fill in the gaps of memory—they still have much to teach us, and we them.

Because siblings can bring each other comfort long after other relationships have receded into the wings of our day-to-day lives.

Because when sibling rancor continues to fester, it can infect our connections to partners, to children, and to friends, overloading them with unrealistic expectations.

Because if we don't at least give the sibling relationship a shot, we'll never know whether or not any part of it was salvageable.

And because siblings, given enough time, might even say "I'm sorry" for the harm they might have caused.

When parents die, leaving a void in the family, there is a tug in the sibling relationship—a gravitational pull—that is undeniable. Even if you despise your sibling and pledge never to see the person again, he or she is, literally and figuratively, *in your blood*—out of sight, perhaps, but not entirely out of mind. Listen to Tracy, forty-four, who as a child was frequently beaten by her mother while her older sister, the "favorite"—with whom Tracy has almost no con-tact—stood by and did nothing:

I once asked a friend who was dumped by her boyfriend what she'd do if he asked to be taken back. She said, "It'd take a thou-sand lunches and dinners before I could trust him again." That's sort of how I feel about my sister—she'd have to convince me that she's contrite. I think it's highly unlikely that we'll make up. Still, you never know. Recently she called me, out of the blue, and I agreed to meet with her. She remembers nothing from our child-hood. Well, not nothing—she did say, "When Mom hit you, I was glad it wasn't me. But I felt guilty." At least she's trying. We'll see.

Settling Sibling Scores

Psychologists Stephen P. Bank and Michael D. Kahn, co-authors of *The Sibling Bond*, would see in this case study an example of what they call "distant identification," in which siblings keep each other at arm's length by being polar opposites or by outright rejection. Such standoffs, say the researchers, often serve as smoke screens for unfinished parent-child business. The danger in prolonging these schisms, however, is that they might be replicated in our other relationships; disavowals and angry cutoffs, when thought of as "solutions," have a way of repeating themselves. For this reason, if for no other, it behooves us to figure out our *unfinished sibling business*.

There are several schools of therapeutic thought as to how serious rifts between adult brothers and sisters might be bridged. One view holds that since the sibling connection is longer than any other, siblings should bend every effort to find *some* basis for communication and at all costs avoid cutoffs. Another view holds that while friendship might not be possible, it's crucial for siblings to understand the source of their rancor so it doesn't trickle down to the next generation.

Preserving the Sibling Bond

Family therapist Karen Gail Lewis, Ed.D., who specializes in sibling relationships, is of the first, more optimistic, school. She says,

> Trite as it sounds, blood is thicker than water. There's something about the connectedness between siblings—that as much as they may not be able to stand each other, they know they're the last

ones from the original family. Siblings are the only people who remember when you were little. They're the historians for the family line; they remember the family jokes, the mythologies, the secrets. Most siblings want that connection.

Dr. Lewis often takes groups of siblings on weekend retreats to hash out such sensitive matters as parental favoritism or negligence. Frequently one sibling will disagree with the others about what happened in the family early on and insist that his or her version of the truth is the correct one. In this instance, the siblings might agree not to discuss a particular topic because it's too painful. "People survive the best way they can," says Dr. Lewis, "and siblings have to respect that." She continues,

> A rule I suggest to siblings is that they make a list of subjects that are off-limits—it might be the parents, or kids, or careers, or politics. Then you can create some commonalities. If you don't have a current life together, then all you're left with is your history.

Fiona, forty-four, is an example of someone who has profited handsomely from sibling therapy. After her parents died, she and her siblings went their separate ways, an estrangement that made none of them happy. At Fiona's suggestion, they decided to enlist the services of a "coach" to steer them through the land mines of their considerable differences—in particular, their disparate reactions to their parents' deaths.

In joint therapy, the siblings began to understand the various childhood roles they had been assigned by their parents and the extent to which their parents had unknowingly pitted them against each other. Fiona, the "brain," was her mother's favorite. Emily, the "athlete," was the father's favorite. Their younger brother, the "problem" who couldn't seem to do anything right, was nobody's favorite.

Because of these roles, the siblings had different parents to lose and, as a consequence, had different issues in the aftermath. Fiona and Emily rebounded from the deaths with relative ease, although there were some lingering resentments between them by virtue of their parents' favoritism. As for their brother, he felt that he was the family outcast, and because of this he took the deaths hardest.

Where once Fiona had no sympathy for her brother, regarding him as "weak," now she thinks of him as a casualty of parental neglect, more to be pitied than scorned. However, the greatest gift of sibling therapy, she says, is that it brought her closer to her sister. "We share the same capacity for insight," says Fiona. "She's the only person I trust and can be myself with. I love my brother and I believe he's doing his best. But Emily and I have become soulmates."

Siblings do not necessarily need the aid of a professional to renegotiate their relationship—frequently they're able to do so on their own. Joyce, forty-nine, and her sister, Gail, forty-one, are a case in point. After their parents died, the two women realized that if they were going to preserve the relationship, they'd have to retire their family roles—Joyce, the mini-mother, and Gail, the doll-like kid sister. Says Joyce,

Gail and I went through a rough stretch because I kept babying her, calling her "clueless" and other teasing nicknames, and telling her what she ought to do. My sister is no fool—for a long time, even in her thirties, she enjoyed the little sister role, because she could get away with murder. But when my folks died she didn't want to be babied anymore; she wanted to be taken seriously. She confronted me daily in torrents of tears, taking umbrage at my teasing. Of course, she was right—I felt terrible—and I apologized. From that time forward, we were best friends.

These sibling renegotiations are examples of what I (borrowing from psychoanalyst Margaret Mahler) call "sibling separation and individuation." When parents die, we need our siblings and our common heritage with them to feel a sense of belonging. But we also need to be recognized by them as unique and autonomous, responsible for our own happiness. It is the similarities that are the bedrock of family loyalty; it is the differences that allow siblings to grow and to respect each other's points of view.

Many adult siblings are able to accomplish this separation-individuation process—this healthy balance between closeness and distance. But some are not, either because there is so much bad blood between them or because one sibling is willing to declare a cease-fire and the other will consider it only when hell freezes over.

Which brings us to the other school of therapeutic thought— how to make peace with the sibling past when the likelihood of reconnection is slim.

Reframing the Sibling Bond

Rapprochement between siblings might be an unreachable ideal. In this case, it is incumbent upon the parties involved at least to clarify the true origin of their enmity and to accept the possibility that the bond might never heal.

Returning to a point made earlier, sibling estrangement doesn't occur in a vacuum; it is usually set into motion by obvious parental favoritism, as was discussed in chapter 4. Dr. Bank sees sibling enmity as a "stolen birthright," which he defines as "the loss of the children's fundamental right to a good relationship—a loss allowed by parental actions and inactions."

Yet siblings in the same family may not all see it this way; one might be the parental defender, another the parental whistle-blower.

Dr. Bank believes that unless siblings comprehend the role their parents (however unwittingly) played in their rifts, it will be difficult for them to patch up their differences. Here the therapeutic goal isn't to force a sibling relationship. Rather, the goal is to recognize that sibling rivalry is not rooted in a brother's or sister's evil intent—it is the harvest of parents who, because of their own troubled histories, did little to encourage sibling solidarity.

When siblings can reframe their hostility, viewing it as the legacy of *their parents'* unfinished emotional business, they can regard one another with greater compassion and form a more balanced picture of what each is capable of giving and what each has suffered. This doesn't get an offending sibling—the one who purloined family treasures, who cheated you in a business deal, who spurned you at your lowest ebb—off the hook. But perceiving such behavior as a desperate survival mechanism helps to lessen its sting.

Nowhere is it written that you have to like your siblings, or spend time with them, or forgive them for grievous wrongs—absolution isn't the point. The *point*, writes Dr. Bank, is to "[take] responsibility for one's relationships and for one's part in keeping misery alive. . . ."

The last person Nicholas, forty-six, would ever want to be stranded on a desert island with is his brother, Sean, forty-four. Where Nicholas is fastidious and charming, Sean could use a shower and some social skills. Where Nicholas is a go-getter, Sean gives new meaning to the words *sloth* and *underachiever*.

There was a time—actually, many times—when these differences nearly brought the brothers to blows. Christmas at their parents' house was a tension-filled affair, as relatives anxiously awaited the inevitable spark that would set off a sibling explosion. The night of their father's death six years ago was the worst, with Nicholas accusing Sean of being the family disgrace, and Sean shouting back that his brother was a phony and a liar. The brothers have not spoken since.

"It scared me how much I hated him," Nicholas recalls of their last meeting. "I was so angry I got chest pains." At his wife's urging, Nicholas went to see his family doctor, who recommended counseling. There, Nicholas was able to trace his and his brother's mutual animosity back to childhood, when their father would constantly berate Sean for not being a good student and not being a good athlete—the areas in which Nicholas excelled—leaving Nicholas to wonder when it would be his turn for punishment.

"This all started with my tyrannical grandfather," says Nicholas. "My father had no role models for anything but violence. I think he saw in my brother a reflection of himself—the loser, the fuckup. I, of course, played this to great advantage. Compared to him, I could only look good."

Nicholas has tried over the years to smooth things over with his brother, but Sean is not interested. And while the door is open, Nicholas holds no hope for brotherly love. Nor, truth be told, does he eagerly welcome it—his brother is a loose cannon. For Nicholas the main event has been to fathom how it could end like this, this horrible parting of the sibling ways, so that it doesn't become a legacy for the next generation. Says Nicholas,

> My brother and I stumbled into the middle of some Eugene O'Neill saga, and I think it killed Sean off emotionally. The best I can do is make sure it doesn't happen with my kids. My wife and I are determined that we do everything humanly possible to help them to become allies.

The Reconstituted Family

Like Nicholas, most of the men and women I interviewed had reinvested their emotional energies in their relationships beyond "home"—their partners, children, and friends. Unlike Nicholas, however, the majority of respondents managed to detach from their families of origin while at the same time maintaining ties to many, if not all, of their relatives.

This family reconstitution usually involved a process of addition and elimination—of building on their positive childhood experiences and attempting to let go of painful aspects of early family life. These respondents tried to concentrate on their similarities to their relatives and to overlook, or at least tolerate, their differences. The result was a blend of the old and the new, as they incorporated their siblings into their separate lives and, with them, carried on certain traditions.

A case in point is Doris, fifty-eight, who is married, and her younger unmarried sister, Annette, fifty-two. One would never guess that the two women are related. Doris is opinionated and earthy, seldom at a loss for words; Annette is prim and demure, as still as a pond—differences that have caused no end of misunderstandings between them. Yet somehow these women, in fits and starts, have managed to be integral parts of each other's lives in the years since their parents died. Says Doris,

> My parents always told me that I should protect my sister and take care of her. So she is always included when we have parties. Sometimes I worry that she'll become too dependent on me. But then I remember how much she has helped me over the years. She was great with my kids when they were growing up—they adore her— and she took care of my parents when they were dying. Even though we're as different as night and day, I feel a very strong, loving connection to her. It is unthinkable to me not to have her in my life.

Other respondents, who came from larger families, remained friendly with some siblings but not others. A few of these people reached the unhappy conclusion that trying to establish ties to a brother or sister who continually rebuffed them was a lesson in self-punishment. Still, giving up on a sibling was a wrenching last resort.

Ellen, forty-two, is the secondborn of three offspring whose parents went through an ugly divorce when she was in elementary school. She is close to her older sister but not to her younger brother, who, despite her entreaties, refuses to have anything to do with her. The reason, she suspects, is that he wants no reminders of their unhappy past. "I can't believe that there will be this legacy of a broken family," she says. "I want us all to triumph over this, but it is not to be. I've had to stop trying to win over my brother—he has basically thrown me away. It's made me appreciate all the more what I *do* have."

Because she is happily married and on exceptionally good terms with her grown children as well as her sister, it is with them that she feels a sense of emotional reciprocity, of family continuity. She explains,

> My sister and I made a vow a long time ago that we're going to keep the best of our family and leave the rest behind. That's why we've worked hard to maintain traditions with each other, and with our kids. Christmas is a very big deal at my house, and Thanksgiving is always at her house. One of us would have to be in the hospital for us not to be together on the holidays.

Custom and Ceremony

As this story illustrates, families are bound not only by blood but also by ritual, the traditions that keep history alive, transcending time and even the people who participate in them. A number of respondents said that they cherish certain family customs and ceremonies, the simplest of them often having the most meaning, as these questionnaire responses demonstrate:

"My sister, who is childless, remembers all the details—the recipes, like Ma's string beans, and the lore. She is our 'culture bearer.' I have done the 'teaching the next generation' part because I have children." (female, forty-six)

"I give my brothers advice, I bake the Thanksgiving desserts and cook the Passover meals. My wife and I function as 'home base' for her family, too." (male, forty-four)

"Because mine is the only 'family' in the traditional way—my sibs aren't married—the rituals have fallen to my husband and me. All the holidays are at our house." (female, thirty-nine)

"My sister and I give each other the unconditional love our parents gave us. But my mother's role as the family matriarch is gone. The larger extended family is gone. Thanksgiving has grown into an even more elaborate family holiday, with new extended family. It's different. Life changes." (female, fifty-four)

The purpose of these and other rituals, says Dr. Evan Imber-Black in her book *The Secret Life of Families*, is "to make and mark transitions for individuals and [the] family." Weddings and christenings celebrate the arrival of new kin; Bar Mitzvahs and graduations celebrate coming-of-age; anniversary parties celebrate the durability of family ties. The paradox of these rituals is that even as they punctuate joyous continuity and change, they are bittersweet reminders of relatives who are no longer around to witness them.

Isabelle, fifty-one, says that never did she miss her parents so much as the day her daughter got married, a wistfulness shared by her son-in-law's mother and father, whose parents were also deceased. In order to include the absent generation symbolically in the

occasion, Isabelle displayed old family photographs in the room
where the wedding reception was to take place. Says Isabelle,

> It was our way of having our parents there to share this special
> day. I remember saying to someone, "I can't believe Mom and
> Dad aren't here." It just didn't make any sense to me. But then it
> struck me that my mother would have been *crazed* by all the details
> of planning this wedding! So it was kind of the best of all worlds—
> having our parents there in spirit, if not in body.

To reiterate, customs and ceremonies usher families into the
future; however, *who* in the family will take it upon himself or herself
to be the prime mover in continuing these customs varies. The respondents who were likeliest to say that they had carried on their
parents' traditions were those who have children (no surprise) and
those who have no siblings (a surprise).

Here Darwinian theory might be lurking amongst the sweet potatoes and cranberry molds. In energetically perpetuating traditions—
especially where *food* is involved—people who have offspring, and
people who are only children, might be more inspired than others
to make the whole *idea* of family inviting, to the benefit of the spe-
cies.

Lucia, fifty-nine, an only child, has been married to the same
man for thirty-five years, and with him has three grown children.
"Keeper of the family flame" doesn't begin to describe her. Not a
birthday goes by, not an anniversary or holiday, without some kind
of festivity at her house that includes her children and grandchildren
and relatives from her husband's side of the family. Says Lucia,

> When I was young I actually had a vision of the kind of family I
> wanted to create. I wanted "home" to have all those corny reso-

nances of "be it ever so humble," and so forth. I wanted my kids to have that, and I wanted them to have each other. Now, a lot of times you have a vision and you can't pull it off. My husband and children, fortunately, were very amenable to it. Our kids and their spouses really like each other—they even take vacations together. So my vision of family has come true, for which I take lavish credit.

As Lucia would be the first to admit, her family is remarkable in its cohesiveness, loyalty, and conviviality. The fact that she even *has* a traditional family—right down to the picket fence outside her door—places her in what is becoming a minority.

The Reinvented Family

In the last thirty years, who and what we consider "family" has undergone a revolution. In his book *Psychotrends*, psychiatrist Shervert H. Frazier, former director of the National Institute of Mental Health (NIMH), says that the traditional nuclear family describes only one in four households. The good old days when Mom stayed home to raise the kids while Dad spent the day toiling elsewhere were never as good as they were cracked up to be, Dr. Frazier asserts. After all, "traditional" families (a twentieth-century cultural blip) consigned mothers to the kitchen and fathers to the margins of their children's lives—hardly an atmosphere of gender equality, of collective jollity and purpose.

Today we see a domestic terrain that would be unrecognizable to our forebears. The number of single-person American households has risen from 10 percent of the population in the 1950s to over 25 percent today (in Sweden, this figure is *40 percent*), making it the fastest-growing household category—and not just because of the swelling ranks of silver-haired widows and widowers.

With the booming divorce rate, below-replacement-level fertility rate, unprecedented numbers of women in the workforce, record-setting out-of-wedlock births, and increasing cultural acceptance of gay and lesbian couples, people are less and less likely to be—or even want to be—part of traditional families.

Instead, Dr. Frazier predicts, our emotional needs will be met by "more new families . . . of the *mind*, not of the genes. The *psychological* family will supplant the biological family." People who are unrelated by blood or marriage are forming what Dr. Frazier calls "fictive families" and "fictive kinships"—that is, "families" of friends. The family is not just being redefined. It is being reinvented.

Many of the men and women I talked to are part of this trend. They have pieced together hybrid families consisting of a select group of treasured friends and relatives. To some respondents, these families of the heart are more rewarding than the families in which they grew up. And the traditions they have created together are richer because they are an elective collaboration.

Several respondents commented that certain family traditions had been tainted by memories of their childhoods when this Christmas or that July Fourth was destroyed by a relative's unseemly behavior. A way to disconnect these rituals from their rueful antecedents was to add new faces and new ways of celebrating with their chosen families.

Every year Marsha, who was raised a nondevout Jew, and her husband, Paul, who was raised a Catholic, have a Passover seder at their house at which friends join the couple and their young children. On Christmas Eve, the couple goes to church to hear Christmas music. Marsha was not close to her mother, although she was to her father; Paul was close to neither of his parents. Yet this couple has observed certain traditions because they provide a kind of stability, a ceremonial anchor. "None of our parents taught us these traditions—we wing it," says Marsha. "But I think they're important. They give me a feeling of belonging I never had as a child."

Every year Susan, who was raised in an abusive family and who has never married, spends Easter with her best friend, Lisa, and Lisa's husband. Joining them is Lisa's brother, who is gay, his partner, and a few neighbors. "Everybody brings a different dish," says Susan. "My job is dessert. I'm also the photographer of record—we always take a group picture." Susan has never regretted not marrying and not having children, because she believes that in her friends she has an ideal family.

What matters most to these people is not family as it is narrowly defined: blood kinship above all other ties. What matters is that they have *a sense of family* with the people they have chosen to love—a characteristic, studies show, that is a hallmark of emotional well-being over the life span. A 1998 nationally representative survey conducted by Fordham University researchers found that as people age, they get happier, regardless of gender, marital status, and other variables. Perhaps the most important reason for this upsurge in contentment, say the investigators, is that adults learn from experience to "select people and situations" that boost their positive emotions and diminish their negative feelings.

Of this capacity to form "psychological families," Glenda Feinsmith, a New York hypno-behavioral psychotherapist who runs support groups for people whose relatives have died of devastating illnesses, has this to say:

> Siblings can't replace for you what you didn't get in childhood. If it's within the original family to create a supportive network for each other, if warmth was always there, it will continue. If it wasn't there, the death of a parent can be a jumping off point where

people can transform themselves and their relationships. The chapter of your childhood is closed. But a new chapter begins.

Passing Through

At the end of his memoir, *Timebends*, Arthur Miller recalls with wonder that one day he and his wife were planting seedlings on their New England property and the next thing he knew, the trees had shot up to sixty feet. Now he was being addressed as "Grandpa" by his grandchildren, while in his mind he thought, "[M]y God, I had hardly begun!" Looking back over his long life, Miller concludes: "[T]he truth, the first truth, probably, is that we are all connected, watching one another."

Most of the men and women who participated in my study spoke of this longing to be connected, literally and metaphorically, to the family of the past, present, and future. If there's one subject we're all experts on, it's our families. And if there's one subject we can agree on, it's that no two people, even if they grew up in the same house, experienced the family in exactly the same way.

Despite our differences, we *are* all connected, because in the beginning, each of us was somebody's child, somebody's "seedling." We can't do a thing to change the families that spawned us. But there's a great deal we *can* do with the lessons we learned in those families—how important it is to be part of things; what it means to matter to someone.

Our children, and those of others, will be our postscript. The manner in which we deal with the aftermath of our own parents' deaths can help them, when the time comes, to adjust to life without us.

11 After We've Gone: Creating a Legacy for the Future

Last year I reached the age my mother was when she died, and since then I've been thinking more about my own mortality. One of the things I think about is, What will I say to myself at the end to make leaving easier? I'll say that I had the most wonderful husband, that I got to contribute to my community, that I did what I set out to do in my career. But mostly I'll say how proud I am of my children, how privileged I was to be their mother. I've tried to teach them to love themselves and each other, and always to give people the benefit of the doubt. To create human beings who will do good in the world is the best legacy anyone could ever leave. That is mine.

—Marilyn, forty-four

When we are very young, our parents define us and, to the best of their ability, gradually prepare us for our launching into adulthood, our leavetaking from childhood. In a thousand ways, by word or deed, they pave the way for our lives without them. If we are lucky, they set these examples: To say those things that ought to be said; to admit to regrettable behavior and make amends; to accept disappointment with a degree of equanimity; to love and to let go; and, at the end, to exit life with a measure of dignity.

If, on the other hand, our parents did not set such examples, in their deaths we might discover the cost to us, and to those we love, of having been denied those examples. It is up to us to profit from this discovery by making necessary changes in our own lives so that unhappy history does not repeat itself.

The people whose voices have been heard in these pages—whose lives and identities have been transformed as a direct result of their parents' absence—are studies in contradiction. Loss and gain are woven into the stories they told me—paradoxes abound.

These adult children have forged, out of sometimes dreadful necessity, new strengths that they hadn't known about, hadn't *needed*, until now. Most of them have experienced a profound sense of solitude, and from it, a greater capacity for intimacy. Lacking a fallback position or the possibility of parental rescue, they have found fulfillment in their own self-reliant industry. Without a parental reference point for themselves, they have become that to their children. And when the chips were down, they found out who their true friends are and how crucially important they are to them.

Jolted into a reassessment of their lives and choices, many of these men and women summoned the ability to go through the painstaking process of altering themselves and of realigning their expectations of others. They became exquisitely aware that time was of the essence, and because of this awareness, wanted to ensure that the years remaining to them would count for something.

These insights—these epiphanies—did not occur to them in one burst of enlightenment, one sudden flash of wisdom. They occurred incrementally, as the years since their parents' deaths went by. Most people eventually reached a point—some invisible border—when they left their childhoods behind and started concentrating in earnest on the future. Little by little, the distant past became less significant to them than the legacies they themselves would leave. They began to imagine what life would be like when they, too, were gone.

Roughly three-quarters of the respondents remarked that they now thought of their mortality in a new way. Fear of death was not on these people's minds—interestingly, only two people mentioned it. Rather, they realized that death was no longer an abstraction—it was all too real—and they wanted to put their own emotional houses in order. Among other things, they said:

"I think more about whether I want to live and die the way my parents did."

"I don't want to end my life with any remorse over things I haven't said or done."

"I feel an urgency to plan ahead so that my passing will be easier for my children."

"I realize that if, by your own life, you do not leave positive memories for others, you will be quickly forgotten."

Of course, not everyone who participated in my project was so poetically introspective. Some respondents didn't want to think about the repercussions of their parents' deaths; they preferred to focus solely on the present. Others said that their work—the output of their professional lives—was their "immortality." Still others harbored the belief that somebody—a child, a sibling, a friend—still owed them something, that they'd been given a raw deal. And then there those who said that nothing good had come of their parents' deaths, that their grief and sadness were unassuaged.

These people were in no frame of mind to consider the possibility that they might not live forever, or to contemplate the impact that their own deaths would have on the people who would survive them. But they were a distinct minority.

The vast majority of women and men I talked to do not want to die without a benevolent trace. They want to be remembered—

if not directly, then indirectly—as having been mentors to their cultural and biological heirs, as having been role models of kindness and optimism, of persevering in the face of adversity.

For example, Sam, fifty-nine, has no children. He never got rich, and no longer obsesses about it—he's just grateful to be happily married and in robust health. What's important to him now is to be well thought of by his nieces and nephews, to live on in their memories as their biggest booster, always good for a joke or a pep talk, their rakish "Uncle Sam."

Rachel, forty-five, is the mother of two grown children. She isn't sure there's an afterlife—she's more interested in making a contribution to future generations. To that end, she and her siblings have established a small research foundation to help find a cure for the illness that took their mother from them.

Ned, fifty-six, whose children visit once or twice a year, finds himself spending more and more time with young colleagues, helping them put their careers on a productive path, giving them a leg up. He considers himself a father figure to his protégés; the door to his office is always open. But he has also started working with inner-city kids, taking them to the park or the library on weekends, showing up at their school plays.

Marcie, sixty-three, a divorcée, wasn't a particularly good parent to her kids when they were growing up; she stashed them with relatives while she pursued her singing career. Now she wants to make up for those lost years. She has come clean to them about her youthful indiscretions and has moved closer to them so that she can be available for conversation, should they wish it, and for baby-sitting for their children, her last shot at mothering.

And Roberta, forty-four, a widow who has no children, has reconnected with her older brother, whom she hadn't seen in years, in order to right the wrongs of their difficult childhoods. She doesn't want what's left of her life to be filled with recriminations; it is more significant to her to have a sense of family, to be involved in the lives of her brother's children, than it is to dwell on ancient history.

These people, and others like them, have been an inspiration to me. They have taught me about survival, about redemption and continuity—everything, in short, that I needed to know to make better sense of my past, my present, and my future.

Final Thoughts

Here's what I have learned about life after parental death—having spent the past two years thinking of little else—and what I have done with that knowledge.

I have never believed in a hereafter, at least not in a religious sense. But I do believe—and, in talking to the men and women who graciously participated in this project, have become convinced—that what happens to us is influenced by the generations that preceded us. How we *respond* to that influence is what matters.

And so I have come to think about my own parents in ways that I did not when I began researching and writing this book. My mother and father were in many respects exemplars of what not to do, how not to behave, especially when it came to childrearing. I do not think that was their intent, even if it ended up being the result.

But all that has begun to feel very long ago, as if it happened to someone else, which, in a sense, it did. I am not the same person I was when I was growing up—not the same person I was when my parents died or have become in the aftermath.

In the years since their deaths, my parents have become more recognizable to me than when they were alive, their influence on me clearer, our similarities and differences crisper, easier to delineate. They had to die for me to see who they were, apart from me, and who I am, apart from them. They had to die for me to fully understand that while I am *of* them, I am *not* them.

In the same unsparing vein, I have thought at length about the influence, good and bad, I have had on my own daughter. In some ways I have been a terrific mother—better at the role, I like to suppose, than my mother was. But in other ways I have fallen short, making monumental mistakes that are all my own.

More times than I can count, I have driven my daughter to distraction. Knowing this, taking responsibility for this, has animated my desire to leave her with a minimum of loose ends, to regard her as a separate individual, to love her with all my heart, and—lovingly—to let her go.

At the same time, I have come to appreciate that, as happened to me when my parents died, it is likely that when I, too, am gone she will be able to see more distinctly her own outlines and fully come into her own.

The supreme irony of our parents' deaths is that only when we are without them do we come face-to-face with the reality of how much growing up we still have to do, how much about ourselves there is left to learn. I'm not sure that anyone ever finishes the job, not altogether—the important thing is to try.

We are the sum not only of our childhoods but also of what we make of ourselves when childhood literally ends. Throughout our lives we can still change, can still make a difference, can still have an effect on the generations to come. Just as we are linked to the past, so, too, are we linked to the future.

Arriving at this conclusion—this feeling of being part of a continuum of love and of loss—has been the most important lesson derived from writing this book, and I didn't get here alone; many generous people accompanied me along the way.

To those unparented men and women who opened their hearts and memories to me, who helped me comprehend the paradoxes of death and renewal, I owe a debt I can never repay. Because of them, endings hold less terror for me.

And to those who are now, or soon will be, confronting their own unparented adulthoods, my greatest wish is that this book will provide them, as it has me, a way to reestablish their emotional moorings; a sense that they are not alone in their struggles; and, above all, the assurance that where they find sorrow, they can, in time, also find hope.

The Parental Loss Questionnaire and Survey Results

Between December 1997 and July 1998, 94 people participated in a mail survey about parental loss in adulthood. Here are the major results of that survey.*

1. **Current Age**

20s	1%
30s	10%
40s	24%
50s	34%
60s or older	31%

2. **Gender**

female	71%
male	29%

3. **Educational Level**

High School graduate	9%
B.A. or B.S.	46%
Master's Degree	29%
Ph.D., M.D., or LL.D.	16%

*Note: In some cases totals exceed 100 percent because of multiple answers or because of rounded numbers. In other cases totals do not add up to 100 percent, either because the percentages were insignificant or a respondent didn't know the answer to a question or left it blank.

4. *Occupational Status*
   Employed   84%
   Homemaker   5%
   Retired   11%

5. *Marital Status*
   Married   70%
   Divorced   15%
   Widowed   5%
   Never married   10%

6. *Childrearing Status*
   Have children   77%
   Do not have children   23%

7. *Sibling Status*
   Have siblings   87%
     Birth Order:
           Youngest   42%
           Middle   16%
           Eldest   38%
   Only Child   13%

8. *How old were you when your mother died?*
   20s   14%
   30s   15%
   40s   29%
   50s   24%
   60s or older   14%
   Median age   45.1

9. *In what ways did your relationship change in the last years of her life?*
   Very close/became friends   30%
   Improved, mellowed   14%
   Warm but roles reversed   15%
   Warm but lived at distance   8%
   Increasingly distant emotionally 11%
   Estranged   11%

10. *How old were you when your father died?*
    20s   16%
    30s   32%

40s   31%
50s   13%
60s or older   3%
Median age   38.0

11. *In what ways did your relationship change in the last years of his life?*
Closer   29%
Mellowed   6%
No change   25%
More distant emotionally   13%
Role reversal   13%
Estranged   5%

12. *At the time of your parent(s)'s death, what was their marital status?*
Married   82%
Widowed   6%
Divorced   14%
Remarried   4%

13. *If one of your parents is still alive, how has your relationship to him or her changed since the death of your other parent?*
Improved   49%
Deteriorated   24%
No change   24%

14. *Did your surviving parent remarry?*
Yes   24%
No   70%

15. *Which sibings(s) were you closest to in childhood?*
Brothers   40%
    older brother   22%
    younger brother   17%
Sisters   32%
    older sister   12%
    younger sister   20%

16. *Why were you close?*
Parents encouraged closeness   5%
Closest in age   17%
Similar values and dispositions   11%
I was parent figure   7%

I looked up to him/her	11%
Affectionate but not close	7%

17. *If your relationship was distant, why was it distant?*

Parents created rivalry, favoritism	12%
Large age difference	19%
Little or nothing in common	16%
Brother a bully, troublemaker	7%
Dysfunctional family	9%

18. *Was one of you a "favorite" of either of your parents?*

Yes	85%
I was Dad's favorite	16%
Brother was Mom's favorite	15%
Sister was Mom's favorite	12%
I was Mom's favorite	10%
Brother was Dad's favorite	6%
Sister was Dad's favorite	6%
I was perceived by sibs as favorite	7%
No	15%
Parents made sure there were no favorites	11%

19. *In what ways has your relationship to your siblings changed since your parent(s) died—are you closer, more distant, or is the relationship unchanged? Please explain.*

Closer to some or all	53%
Drifted away or estranged	23%
Little or no change	19%

20. *If you are an only child, how has your relationship to extended family been affected?*

Not affected	17%
Little or no family	42%
Closer to aunt or uncle	16%
Virtually no relationship	17%

21. *Did one sibling inherit more than another?*

No; nothing to inherit, other reasons	52%
Yes	23%
Equally divided	17%

22. *In what way, if at all, did the terms of your deceased parent's will, or disposition of his or her belongings, cause problems for you?*
    No major problems   80%
    Significant problems   20%

23. *How, if at all, did the terms of the will and disposition of belongings cause problems for your siblings?*
    No problems   70%
    Caused problems   7%

24. *If one or both of your parents are deceased, what are your overriding feelings about being an "adult orphan"?*
    Positive feelings   51%
    Ambivalent feelings   27%
    Negative feelings (anger or ongoing sadness)   22%

25. *Who in your family of origin—including grandparents, aunts and uncles, cousins, as well as siblings—are you closest to now?*
    Sibling(s)   56%
    Aunt or uncle   16%
    Not close to any   15%
    Cousins   12%
    Surviving parent   13%

26. *Why are you close?*
    Always close   23%
    Shared history, familiarity   20%
    The relative appreciates me, is supportive   13%

27. *How has your marriage or romantic attachment—or the absence of a partner—been affected by your parent(s)'s death?*
    Improved   39%
    Deteriorated   17%
    Not affected   31%

28. *Since your parent's death, have you made any career changes?*
    Yes   50%
    No   45%

29. *If so, is this a direct result of the death?*
    Yes   69%
    No   31%

30. *If you have children, how has your relationship to them changed since the death of your parent?*
    Changed   54%
    No change   47%

31. *If you have no children, how do you feel about being the last of your line at this stage of your life?*
    Okay or resigned or childless by choice   63%
    Unsettled, horrible   32%
    Still plan to have or adopt   14%

32. *In what ways, if any, have your friendships changed since the deaths of your parents?*
    Changed   53%
    No change   48%

33. *Looking back on your parents' deaths, what, if anything, was left unsaid between you and the parent?*
    Nothing   45%
    Wish I'd thanked them, shown appreciation   15%
    Wish we'd talked more, had better relationship   12%
    Everything; parent didn't express love or concern or was   20%
    neglectful

34. *When your parents died did you seek help from a therapist, support group, pastoral counselor, other?*
    Yes   49%
    No   48%

35. *Did this help you to come to terms with unfinished business with your parents and if so, how?*
    Helped me be more objective, insights about parent   28%
    Helped me redefine myself   9%
    Helped me give up anger   9%
    Still working on it   17%
    Helped me work through grief   20%

36. *What, if anything, positive came out of your loss?*
    Discovered my strengths, wiser, can concentrate on self,
    I'm a better parent, set me free   62%
    I understand them better, greater sympathy, less angry at   21%

I rose above family strife, I'm a good person despite their
low opinion   12%
Nothing; part of life   15%

37. *In what ways have you and/or your siblings "stepped into the shoes" of
    your deceased parent—for example, by giving advice, or maintaining
    family ties, or keeping traditions such as specific holiday meals?*
    Have   48%
    Have not   49%

38. *Do you now think of your mortality in a new way?*
    Yes   73%
    No   26%

Notes

Unattributed quotations are from interviews conducted by the author.

Introduction

p. xxxiii "...76 million baby boomers..." See Landon Y. Jones, *Great Expectations: America and the Baby Boom Generation*, N.Y.: Ballantine, 1986.

p. xlv " 'teaches the steadiest minds to waver.' " Sophocles, *Antigone*, l. 563, c. 442 BC.

Chapter 1: Point of Departure: When One Parent Dies

p. 10 " 'Please, sir, I want some more.' " From *Oliver Twist*, by Charles Dickens, 1838.

p. 10 " 'a fatherless or motherless child.' " *The Compact Edition of the Oxford English Dictionary*, Glasgow and N.Y.: Oxford University Press, 1971, p. 2011.

p. 10 " 'deprived by death of one...' " *Merriam-Webster's Collegiate Dictionary*, 10th ed., Springfield, Mass.: Merriam-Webster, Inc., 1995, p. 821.

p. 10 " 'funerals are always occasions for pious lying.' " I. F. Stone, "We All Had a Finger on That Trigger," *I. F. Stone's Weekly*, December 9, 1963.

p. 11 "...all-time high of 76.5 years..." "Births and Deaths: Preliminary Data for 1997," by Stephanie J. Ventura, M.A.; Robert N. Anderson, Ph.D.; et al., *National Vital Statistics Report*, vol. 47, No. 4, Hyattsville, Md.: U.S. Department of Health and Human Services, Centers for Disease Control and Prevention, National Center for Health Statistics, October 7, 1998, p. 5.

p. 11 "As social historian Philippe Ariès..." *Western Attitudes Toward*

Death: From the Middle Ages to the Present, by Philippe Ariès (translated by Patricia M. Ranum), Baltimore and London: Johns Hopkins University Press, 1974, p. 13.

p. 11 " ' . . . dare not utter its name.' " Ibid.

p. 11 ". . . occur when one is alone . . . 'hushed up.' " Ibid., p. 87.

p. 11 "The first systematic study of the psychodynamic reactions of adult offspring . . ." "Adults' Reactions to the Death of a Parent: A Preliminary Study," by Dennis P. Malinak, M.D., Michael F. Hoyt, Ph.D.; and Virginia Patterson, M.A., *American Journal of Psychiatry* 136:9, September 1979, pp. 1152–56.

p. 11 " 'so painful that we as researchers and clinicians. . . .' " "The Impact of Parental Death on Middle Aged Children," by Miriam S. Moss and Sidney Z. Moss, *Omega,* vol. 14(1), 1983–1984, p. 66.

p. 12 " 'disenfranchised grief.' " "Disenfranchised Grief," paper presented by Kenneth J. Doka, Ph.D., to a symposium on Death Education of the Foundation of Thanatology, New York, April 25, 1985. See also, *Disenfranchised Grief,* by Kenneth J. Doka, Ph.D., Lexington, Mass.: Lexington Press, 1989.

p. 13 " 'Death Wish' . . . parent-child conflict plays a huge role. . . ." *Born to Rebel: Birth Order, Family Dynamics, and Creative Lives,* by Frank J. Sulloway, New York: Vintage Books, Random House, Inc., 1997, p. 122. See also, *Freud: A Life for Our Time,* by Peter Gay, N.Y.: Anchor Books, Doubleday, 1989, pp. 112–13.

p. 14 ". . . aggressive themselves . . . identifying with the other . . ." *The Bonds of Love: Psychoanalysis, Feminism, and the Problem of Domination,* by Jessica Benjamin, N.Y.: Pantheon Books, 1988, pp. 28, 54–82.

p. 14 ". . . life, death, and the mother-father-child triangle . . ." Ibid.

p. 14 ". . . repress their painful memories . . . subconsciousness . . ." Gay, *Freud,* p. 96.

p. 14 " 'repetition compulsion.' " Gay, *Freud,* pp. 400–402. See also, *The Drama of the Gifted Child: The Search for the True Self,* by Alice Miller, N.Y.: Basic Books, 1981, pp. 76–83.

p. 15 " 'triangulation.' " For a discussion of "triangling," see Michael E. Kerr and Murray Bowen, *Family Evaluation: An Approach Based on Bowen Theory,* N.Y.: W. W. Norton, 1988, pp. 134–162.

p. 15 " 'attachment behavior.' " *A Secure Base: Parent-Child Attachment and Healthy Human Development,* by John Bowlby, N.Y.: Basic Books, Inc., 1988, p. 27.

p. 15 ". . . can confidently go out into the world . . . take for granted . . ." Ibid., p. 11.

p. 16 ". . . the child has 'internalized' it and made it his or her own." Ibid., p. 46.

p. 16 "Contrary to Freudian theory . . . boost the odds of survival." *At-*

tachment and Loss, Vol. III, *Loss: Sadness and Depression*, by John Bowlby, N.Y.: Basic Books, Inc., 1980, pp. 40–41.

p. 16 ". . . depending on his or her 'disposition' . . . one of three insecure ways . . ." Ibid., pp. 202–207.

p. 16 " 'compulsive caregiving.' " Ibid., pp. 207, 222.

p. 16 " 'anxious and ambivalent.' " Ibid., pp. 218–19.

p. 16 " 'independence of affectional ties.' " Ibid., pp. 224–25.

p. 16 " 'working models.' " Ibid. pp. 229–30.

p. 16 " 'insecurely attached' children learn to distrust.' " Ibid., p. 230.

p. 18 "This mutual need was examined by Margaret Hellie Huyck and Susan Frank . . ." "Midlife Parental Imperatives," by Margaret Hellie Huyck, in Richard A. Kalish, ed., *Midlife Loss: Coping Strategies*, Newbury Park, Calif.: Sage Publications, 1989, pp. 123–144.

p. 18 "The most important finding . . . *looked to the other for validation* . . ." Ibid., pp. 140–141.

p. 18 " '[T]he issue,' writes Benjamin, 'is not how we become free . . .' " Benjamin, *The Bonds of Love*, p. 18.

p. 19 ". . . a 'dialogue' with the parent that had been 'derailed . . .' " *No Voice Is Ever Wholly Lost*, by Louise J. Kaplan, N.Y.: Simon & Schuster, 1995, pp. 22, 25, citing René Spitz, "The Derailment of Dialogue," *Journal of the American Psychoanalytic Association* 12: 1964, pp. 752–75.

p. 19 " 'However old or young a person is when a parent dies.' " Kaplan, *No Voice Is Ever Wholly Lost*, p. 99.

Chapter 2: The Relationship to the Remaining Parent

p. 26 "In 1900, only about 10 percent . . . climbed to 47 percent." "Parent-Child Relations in Later Life: Trends and Gaps in Past Research," by Gunhild O. Hagestad, in Jane B. Lancaster, Jeanne Altmann, Alice S. Rossi, and Lonnie R. Sherrod, eds., *Parenting Across the Lifespan: Biosocial Dimensions*, Hawthorne, N.Y.: Aldine de Gruyter, 1987, p. 406.

p. 26 "According to a 1997 national survey conducted for the . . . [AARP] . . ." "AARP Independent Living *Excel* Insert: Tabulation Report July 30–August 19, 1997," Excel: ICR's Twice Weekly National Telephone Omnibus Service, conducted for the AARP by International Communications Research, Media, Pa.

p. 27 "In 1997, 2.3 million Americans died . . ." *Births and Deaths: Preliminary Data for 1997*, by Stephanie J. Ventura, M.A., Robert N. Anderson, Ph.D., et al., National Vital Statistics Reports from the Centers for Disease Control and Prevention, National Center for Health Statistics, vol. 47, no. 4, October 7, 1998, p. 5.

p. 27 ". . . the age-adjusted death rate . . . twice as high for men . . ." Ibid., p. 6.

p. 28 " 'Over and over again [my father] recounted for me . . .' " *Patrimony: A True Story*, by Philip Roth, N.Y.: Simon & Schuster, 1991, p. 36.

p. 28 ". . . overbearing 'stubbornness.' " Ibid.

p. 28 ". . . Roth's own . . . 'physical estrangement.' " Ibid., p. 152.

p. 28 " 'It wasn't that I hadn't understood that the connection. . . .' " Ibid., p. 129.

p. 34 ". . . interdependencies . . . survival dependencies . . . excessive dependencies . . ." "The Adult Child and Older Parents," by Robert A. Lewis, in Timothy H. Brubaker, ed., *Family Relationships in Later Life*, 2nd ed., Newbury Park, Calif.: Sage Publications, 1990, pp. 71–72.

p. 34 ". . . 'dependencies' between middle-aged progeny and their aging parents . . ." Ibid., p. 73.

p. 34 "During this stage, parent-child problems . . ." Ibid., pp. 73, 77–78.

p. 35 ". . . many parents would rather call upon a friend or sibling . . ." See, "Family Support in Relation to Health Problems of the Elderly," by Victor R. Cicirelli, in Brubaker, ed., *Family Relationships in Later Life*, pp. 211–27.

p. 35 "Researchers have found that when relationships between people are healthy . . ." "The Process and Mechanics of Social Support," by Stevan E. Hobfoll and Joseph P. Stokes, in S. W. Duck, ed., *Handbook of Personal Relationships*, London: John Wiley & Sons, Ltd., 1988, p. 515.

p. 37 " 'From both generations I hear stories . . .' " *Another Country: Navigating the Emotional Terrain of Our Elders*, by Mary Pipher, Ph.D., N.Y.: Riverhead Books, Penguin Putnam Inc., 1999, p. 7.

p. 38 ". . . the relationship might actually warm up." Cicirelli, in Brubaker, ed., *Family Relationships in Later Life*, p. 224, citing Siliman, R. A.; Fletcher, R. H.; Earp, J. L.; et al., "Families of Elderly Stroke Patients: Effects of Home Care," *Journal of the American Geriatrics Society* 34, 1986, pp. 643–48.

p. 38 "Studies show that aging parents would *like* to see or hear from . . ." "Parent-Child Relations in Later Life: Trends and Gaps in Past Research," by Gunhild O. Hagestad, in Lancaster, et al., eds., *Parenting Across the Lifespan*, p. 416, citing Hawkinson, W., "Wish, Expectancy, and Practice in the Interaction of Generations," in A. Rose and W. Peterson, eds., *Older People and Their Social World*, Philadelphia, Pa.: F. A. Davis Co., 1965.

p. 38 ". . . a 'demilitarized zone,' silently agreeing not to disagree." Hagestad, in *Parenting Across the Lifespan*, p. 414.

p. 39 ". . . sons tend to demonstrate filial devotion *instrumentally* . . ." Ibid., p. 420, citing House, J. S., *Work Stress and Social Support*, Reading, Mass.: Addison-Wesley, 1981.

p. 40 "Women have traditionally been 'kin-keepers' . . ." *Of Human Bond-*

ing: Parent-Child Relations Across the Life Course, by Alice S. Rossi and Peter H. Rossi, Hawthorne, N.Y.: Aldine de Gruyter, 1990, p. 197.

p. 41 "Most sons are tacitly encouraged . . . *unlike their mothers . . .*" *The Reproduction of Mothering: Psychoanalysis and the Sociology of Gender,* by Nancy J. Chodorow, Berkeley, Calif.: University of California Press, 1978, pp. 96-97.

p. 41 "The majority of the middle-aged fathers I interviewed. . . ." *Women and Their Fathers: The Sexual and Romantic Impact of the First Man in Your Life,* by Victoria Secunda, N.Y.: Delta Books, 1993.

p. 42 " 'Maternal gatekeeping,' wherein Mom knows best . . ." See "Father Influences Viewed in a Family Context," by Frank A. Pederson, in Michael E. Lamb, ed., *The Role of the Father in Child Development,* 2nd ed., N.Y.: A Wiley-Interscience Publication, John Wiley and Sons, 1981, p. 303. See also Ross D. Parke, *Fathers,* Cambridge, Mass.: Harvard University Press, 1981.

p. 42 " 'A man who has been the indisputable favorite . . .' " *The Life and Work of Sigmund Freud: The Formative Years and the Great Discoveries 1856–1900,* by Ernest Jones, M.D., vol. 1, N.Y.: Basic Books, 1953, p. 5.

p. 44 ". . . an estimated *78 percent of American caregivers are women.*" "Assistance for Caregivers" brochure, Children of Aging Parents (CAPS), 1609 Woodbourne Road, Suite 302A, Levittown, PA 19057. (For further information, call 1-800-227-7294.)

p. 46 "As researchers on 'social comparison' have discovered . . ." "Sibling Deidentification and Split-Parent Identification: A Family Tetrad," by Frances Fuchs Schacter, in Lamb, Michael E., and Sutton-Smith, Brian, eds., *Sibling Relationships: Their Nature and Significance Across the Lifespan,* Hillsdale, N.J.: Erlbaum, 1982, p. 133–34.

p. 46 "But if parents lavish unambiguous preference . . ." "The Separate Worlds of Teenage Siblings: An Introduction to the Study of the Nonshared Environment and Adolescent Development," by David Reiss; Robert Plomin; and E. M. Hetherington, et al., in Hetherington, E.M., Reiss, D. and Plomin, R. eds., *Separate Social Worlds of Siblings: The Impact of Nonshared Environment on Development,* Hillsdale, N.J.: Erlbaum, 1993, p. 96.

p. 47 "Authorities on the sibling relationship . . ." See *Siblings in Therapy: Life Span and Clinical Issues,* Kahn, Michael D., and Karen Gail Lewis, eds., New York and London: W. W. Norton & Company, 1988.

p. 47 "Sulloway's thesis, based on over twenty years of research, is that parental 'resources' . . ." *Born to Rebel: Birth Order, Family Dynamics, and Creative Lives,* by Frank J. Sulloway, N.Y.: Vintage Books, Random House, Inc., 1997, p. xiv.

p. 48 " 'The story of sibling differences . . . and any perceived biases in it.' " Ibid., p. xv.

p. 48 "No social injustice is felt more deeply . . ." Ibid.

p. 50 ". . . adult children of separated or divorced parents see their parents less often—up to *36 percent less often . . .*" "Interaction and Living Arrangements of Older Parents and Their Children: Past Trends, Present Determinants, Future Implications," by Eileen M. Crimmins and Dominque G. Ingegneri, *Research on Aging*, vol. 12, no. 1, March 1990, p. 23.

Chapter 3: Voices from the Grave: Legacies and Loyalties

p. 57 " '[T]he psychodynamic work of mourning. . . .' " "Loss as a Metaphor for Attachment," by George E. Vaillant, *The American Journal of Psychoanalysis*, Vol. 45, No. 1, 1985, p. 59.

p. 65 " 'You imagine their gratitude . . .' " *Making the Most of Your Money*, by Jane Bryant Quinn, N.Y.: Simon & Schuster, 1997, p. 96.

p. 65 ". . . attempt to posthumously control . . . through the employment of 'conditional bequests' . . ." *The Complete Book of Wills & Estates*, by Alexander A. Bove, Jr., N.Y.: Henry Holt and Company, 1989, pp. 79–92.

p. 65 "Not all of these 'conditions,' and others similar to them, are unreasonable . . ." I am grateful to psychologist and financial planner Kenneth O. Doyle, Ph.D., associate professor at the University of Minnesota School of Journalism and Mass Communication, for explaining the wisdom of certain "conditions" that might protect an adult child—as, for instance, establishing a trust that, in the event of a child's divorce, would be safeguarded.

p. 66 "Kenneth J. Doka, Ph.D., . . . has studied how inheritance disagreements . . ." "The Monkey's Paw: The Role of Inheritance in the Resolution of Grief," by Kenneth J. Doka, *Death Studies* 16, 1992, pp. 45–58.

p. 71 "Susan C. Vaughan . . . author of *The Talking Cure* . . ." *The Talking Cure: The Science Behind Psychotherapy*, by Susan C. Vaughan, M.D., N.Y.: G. P. Putnam's Sons, 1997.

p. 72 "Family therapist Evan Imber-Black . . . has examined the effect upon families of 'dangerous secrets' . . ." *The Secret Life of Families: Truth-Telling, Privacy, and Reconciliation in a Tell-All Society*, by Evan Imber-Black, Ph.D., N.Y.: Bantam Books, 1998, pp. 17–19.

p. 75 "Six percent of the respondents lost their parents to suicide . . ." For a discussion of the impact of parental suicide on families, see "Survivor Family Relationships: Literature Review," by John L. McIntosh, in *Suicide and Its Aftermath: Understanding and Counseling the Survivors*, Edward J. Dunne, John L. McIntosh, and Karen Dunne-Maxim, eds., N.Y.: W. W. Norton & Company, 1987, pp. 73–84. See also, "Reconsidering the Role of Hostility in Completed Suicide: A Life-Course Perspective," by Paul R. Duberstein, Larry Seidlitz, and Yeates Conwell, in *Psychoanalytic Perspectives on Developmental Psychology*, Joseph M. Masling and Robert F. Bornstein, eds., Washington, D.C.: American Psychological Association, 1996, pp. 257–323.

p. 77 ". . . homicide can 'kill' on many levels . . ." For a discussion of the short-term and long-term impacts of homicide on surviving families, see "Family Reaction to Homicide," by Ann Wolbert Burgess, R.N., D.N.Sc., *American Journal of Orthopsychiatry* 45(3), April 1975, pp. 391–398.

Chapter 4: Realigned Family Ties: Siblings and Only Children

p. 85 " 'I used to think the world divided between those who have children . . .' " *And When Did You Last See Your Father? A Son's Memoir of Love and Loss,* by Blake Morrison, N.Y.: Picador, 1995, pp. 205–206.

p. 87 ". . . more recently (1959), writer Jack Douglas quipped . . ." *My Brother Was an Only Child,* by Jack Douglas, N.Y.: Dutton, 1959.

p. 87 " 'only a bit-part in the drama of sibling differences.' " *Separate Lives: Why Siblings Are So Different,* by Judy Dunn and Robert Plomin, N.Y.: Basic Books, HarperCollins Publishers, 1990, p. 85.

p. 87 "The other caveat is that 'emotionally corrective experiences' " "The Social Transmission of Parental Behavior: Attachment Across Generations," by Margaret H. Ricks, in *Growing Points of Attachment Theory and Research,* Inge Bretherton and Everett Waters, eds., Monographs of the Society for Research in Child Development, Vol. 50, Nos. 1–2, Chicago: University of Chicago Press, 1985, pp. 226–27.

p. 88 "For it is *within* the family that children first learn . . . how to negotiate conflict . . ." *Family Constellation: Its Effects on Personality and Social Behavior,* 3rd ed., by Walter Toman, N.Y.: Springer, 1976, p. 79.

p. 88 "*Firstborns,* Sulloway has found, tend to be 'assertive, socially dominant, ambitious . . .' " *Born to Rebel: Birth Order, Family Dynamics, and Creative Lives,* by Frank J. Sulloway, N.Y.: Vintage Books, 1997, p. xiv.

p. 88 "From earliest childhood, they try to avoid conflict with their parents, . . ." Ibid., pp. 21, 121.

p. 88 ". . . guarding their own special family standing." Ibid., p. xiv.

p. 88 "In childhood, firstborns tend to be larger . . ." Ibid., p. 68–69.

p. 88 "They are also more 'emotionally intense' . . ." Ibid., p. 70.

p. 88 ". . . and 'tough-minded' . . ." Ibid. p. 302.

p. 88 ". . . they savor the status quo." Ibid., p. 98.

p. 88 "But should a sibling appear on the scene . . ." Ibid., pp. 68–69.

p. 88 ". . . they often are leaders . . ." Ibid., p. 69.

p. 88 ". . . and high achievers." Ibid., p. 21.

p. 88 "And if they can hang on to their privileged status for six or more years . . ." Ibid., p. 22.

p. 89 ". . . secondborns tend to be diplomats . . . how to curry favor." Ibid., p. 55, citing Adler, Alfred, *Children* 3, 1928, pp. 14–52.

p. 89 "They find a skill or talent . . . a 'niche' . . ." Sulloway, *Born to Rebel*, p. 95.

p. 89 "The strategy for secondborns is to be *different* . . ." Ibid., p. 98.

p. 89 "A solution to this problem . . . is *diversification*." Ibid., p. 106.

p. 90 "(These also-rans . . . are often late bloomers . . .)" Ibid., pp. 357, 439.

p. 91 ". . . 'open[ness] to radical innovations,' . . ." Ibid., p. 357.

p. 91 "Lastborns . . . uncomplaining followers." Sulloway, *Born to Rebel*, p. 69.

p. 91 "They frequently get coddling from everyone . . ." Ibid., pp. 303, 305.

p. 91 ". . . middleborn children . . . the Darwinian 'losers.' " Ibid., p. 305.

p. 91 ". . . parents tend to favor . . . the oldest . . . the youngest . . ." Ibid.

p. 91 ". . . middleborns are *themselves* 'displaced' . . ." "Children of Alcoholics: Their Sibling World," by Rosalie C. Jesse, in *Siblings in Therapy: Life Span and Clinical Issues*, Michael D. Kahn and Karen Gail Lewis, eds., N.Y.: W. W. Norton & Company, 1988, p. 246.

p. 91 "As a result, they tend to be more loosely attached to their parents . . ." *The Birth Order Book*, by Dr. Kevin Leman, N.Y.: Dell Publishing Co., 1985, p. 120.

p. 93 "The disadvantages . . . often raised in single-parent homes." "Differential Parental Investment: Its Effects on Child Quality and Status Attainment," by Judith Blake, in *Parenting Across the Lifespan: Biosocial Dimensions*, Jane B. Lancaster, et al., eds., N.Y.: Aldine de Gruyter, 1987, p. 356.

p. 93 "According to Sulloway . . . *much more conflict* . . ." Sulloway, *Born to Rebel*, Notes, p. 489.

p. 93 ". . . parents of only children tend to be well educated with lofty IQs." *The Limits of Family Influence: Genes, Experience, and Behavior*, by David C. Rowe, N.Y.: Guilford Press, 1994, p. 159.

p. 93 "In a review of the psychological literature on only children, Toni Falbo. . . . 'locus of control.' " "Only Children in America," by Toni Falbo, in *Sibling Relationships: Their Nature and Significance Across the Lifespan*, Michael E. Lamb and Brian Sutton-Smith, eds., Hillsdale, N.J.: Lawrence Erlbaum Associates, 1982, p. 294.

p. 94 ". . . only children, because they have their parents' undivided attention . . ." Ibid.

p. 94 ". . . only children 'acquire a more trusting style of interaction.' " Ibid., p. 296.

p. 94 ". . . the most predictable characteristic of only children . . . so *unpredictable*." Sulloway, *Born to Rebel*, p. 204.

p. 94 ". . . onlies are more open to experience." Ibid., p. 205, Notes, p. 503.

p. 94 ". . . onlies are the most consistently emotionally stable. . . ." "Life Span Personality Stability in Sibling Status," by B. G. Rosenberg, in Lamb et al., eds., *Sibling Relationships*, p. 172.

p. 94 ". . . identifying with both parents . . ." Ibid., p. 217.

p. 94 " 'A child who cannot count on parental investment . . .' " Sulloway, *Born to Rebel*, p. 90.

p. 96 " 'family systems theory.' " *Family Evaluation: An Approach Based on Bowen Theory*, by Michael E. Kerr and Murray Bowen, N.Y.: W. W. Norton & Company, 1988, p. viii.

p. 96 " 'The family is a unit because it operates as a system . . . to the responses of others to him, etc.' " Ibid., p. 10.

p. 96 "Triangles are the 'molecule' . . ." Ibid., p. 134.

p. 96 ". . . the third person suddenly becomes important, drawn in to 'stabilize' . . ." Ibid., p. 135.

p. 96 ". . . this is called 'triangling' . . ." Ibid., p. 134.

p. 96 ". . . people *function* in response to the functioning . . . ." p. 142.

p. 97 "Indeed, scapegoating . . ." Ibid., pp. 137–38.

p. 98 " 'Once the emotional circuitry . . . play lives on through the generations.' " Ibid., p. 135.

p. 99 ". . . says psychotherapist Dr. Jane Greer, co-author of *Adult Sibling Rivalry*." *Adult Sibling Rivalry: Understanding the Legacy of Childhood*, by Dr. Jane Greer with Edward Myers, N.Y.: Crown Publishers, Inc., 1992.

p. 103 "Investigators have found that older and younger siblings prefer middleborns . . ." "Sibling Influence Throughout the Lifespan," by Victor G. Cicirelli, in Lamb et al., eds., *Sibling Relationships*, p. 275.

p. 104 "Many researchers have found that sibling attachments post–parental death . . ." See "Important Variables in Adult Sibling Relationships: A Qualitative Study," by Helgola G. Ross and Joel I. Milgram, in Lamb et al., eds., *Sibling Relationships*, p. 230–31.

p. 105 ". . . (studies on human development have found that the older siblings get . . .)" See Dunn and Plomin, *Separate Lives*, pp. 115–134.

p. 107 "In their book *Of Human Bonding*. . . . a sense of 'kinship obligation' . . ." *Of Human Bonding: Parent-Child Relations Across the Life Course*, by Alice S. Rossi and Peter H. Rossi, N.Y.: Aldine de Gruyter, 1990, p. 216.

p. 107 ". . . reduced when parents have emotional troubles. . . . But when parents are happily married . . ." Ibid., pp. 230–35, 268, 290.

p. 109 " '[A]voidance may . . . allow siblings to find strengths . . .' " Ross and Milgram, in Lamb et al., eds., *Sibling Relationships*, p. 248.

p. 109 "In one such investigation, Victor G. Cicirelli. . . ." "Sibling Influence Throughout the Lifespan," by Victor G. Cicirelli, in Lamb et al., eds., *Sibling Relationships*, p. 274.

p. 109 ". . . a form of 'attachment' behavior . . ." Ibid., p. 282.

p. 111 "Onlies so identify with parents . . . main problem often is learning . . ." "Life Span Personality Stability in Sibling Status," by B. G. Rosenberg, in Lamb et al., eds., *Sibling Relationships*, p. 220.

Chapter 5: Changes of Heart: Effect on Romantic Partnerships

p. 119 "Numerous psychological pundits . . . a hallmark of adulthood is the ability to detach . . ." *A Secure Base: Parent-Child Attachment and Healthy Human Development*, by John Bowlby, N.Y.: Basic Books, Inc., 1988, p. 163.

p. 119 "By reattachment, these theorists are talking about . . ." See *The Wisdom of the Ego*, by George E. Vaillant, Cambridge, Mass.: Harvard University Press, 1993, pp. 147–49.

p. 120 ". . . when people marry, they inevitably bring with them the templates. . . ." *Attachment and Loss*, Vol. III, *Loss: Sadness and Depression*, by John Bowlby, N.Y.: Basic Books, Inc., 1980, p. 235.

p. 123 "In a study of long-term changes . . . Joan Delahanty Douglas examined forty adults. . . ." "Patterns of Change Following Parent Death in Midlife Adults," by Joan Delahanty Douglas, *Omega*, vol. 22(2), 1990–1991, pp. 123–37.

p. 124 "Over half . . . experienced a 'marital upheaval' . . ." Ibid., pp. 132, 134.

p. 127 "Yet they, too, can find connubial contentment." See "Attachments Across the Life Span," by Mary D. Salter Ainsworth, *Bulletin of the New York Academy of Medicine*, vol. 61, no. 9, November 1985, pp. 792–812.

p. 127 "These were among the conclusions arrived at by Margaret H. Ricks . . ." "The Social Transmission of Parental Behavior: Attachment Across Generations," by Margaret H. Ricks, in *Growing Points of Attachment Theory and Research*, Inge Bretherton and Everett Waters, eds., Chicago: University of Chicago Press, 1985, pp. 211–27.

p. 127 "These women had remarkably sturdy bonds not only to their husbands . . . *husbands' families*." Ibid., p. 223.

p. 127 "The women were able to reframe their parents' treatment of them . . ." Ibid., pp. 224–27. See also "Attachment Theory: Retrospect and Prospect," by Inge Bretherton, in Bretherton et al., eds., *Growing Points of Attachment Theory and Research*, p. 23.

p. 131 ". . . psychologist Debra Umberson . . . found four 'themes' of marital 'decline' . . ." "Marriage as Support or Strain? Marital Quality Following the Death of a Parent," by Debra Umberson, *Journal of Marriage and the Family*, 1995, pp. 709–23.

p. 131 "The spouses were unable to provide . . . bounce back quickly from the loss." Ibid., p. 719.

p. 136 ". . . Anthony Storr believes that the capacity to be alone is . . . as 'therapeutic' . . ." *Solitude: A Return to the Self*, by Anthony Storr, N.Y.: The Free Press, Macmillan, Inc., 1988, p. 29.

p. 136 " 'If we did not look to marriage as the principal source of happiness . . . end in tears.' " Ibid., p. xiv.

p. 136 " 'Intimate attachments are *a* hub . . . not necessarily *the* hub.' " Ibid., p. 15.

Chapter 6: Parenthood Reconsidered: On Having, and Not Having, Children

p. 146 ". . . children tend to discuss personal matters with their mothers much more than with fathers . . ." *Of Human Bonding: Parent-Child Relations Across the Life Course*, by Alice S. Rossi and Peter H. Rossi, N.Y.: Aldine de Gruyter, 1990, p. 257.

p. 146 ". . . a pattern of intimacy that continues into the offspring's middle age." Ibid., pp. 277–279.

p. 146 " 'It is when children have married and are rearing children . . . may be demonstrated.' " Ibid., p. 337.

p. 146 "Those in the Rossi study who had loving attachments . . . tended to form families that were similar . . ." Ibid., p. 359.

p. 147 "Whereas those who had thorny relationships . . . correspondingly *stronger* commitments to the people they chose . . ." Ibid., p. 235.

p. 149 "Studies show . . . that parents of young children are expected to act like grown-ups . . ." "Models of Midlife," by Margaret Hellie Huyck, in Kalish, Richard A., ed., *Midlife Loss: Coping Strategies*, Newbury Park, Calif.: Sage Publications, 1989, pp. 28–29, citing Gutmann, D. L., *Reclaimed Powers: Toward a New Psychology of Men and Women in Later Life*, N.Y.: Basic Books, 1987.

p. 149 ". . . stress . . . is a 'life-force dynamic' . . ." "Stress and Loss in Middle Age," by David A. Chiriboga, in Kalish, ed., *Midlife Loss*, p. 46.

p. 149 ". . . the survivors must 'reformulate' themselves." Ibid., p. 56.

p. 156 "In her book *The Bonds of Love*, psychoanalyst Jessica Benjamin . . . engage in a *mutual* relationship . . ." *The Bonds of Love: Psychoanalysis, Feminism, and the Problem of Domination*, by Jessica Benjamin, N.Y.: Pantheon Books, 1988, pp. 24–28.

p. 157 ". . . children form 'prototypes,' based on their experiences with their parents . . ." *The Talking Cure: The Science Behind Psychotherapy*, by Susan C. Vaughan, M.D., N.Y.: G. P. Putnam's Sons, 1997, pp. 81–83.

p. 157 " 'Without disapproval, the child cannot be educated . . . deflated negative emotion.' " Ibid., pp. 115–16.

p. 157 "But children who have experienced only parental . . . allow their children to control their emotions for them . . ." Ibid., pp. 132–33.

p. 158 ". . . children's attachment behaviors tend to persist into adulthood . . ." Bowlby, *A Secure Base*, pp. 126, 129–30.

p. 158 "Adult children can then change their attachment 'styles' . . ." Ibid., pp. 125–27.

p. 158 "The key to this altered parenting style . . . develop an understanding of why their parents might have felt compelled . . ." Ibid., p. 139.

p. 158 " 'It is not . . . a question of the parents committing no faults . . .' " *The Development of Personality: Papers on Child Psychology, Education, and Related Subjects*, by C. G. Jung, vol. 17 of the Collected Works of C. G. Jung, Bollingen Series XX, translated by R. F. C. Hull, N.Y.: Pantheon Books, 1954, p. 79.

p. 165 "Throughout the millennia, says Frank J. Sulloway . . . laterborns have typically been less inclined . . ." Sulloway, *Born to Rebel*, Appendix 10, p. 433.

p. 165 " 'Freed from the special obligations of parental duties. . . . assisting close relatives.' " *On Human Nature*, by Edward O. Wilson, Cambridge, Mass.: Harvard University Press, 1978, pp. 144–45.

p. 166 " '[W]hat does it mean to think about the death . . . if there is no next of kin?' " *Bequest & Betrayal: Memoirs of a Parent's Death*, by Nancy K. Miller, N.Y. and Oxford: Oxford University Press, 1996, p. 11.

p. 166 "One of the things that can happen . . . is the handing down of one's ideas . . . in the form of art, as Simone de Beauvoir . . ." Ibid., p. 41.

p. 166 " 'Some of the psychological readjustments . . . act as a model or mentor to the young.' " *The Meanings of Age: Selected Papers of Bernice L. Neugarten*, edited and with a foreword by Dail A. Neugarten, Chicago and London: University of Chicago Press, 1996, p. 187.

Chapter 7: Achievement: Reappraised Careers

p. 171 "This was certainly the case for McCourt . . . a harrowing account of his father's abandonment . . ." *Angela's Ashes: A Memoir*, by Frank McCourt, N.Y.: Scribner, 1996.

p. 171 " 'If I hadn't written [it] . . . I would have died howling.' " "Why You Must Get Your Story Out," by Victoria Secunda, *New Choices*, June 1997, p. 57.

p. 173 "In her book . . . Martha A. Robbins argues that women's 'unconscious loyalty bonds' . . ." *Midlife Women and Death of Mother: A Study of Psychohistorical and Spiritual Transformation*, by Martha A. Robbins, N.Y.: Peter Lang, 1990, American University Studies Series VIII, Psychology, vol. 8, p. 131.

p. 173 ". . . might put a crimp in their own aspirations." Ibid., p. 125.

p. 173 "In her study Robbins found . . . more saddened by their mothers' culturally constrained lives . . ." Ibid., p. 150–51.

p. 173 ". . . angry that their mothers hadn't somehow managed to surmount . . ." Ibid., p. 209.

p. 173 "These two emotions . . . allowed the women to 'differentiate' . . . through 'meaningful work.' " Ibid., p. 94.

p. 174 " 'Lick the world!' Willy Loman commands . . . 'You guys together . . . lick the civilized world.' " *Death of a Salesman*, by Arthur Miller, N.Y.: Viking Press, 1949, 1973, p. 64.

p. 174 "In a study of adult brothers and sisters by Helgola G. Ross. . . ." "Important Variables in Adult Sibling Relationships: A Qualitative Study," by Helgola G. Ross and Joel I. Milgram, in *Sibling Relationships: Their Nature and Significance Across the Lifespan*, Michael E. Lamb and Brian Sutton-Smith, eds., Hillsdale, N.J.: Lawrence Erlbaum Associates, 1982, pp. 232–33.

p. 174 ". . . tagging them with such labels as 'stupid' or 'intelligent.' " Ibid., p. 236.

p. 174 " 'From childhood to old age . . . dimension of rivalry *par excellence.*' " Ibid., pp. 236–37.

p. 175 "(In contrast . . . they take pleasure in . . . each other's attainments.)" Ibid., p. 237.

p. 180 "In a book titled *Parental Loss and Achievement . . .*" *Parental Loss and Achievement*, by Marvin Eisenstadt, André Haynal, Pierre Rentchnick, and Pierre de Senarclens, Madison, Conn.: International Universities Press, 1989.

p. 180 "Psychologist Marvin Eisenstadt . . . conducted a study of eminence, or 'genius' . . ." Ibid., pp. 5, 20.

p. 180 "Of the 573 'greats' studied . . . adult orphanhood rate . . . was remarkably high." Ibid., pp. 7, 10–11.

p. 180 "Eisenstadt concluded that for certain gifted people . . ." Ibid., pp. 25–27.

p. 184 "In a study called 'My Children and Me . . .' " "My Children and Me: Midlife Evaluations of Grown Children and of Self," by Carol D. Ryff, Young Hyun Lee, et al., *Psychology and Aging*, vol. 9, no. 2, 1994, pp. 195–205.

p. 190 "Psychiatrist George E. Vaillant must have had people like Deborah and Thelma in mind . . ." *The Wisdom of the Ego*, by George E. Vaillant, Cambridge, Mass.: Harvard University Press, 1993.

p. 190 "Drawing on data . . . he argues that a midlife work renaissance . . ." Ibid., p. 189.

p. 190 "The men and women . . . who failed to achieve what he calls 'career consolidation'—which he defines as . . ." Ibid., pp. 149–150.

p. 190 ". . . were those who were either 'explosive' or smouldered within . . ." Ibid., p. 189.

p. 191 ". . . failed to attract mentors." Ibid.

p. 191 " 'To grow,' Vaillant writes, 'we need to feel enriched by those we have loved.' " Ibid., p. 181.

p. 191 "If we have internalized only our parents' criticism . . . and have not formed lasting relationships outside the family. . . ." Ibid., pp. 148–49, 347–48.

p. 191 "But if, as Vaillant suggests, we can find people who believe in us. . . . internalize *their* voices instead . . ." Ibid., pp. 150, 345, 352.

p. 192 " 'Even those who have the happiest relationships with others . . . to complete their fulfillment.' " *Solitude: A Return to the Self,* by Anthony Storr, N.Y.: Free Press, Macmillan, Inc., 1988, p. 75.

Chapter 8: Friendships Reassessed

p. 198 ". . . countless investigators have found that peers outside the family . . ." *Separate Lives: Why Siblings Are So Different,* by Judy Dunn and Robert Plomin, N.Y.: Basic Books, HarperCollins Publishers, 1990, pp. 118–25.

p. 198 "*Who* we choose as friends has a lot to do with temperament . . ." "Roundtable: What Is Temperament? Four Approaches," by H. Hill Goldsmith, Arnold H. Buss, Robert Plomin, et al., *Child Development* 58, 1987, pp. 519–20.

p. 199 "According to UCLA psychologist Shelley E. Taylor's book . . ." *Positive Illusions: Creative Self-Deception and the Healthy Mind,* N.Y.: Basic Books, HarperCollins Publishers, 1989, p. 135.

p. 199 "When friends criticize us . . . to mend our offending ways." Ibid.

p. 200 "In his studies, psychologist Abraham Tesser has found . . . *they cannot be rivals* . . ." Ibid., p. 136, citing Tesser, A. and Campbell, J., (1980), "Self-Definition: The Impact of the Relative Performance and Similarity of Others," *Social Psychology Quarterly* 43, pp. 341–47, and Tesser, A., and Campbell, J. (1982), "Self-Evaluation Maintenance and the Perception of Friends and Strangers," *Journal of Personality* 50, pp. 261–79.

p. 200 "Of the 4,000-plus respondents, *86 percent* . . ." "The *New Woman* Friendship Report: What Friends Mean to Us," by Victoria Secunda, *New Woman,* August 1992, pp. 72–75.

p. 201 "These are among the questions that psychologists Stevan E. Hobfoll and Joseph P. Stokes . . ." "The Process and Mechanics of Social Support," by Stevan E. Hobfoll and Joseph P. Stokes, in *Handbook of Personal Relationships,* S. W. Duck, ed., London: John Wiley & Sons Ltd., 1988, pp. 497–517.

p. 201 ". . . 'social support,' which they define as the people in our lives who provide . . ." Ibid., p. 499.

p. 201 ". . . when we are threatened with loss, we invest in 'other resources' . . ." Ibid., p. 500.

p. 201 " *'it extends the self and what the self can achieve alone.'* " Ibid., p. 502.

p. 201 "Key to the effectiveness . . . is the perceived motive behind it." Ibid., p. 509.

p. 201 "Studies show that men are less likely than women . . ." Ibid., p. 512.

p. 201 "Men might occasionally unburden themselves to one or two buddies . . ." Ibid., p. 514.

p. 201 "As they age, men increasingly prize friendship . . . usually to their families." "Age and Gender Dimensions of Friendship," by Margery Fox, Margaret Gibbs, and Doris Auerbach, *Psychology of Women Quarterly* 9, 1985, pp. 497–98.

p. 201 "Women, on the other hand, tend to be more 'expressive'. . . ." Ibid., p. 498.

p. 205 ". . . 'I tell my clients all the time, "It's very possible to live a long and happy life . . ." ' " Secunda, "The New Woman Friendship Report," August 1992, p. 74.

p. 209 "According to University of California psycholgist Karen Rook . . . be in 'synch' in terms of what is happening . . ." "The Pleasures and Problems of Friendship," by Karen Rook, in *Every Woman's Emotional Well-Being*, Carol Tavris, ed., N.Y.: Doubleday, 1986, pp. 124–25.

p. 210 "A 'friend of the heart' . . . 'perceives me as one of the better versions of myself. . . .' " *Families*, by Jane Howard, N.Y.: Simon and Schuster, 1978, p. 263.

p. 214 "In his research, he has found that people who quickly reject . . ." *Attachment and Loss*, Vol. III, *Loss: Sadness and Depression*, by John Bowlby, N.Y.: Basic Books, 1980, p. 219.

p. 215 " 'Friendship is a complementary quality . . . jollying along the sluggish.' " *Pleasures of a Tangled Life*, by Jan Morris, N.Y.: Random House, 1989, p. 207.

p. 216 " 'The best of all friendships are the ones . . . the fires of love alive.' " Ibid., p. 209.

Chapter 9: Unfinished Business: Coming to Terms with the Past

p. 221 "In an illuminating article titled 'The Myths of Coping with Loss' . . ." "The Myths of Coping with Loss," by Camille B. Wortman and Roxane Cohen Silver, *Journal of Consulting and Clinical Psychology*, vol. 57, no. 3, 1989, pp. 349–357.

p. 222 ". . . they bounce back more quickly than is generally supposed." Ibid., p. 350.

p. 222 "Nor is the lack of grief . . . 'disordered mourning'. . . ." Ibid.

p. 222 ". . . the absence of grief might be a sign of strength." Ibid., p. 354.

p. 222 "This is especially true in the event of a traumatizing . . ." Ibid., p. 352.

p. 222 "They might never . . . reach a true 'state of resolution.' " Ibid., p. 353.

p. 222 "The expectation that they 'must' do so . . ." Ibid., p. 355.

p. 222 " '[O]utsiders may minimize the length of time . . . destruction of future hopes and plans. . . .' " Ibid., p. 355.

p. 227 ". . . how we relate to the world is established in infancy and early childhood." *The Talking Cure: The Science Behind Psychotherapy*, by Susan C. Vaughan, M.D., N.Y.: G. P. Putnam's Sons, 1997, pp. 104–105.

p. 227 "Based on thousands of interactions. . . ." Ibid., p. 98.

p. 227 ". . . these perceptions—or 'prototypes' . . ." Ibid., pp. 85–86.

p. 228 "In this way, our previously negative images . . . neurons in our brains can be literally 'rewired.' " Ibid., p. 4.

p. 234 " 'Realization entails understanding our parents' . . . a person with whom you can deal." *Bequest & Betrayal: Memoirs of a Parent's Death*, by Nancy K. Miller, N.Y. and Oxford: Oxford University Press, 1996, p. 6.

p. 234 "In an article titled 'Creating a Participant Text' . . ." "Creating a Participant Text: Writing, Multiple Voices, Narrative Multiplicity," by Peggy Penn, M.S.W., and Marilyn Frankfurt, M.S.W., *Family Process*, vol. 33, no. 3, September 1994, pp. 217–31.

p. 238 " 'In the end . . . one has to make sense of one's own life . . .' " *Solitude: A Return to the Self*, by Anthony Storr, N.Y.: Free Press, Macmillan, Inc., 1988, p. 92.

p. 239 "According to Carl Jung . . . 'greatest unfolding' . . . the 'real motivations . . . discoveries are made.' " *The Development of Personality: Papers on Child Psychology, Education, and Related Subjects*, by C. G. Jung, vol. 17 of the *Collected Works of C. G. Jung*, Bollingen Series XX, translated by R. F. C. Hull, Pantheon Books, 1954, p. 193.

p. 239 "These epiphanies . . . 'are gained only through the severest shocks.' " Ibid.

p. 239 ". . . look inside themselves for 'self-hood.' " Ibid., p. 197.

p. 239 "In their longitudinal studies . . . Mary Main and Nancy Kaplan . . . 'very secure parents' . . ." "Security in Infancy, Childhood, and Adulthood: A Move to the Level of Representation," by Mary Main and Nancy Kaplan, in *Growing Points of Attachment Theory and Research*, Inge Bretherton and Everett Waters, eds., Chicago: University of Chicago Press, 1985, p. 96.

Chapter 10: *A New Sense of Family*

p. 246 "Psychologists Stephen P. Bank and Michael D. Kahn . . . an example of what they call 'distant identification' . . ." *The Sibling Bond*, by Stephen P. Bank and Michael D. Kahn, N.Y.: Basic Books, 1982, p. 84.

p. 246 ". . . keep each other at arm's length by being polar opposites. . . . smoke screens for unfinished parent-child business." Ibid., pp. 105–106.

p. 249 "These sibling renegotiations . . . (borrowing from psychoanalyst Margaret Mahler) call 'sibling separation and individuation.'" *The Psychological Birth of the Human Infant*, by Margaret Mahler, Fred Pine, and Anni Bergman, N.Y.: Basic Books, 1975.

p. 249 "It is the similarities that are the bedrock of . . . the differences that allow siblings to grow . . ." For a discussion of "partial identification," where siblings acknowledge their similarities and differences, see Bank and Kahn, *The Sibling Bond*, pp. 84–111.

p. 249 "Dr. Bank sees sibling enmity as a 'stolen birthright'. . . ." "The Stolen Birthright: The Adult Sibling in Individual Therapy," by Stephen P. Bank, in *Siblings in Therapy: Life Span and Clinical Issues*, Michael D. Kahn and Karen Gail Lewis, eds., N.Y.: W. W. Norton & Company, 1988, pp. 341–355.

p. 249 ". . . 'the loss of the children's fundamental right . . .'" Ibid., p. 342.

p. 250 "Dr. Bank believes that unless siblings comprehend the role their parents . . . played in their rifts . . ." Ibid., p. 346.

p. 250 "Rather, the goal is to recognize . . . the harvest of parents who, because of their own troubled histories . . ." Ibid., p. 354.

p. 250 "When siblings can reframe their hostility, viewing it as the legacy of *their parents'* unfinished emotional business . . ." Ibid., p. 353.

p. 250 "The *point*, writes Dr. Bank, is to " '[take] responsibility for one's relationships . . .'" Ibid., p. 350.

p. 254 "The purpose of these and other rituals . . . 'is to make and mark transitions for individuals . . .'" *The Secret Life of Families: Truth-Telling, Privacy, and Reconciliation in a Tell-All Society*, by Evan Imber-Black, Ph.D., N.Y.: Bantam Books, 1998, p. 143.

p. 254 "Weddings and christenings . . . Bar Mitzvahs . . . anniversary parties. . . ." See "Rituals and the Healing Process," by Evan Imber-Black, in *Living Beyond Loss: Death in the Family*, Froma Walsh and Monica McGoldrick, eds., N.Y.: W. W. Norton & Company, 1991, pp. 216–17.

p. 256 "In his book *Psychotrends*, psychiatrist Shervert H. Frazier . . ." *Psychotrends: What Kind of People Are We Becoming?* by Shervert H. Frazier, M.D., N.Y.: Simon & Schuster, 1994.

p. 256 ". . . traditional nuclear family describes only one in four households." Ibid., p. 95.

p. 256 "After all, 'traditional' families . . . consigned mothers to the kitchen . . . ' " Ibid., pp. 96–97.

p. 256 "The number of single-person American households . . . is 40 percent . . ." Ibid., p. 109.

p. 257 "Instead . . . 'more new families . . . of the *mind*, not of the genes . . . supplant the biological family.' " Ibid., p. 90.

p. 257 "People who are unrelated . . . forming what Dr. Frazier calls 'fictive families' and 'fictive kinships' . . ." Ibid., p. 114.

p. 257 "The family . . . is being reinvented." Ibid., pp. 98–99.

p. 257 "A way to disconnect these rituals from their rueful antecedents . . ." See Imber-Black, in *Living Beyond Loss*, p. 217.

p. 258 "A 1998 nationally representative survey conducted by Fordham . . ." "The Effect of Age on Positive and Negative Affect: A Developmental Perspective on Happiness," by Daniel K. Mroczek and Christian M. Kolarz, *Journal of Personality and Social Psychology*, vol. 75, no. 5, November 1998, pp. 1333–49.

p. 258 ". . . adults learn from experience to 'select people and situations' . . ." Ibid.

p. 259 "At the end of his memoir, *Timebends*, Arthur Miller . . ." *Timebends: A Life*, by Arthur Miller, N.Y.: Penguin Books, 1995, p. 598.

p. 259 "Now he was being addressed as 'Grandpa' . . . '[M]y God, I had hardly begun!' " Ibid.

p. 259 "[T]he truth, the first truth, probably . . . watching one another.' " Ibid., p. 599.

Bibliography

AARP (American Association of Retired Persons), "AARP Independent Living *Excel* Insert: Tabulation Report July 30–August 19, 1997," Excel: ICR's Twice Weekly National Telephone Omnibus Service, Conducted for the AARP by International Communications Research, Media, PA.

Ainsworth, Mary D. Salter, "Patterns of Infant-Mother Attachment: Antecedents and Effects of Development," pp. 771–91, and "Attachments Across the Life Span," pp. 792–812, *Bulletin of the New York Academy of Medicine* 61, No. 9, November, 1985.

Angel, Marc D., Ph.D., *The Orphaned Adult: Confronting the Death of a Parent*, N.Y.: Insight Books, Human Sciences Press, 1987.

Ariès, Phillippe, *Western Attitudes Toward Death: From the Middle Ages to the Present*, trans. by Patricia M. Ranum, Baltimore and London: Johns Hopkins University Press, 1974.

Bahr, Stephen J., and Evan T. Peterson, eds., *Aging and the Family*, Lexington, Mass.: Lexington Books, 1989.

Bank, Stephen P., and Michael D. Kahn, *The Sibling Bond*, N.Y.: Basic Books, 1982.

Beechem, Michael H., Cybil Anthony, and James Kurtz, "A Life Review Interview Guide: A Structured Systems Approach to Information Gathering,"

The International Journal of Aging and Human Development, vol. 46, no. 1, 1998, pp. 25–44.

Benjamin, Jessica, *The Bonds of Love: Psychoanalysis, Feminism, and the Problem of Domination*, N.Y.: Pantheon Books, 1988.

Bove, Alexander A., Jr., *The Complete Book of Wills and Estates*, N.Y.: Henry Holt and Company, 1989.

Bower, Anne R., Ph.D., "The Adult Child's Acceptance of Parent Death," *Omega*, special issue: Kinship and Bereavement in Later Life, August 1997, vol. 35, no. 1, pp. 67–96.

Bowlby, John, *A Secure Base: Parent-Child Attachment and Healthy Human Development*, N.Y.: Basic Books, 1988.

——, *Attachment and Loss* Vol. III, *Loss: Sadness and Depression*, N.Y.: Basic Books, Inc., 1980.

Bretherton, Inge, and Everett Waters, eds., *Growing Points of Attachment Theory and Research*, Monographs of the Society for Research in Child Development Serial No. 209, vol. 50, nos. 1–2, Chicago: University of Chicago Press, 1985.

Brubaker, Timony H., ed., *Family Relationships in Later Life*, 2nd ed., Newbury Park, Calif.: Sage Publications, 1990.

Burgess, Ann Wolbert, R.N., D.N.Sc., "Family Reaction to Homicide," *American Journal of Orthopsychiatry* 45(3), April 1975, pp. 391–98.

Burke, Peter J., "Identity Processes and Social Stress," *American Sociological Review*, vol. 56, 1991, pp. 836–49.

Chodorow, Nancy J., *The Reproduction of Mothering: Psychoanalysis and the Sociology of Gender*, Berkeley, Calif.: University of California Press, 1978.

Cohen, Steven Z., and Bruce Michael Gans, *The Other Generation Gap: The Middle-Aged and Their Aging Parents*, N.Y.: Dodd Mead and Company, 1988.

Crimmins, Eileen M., and Dominique G. Ingegneri, "Interaction and Living Arrangements of Older Parents and Their Children: Past Trends, Present

Determinants, Future Implications," *Research on Aging*, vol. 12, no. 1, March 1990, pp. 3–35.

Daniels, Norman, *Am I My Parents' Keeper? An Essay on Justice Between the Young and the Old*, N.Y.: Oxford University Press, 1988.

Davenport, Donna S., "The Functions of Anger and Forgiveness: Guidelines for Psychotherapy With Victims," *Psychotherapy*, vol. 28, no. 1, Spring 1991, pp. 140–44.

Doka, Kenneth J., "The Monkey's Paw: The Role of Inheritance in the Resolution of Grief," *Death Studies*, *16*, 1992, pp. 45–58.

———, *Disenfranchised Grief*, Lexington, Mass.: Lexington Press, 1989.

Douglas, Joan Delahanty, "Patterns of Change Following Parent Death in Midlife Adults," *Omega*, vol. 22(2), 1990–1991, pp. 123–37.

Duberstein, Paul R., Ph.D.; Yeates Conwell, M.D.; and Christopher Cox, Ph.D., "Suicide in the Widowed: A Psychological Autopsy Comparison of Recently and Remotely Bereaved Elders," 1996 (paper).

Duberstein, Paul. R.; Larry Seidlitz; and Yeates Conwell, "Reconsidering the Role of Hostility in Completed Suicide: A Life-Course Perspective," in *Psychoanalytic Perspectives on Developmental Psychology*, in Joseph M. Masling and Robert F. Bornstein, eds., Washington, D.C.: American Psychological Association, 1996, pp. 257–323.

Dunn, Judy, and Robert Plomin, *Separate Lives: Why Siblings Are So Different*, N.Y.: Basic Books, HarperCollins Publishers, 1990.

Dunne, Edward J.; John L. McIntosh; and Karen Dunne-Maxim, eds., *Suicide and Its Aftermath: Understanding and Counseling the Survivors*, N.Y.: W. W. Norton & Company, 1987.

Edelman, Hope, *Motherless Daughters: The Legacy of Loss*, N.Y.: Delta, 1995.

Eichorn, Dorothy H.; John A. Clausen; Norma Haan; Marjorie P. Honzik; and Paul H. Mussen, eds., *Present and Past in Middle Life*, N.Y.: Academic Press, Harcourt Brace Jovanovich, Publishers, 1981.

Eisenstadt, Marvin; André Haynal; Pierre Rentchnick; and Pierre de Senar-clens, *Parental Loss and Achievement*, Madison, Conn.: International Universities Press, Inc., 1989.

Epstein, Helen, *Where She Came From: A Daughter's Search for Her Mother's History*, Boston, Mass.: Little, Brown and Company, 1997.

Erikson, Erik H., *Identity and the Life Cycle*, N.Y.: W. W. Norton and Company, 1979.

Fox, Margery; Margaret Gibbs; and Doris Auerbach, "Age and Gender Dimensions of Friendship," *Psychology of Women Quarterly* 9, 1985, pp. 489–502.

Frazier, Shervert H., M.D., *Psychotrends: What Kind Of People Are We Becoming?* N.Y.: Simon & Schuster, 1994.

Freud, "Mourning and Melancholia" (1917), in *The Standard Edition of the Complete Psychological Works of Sigmund Freud*, vol. 14, J. Strachey, ed., London: Hogarth Press, 1963.

Gay, Peter, *Freud: A Life for Our Time*, N.Y.: Anchor Books, Bantam Doubleday Dell Publishing Group, Inc., 1989.

Goldsmith, Barbara, *Johnson v. Johnson*, N.Y.: Alfred A. Knopf, 1987.

Goldsmith, H. Hill; Arnold H. Buss; Robert Plomin; Mary Klevjord Rothbart; Alexander Thomas and Stella Chess; Robert A. Hinde; and Robert B. McCall, "Roundtable: What Is Temperament? Four Approaches," *Child Development* 58, 1987, pp. 505–29.

Graham-Bermann, Sandra A., "Siblings in Dyads: Relationships Among Perceptions and Behavior," *The Journal of Genetic Psychology* 152(2), June 1991, pp. 207–16.

Greenberg, Vivian E., *Children of a Certain Age*, N.Y.: Lexington Books, 1994.

Greer, Jane, with Edward Myers, *Adult Sibling Rivalry: Understanding the Legacy of Childhood*, N.Y.: Crown Publishers, Inc., 1992.

Heilbrun, Carolyn G., *The Last Gift of Time: Life Beyond Sixty*, N.Y.: Dial Press, 1997.

Hobfoll, Stevan E., and Joseph P. Stokes, "The Process and Mechanics of Social Support," in *Handbook of Personal Relationships*, S. W. Duck, ed., London: John Wiley & Sons Ltd., 1988, pp. 497–517.

Hoffman, Lois Wladis, "The Influence of the Family Environment on Personality: Accounting for Sibling Differences," *Psychological Bulletin*, vol. 110, no. 2, 1991, pp. 187–203.

Holmes, Thomas H., and Richard H. Rahe, "The Social Readjustment Rating Scale," *Journal of Psychosomatic Research*, vol. 11, 1967, pp. 213–18.

House, James S.; Karl R. Landis; and Debra Umberson, "Social Relationships and Health," *Science* 29, vol. 241, July 1988, pp. 540–545.

Howard, Jane, *Families*, N.Y.: Simon & Schuster, 1978.

Imber-Black, Evan, Ph.D., *The Secret Life of Families: Truth-Telling, Privacy, and Reconciliation in a Tell-All Society*, N.Y.: Bantam Books, 1998.

Jones, Ernest, M.D., *The Life and Work of Sigmund Freud, Volume I: The Formative Years and the Great Discoveries 1856–1900*, N.Y.: Basic Books, Inc., 1953.

Jung, C.G., *Psychological Types*, A revision by R.F.C. Hull of the Translation by H.G. Baynes, Bollingen Series XX, The Collected Works of C.G. Jung, Vol. 6, Sir Herbert Read et al., eds., Princeton, N.J.: Princeton University Press 1971.

————, *The Undiscovered Self*, Translated from the German by R.F.C. Hull, Boston, Mass.: Little, Brown and Company, 1957, 1958.

————, *The Development of Personality: Papers on Child Psychology, Education, and Related Subjects*, Vol. 17 of the Collected Works of C.G. Jung, Bollingen Series XX, translated by R.F.C. Hull, N.Y.: Pantheon Books, 1954.

Kahn, Michael D., and Karen Gail Lewis, eds., *Siblings in Therapy: Life Span and Clinical Issues*, N.Y.: W. W. Norton & Company, 1988.

Kalish, Richard A., ed., *Midlife Loss: Coping Strategies*, Newbury Park, CA: Sage Publications, 1989.

Kaplan, Louise J., *No Voice Is Ever Wholly Lost*, N.Y.: Simon & Schuster, 1995.

Kerr, Michael E., and Murray Bowen, *Family Evaluation: An Approach Based on Bowen Theory*, N.Y.: W. W. Norton & Co., 1988.

Koch, Thomas, *Mirrored Lives: Aging Children and Elderly Parents*, N.Y.: Praeger Publishers, 1990.

Lamb, Michael E., and Brian Sutton-Smith, eds., *Sibling Relationships: Their Nature and Significance Across the Lifespan*, Hillsdale, N.J.: Lawrence Erlbaum Associates, 1982.

Lancaster, Jane. B., Jeanne Altmann, Alice S. Rossi, and Lonnie R. Sherrod, eds., *Parenting Across the Life Span: Biosocial Dimensions*, Hawthorne, N.Y.: Aldine de Gruyter, 1987.

Malcolm, Janet, *Psychoanalysis: The Impossible Profession*, N.Y.: Vintage Books, 1982.

Malinak, Dennis, M.D., Michael F. Hoyt, Ph.D., and Virginia Patterson, M.A., "Adults' Reactions to the Death of a Parent: A Preliminary Study," *American Journal of Psychiatry*, 136:9, September 1979, pp. 1152–56.

McIntosh, John L., Ph.D., "Generational Analyses of Suicide: Baby Boomers and 13ers," *Suicide and Life-Threatening Behavior*, vol. 24(4), Winter 1994, pp. 334–42.

———, "Review Article: Control Group Studies of Suicide Survivors: A Review and Critique," *Suicide and Life-Threatening Behavior*, vol. 23(2), Summer 1993, pp. 146–61.

McKenna, David, *When Our Parents Need Us Most*, Wheaton, Ill.: H. Shaw Publishers, 1994.

Miller, Alice, *The Drama of the Gifted Child: The Search for the True Self*, N.Y.: Basic Books, 1981.

Miller, Arthur, *Timebends: A Life*, N.Y.: Penguin Books, 1995.

———, *Death of a Salesman*, N.Y.: Viking Press, 1949, 1973.

Miller, Nancy K., *Bequest & Betrayal: Memoirs of a Parent's Death*, N.Y. and Oxford: Oxford University Press, 1996.

Morris, Jan, *Pleasures of a Tangled Life*, N.Y.: Random House, 1989.

Morrison, Blake, *And When Did You Last See Your Father? A Son's Memoir of Love and Loss*, N.Y.: Picador, 1995.

Moss, Miriam S., and Sidney Z. Moss, "The Impact of Parental Death on Middle Aged Children," *Omega*, vol. 14(1), 1983–1984, pp. 65–75.

Moss, Miriam S.; Nancy Resch; and Sidney Z. Moss, "The Role of Gender in Middle-Aged Children's Responses to Parent Death," *Omega*, vol. 35, no. 1, August 1997, pp. 43–65.

Mroczek, Daniel K., and Christian M. Kolarz, "The Effect of Age on Positive and Negative Affect: A Developmental Perspective on Happiness," *Journal of Personality and Social Psychology*, vol. 75, no. 5, November 1998, pp. 1333–49.

Myers, Edward, *When Parents Die: A Guide for Adults*, rev. ed., N.Y.: Penguin Books, 1997.

Neugarten, Bernice L., ed., *Middle Age and Aging: A Reader in Social Psychology*, Chicago: University of Chicago Press, 1968.

Neugarten, Dail A., ed., *The Meanings of Age: Selected Papers of Bernice L. Neugarten*, Chicago: University of Chicago Press, 1996.

Orbuch, Terri L.; James S. House; Richard P. Mero, et al., "Marital Quality Over the Life Course," *Social Psychology Quarterly*, vol. 59, no. 2, 1996, pp. 162–71.

Parkes, Colin Murray, and Robert S. Weiss, *Recovery from Bereavement*, N.Y.: Basic Books, Inc., 1983.

Penn, Peggy, M.S.W., and Marilyn Frankfurt, M.S.W., "Creating a Participant Text: Writing, Multiple Voices, Narrative Multiplicity," *Family Process*, vol. 33, no. 3, September 1994, pp. 217–31.

Perkins, H. Wesley, and Lynne B. Harris, "Familial Bereavement and Health in Adult Life Course Perspective," *Journal of Marriage and the Family* 52, February 1990, pp. 233–41.

Pipher, Mary, Ph.D., *Another Country: Navigating the Emotional Terrain of Our Elders*, N.Y.: Riverhead Books, Penguin Putnam, Inc., 1999.

Plomin, Robert, and Denise Daniels, "Why Are Children in the Same Family So Different from One Another?" *Behavioral and Brain Sciences* 10, 1987, pp. 1–60.

Pollock, George H., "The Mourning Process and Creative Organizational Change," *Journal of the American Psychoanalytic Association* 25, 1977, pp. 3–34.

Quinn, Jane Bryant, *Making the Most of Your Money*, N.Y.: Simon & Schuster, 1997.

Rando, Therese A., Ph.D., *Treatment of Complicated Mourning*, Champaign, Ill: Research Press, 1993.

Robbins, Martha A., *Midlife Women and Death of Mother: A Study of Psycho-historical and Spriritual Transformation*, N.Y.: Peter Lang, 1990 (American University Studies Series VIII, Psychology, vol. 8).

Rook, Karen, "The Pleasures and Problems of Friendship," in *Every Woman's Emotional Well-Being*, Carol Tavris, ed., N.Y.: Doubleday, 1986.

Rossi, Alice S., and Peter H. Rossi, *Of Human Bonding: Parent-Child Relations Across the Life Course*, Hawthorne, N.Y.: Aldine de Gruyter, 1990.

Roth, Philip, *Patrimony: A True Story*, N.Y.: Simon & Schuster, 1991.

Rothenberg, Rose-Emily, "The Orphan Archetype," *Psychological Perspectives* 14, Fall 1983, pp. 181–94.

Rowe, David C., *The Limits of Family Influence: Genes, Experience, and Behavior*, N.Y.: Guilford Press, 1994.

Ryff, Carol D.; Young Hyun Lee; Marilyn J. Essex; and Pamela S. Schmutte, "My Children and Me: Midlife Evaluations of Grown Children and of Self," *Psychology and Aging*, vol. 9, no. 2, 1994, pp. 195–205.

Scarr, Sandra, and Kathleen McCartney, "How People Make Their Own Environments: A Theory of Genotype ⟶ Environment Effects," *Child Development* 54, 1983, pp. 424–435.

Scharlach, Andrew E., Ph.D. and Karen I. Fredriksen, M.S.W., "Reactions to the Death of a Parent During Midlife," *Omega*, vol. 27, no. 4, 1993, pp. 307–319.

Schmutte, Pamela S., and Carol D. Ryff, "Success, Social Comparison, and Self-Assessment: Parents' Midlife Evaluations of Sons, Daughters, and Self," *Journal of Adult Development*, vol. 1, no. 2, 1994, pp. 109–26.

Secunda, Victoria, *When Madness Comes Home: Help and Hope for the Families of the Mentally Ill*, N.Y.: Hyperion, 1998.

———, *Women and Their Fathers: The Sexual and Romantic Impact of the First Man in Your Life*, N.Y.: Delta, 1993.

———, *When You and Your Mother Can't Be Friends: Resolving the Most Complicated Relationship of Your Life*, N.Y.: Delta, 1991.

———, "Why You Must Get Your Story Out," *New Choices*, June 1997, pp. 54–57.

———, "The New Woman Friendship Report," *New Woman*, August 1992, pp. 72–75.

Shapiro, Ester R., *Grief as a Family Process: A Developmental Approach to Clinical Practice*, N.Y.: Guilford Press, 1994.

Silver, Roxane L.; Cheryl Boon; and Mary H. Stones, "Searching for Meaning in Misfortune: Making Sense of Incest," *Journal of Social Issues*, vol. 39, no. 2, 1983, pp. 81–102.

Smith, J. Walker, and Ann Clurman, *Rocking the Ages: The Yankelovich Report on Generational Marketing*, N.Y.: HarperBusiness, 1997.

Snyder, C. R., Cheri Harris; John R. Anderson et al., "The Will and the Ways: Development and Validation of an Individual-Differences Measure of Hope," *Journal of Personality and Social Psychology*, vol. 60, no. 4, 1991, pp. 570–85.

Snyder, C. R.; Lori M. Irving; and John R. Anderson, "Hope and Health," in *Handbook on Social and Clinical Psychology: The Health Perspective*, C. R. Snyder and D. R. Forsyth, eds., Elmsford, N.Y.: Pergamon Press, 1991, pp. 285–305.

Stewart, Abigail J., "Rethinking Middle Age: Learning from Women's Lives," invited address, Eastern Psychological Association, April 1, 1995.

Stocker, Clare; Judy Dunn; and Robert Plomin, "Sibling Relationships: Links with Child Temperament, Maternal Behavior, and Family Structure," *Child Development* 60, 1989, pp. 715–27.

Storr, Anthony, *The Integrity of the Personality*, N.Y.: Ballantine Books, 1992.

————, *Solitude: A Return to the Self*, N.Y.: Free Press, Macmillan, Inc., 1988.

Sulloway, Frank J., *Born to Rebel: Birth Order, Family Dynamics, and Creative Lives*, N.Y.: Vintage Books, Random House, Inc., 1997.

————, "Birth Order and Evolutionary Psychology: A Meta-analytic Overview," *Psychological Inquiry* 6, 1995, pp. 75–80.

Taylor, Shelley E., *Positive Illusions: Creative Self-Deception and the Healthy Mind*, N.Y.: Basic Books, HarperCollins Publishers, 1989.

Toman, Walter, *Family Constellation: Its Effect on Personality and Social Behavior*, 3rd ed., N.Y.: Springer Publishing Company, Inc., 1976.

Trillin, Calvin, *Messages from My Father*, N.Y.: Farrar, Straus and Giroux, 1996.

Umberson, Debra, "Marriage as Support or Strain? Marital Quality Following the Death of a Parent," *Journal of Marriage and the Family*, 1995, pp. 709–23.

————, "Relationships Between Adult Children and Their Parents: Psychological Consequences for Both Generations," *Journal of Marriage and the Family* 54, August 1992, pp. 664–74.

Umberson, Debra, and Toni Terling, "The Symbolic Meaning of Relationships: Implications for Psychological Distress Following Relationship Loss," *Journal of Social and Personal Relationships*, vol. 14, no. 6, December 1997, pp. 723–44.

Umberson, Debra, and Meichu D. Chen, "Effects of a Parent's Death on Adult Children: Relationship Salience and Reaction to Loss," *American Sociological Review*, vol. 59, February 1994, pp. 152–68.

Vaillant, George E., *The Wisdom of the Ego*, Cambridge, Mass.: Harvard University Press, 1993.

———, "Loss as a Metaphor for Attachment," *The American Journal of Psychoanalysis*, vol. 45, no. 1, 1985, pp. 59–67.

Vaughan, Susan C., *The Talking Cure: The Science Behind Psychotherapy*, N.Y.: G. P. Putnam's Sons, 1997.

Viorst, Judith, *Necessary Losses: The Loves, Illusions, Dependencies and Impossible Expectations That All of Us Have to Give Up in Order to Grow*, N.Y.: Fawcett Gold Medal, Ballantine Books, 1987.

Walsh, Froma, and Monica McGoldrick, eds., *Living Beyond Loss: Death in the Family*, N.Y.: W. W. Norton & Company, 1991.

Weiss, Robert, "Loss and Recovery," *Journal of Social Issues* 44(3), 1988, pp. 37–52.

Wilson, Douglas L., *Honor's Voice: The Transformation of Abraham Lincoln*, N.Y.: Alfred A. Knopf, 1998.

Wilson, Edward O., *On Human Nature*, Cambridge, Mass.: Harvard University Press, 1978.

Winnicott, Claire, et al., eds., *Deprivation and Delinquency*, London: Tavistock Publications, 1984.

Wortman, Camille B., and Roxane Cohen Silver, "The Myths of Coping with Loss," *Journal of Consulting and Clinical Psychology*, vol. 57, no. 3, 1989, pp. 349–57.

Ziller, Robert C., and Betty J. Stewart-Dowdell, "Life After Parental Death: Monitoring a Child's Self-Concept Before and After Family Violence," *Death Studies* 15, 1991, pp. 577–86.

Index